Praise for
CROSSING THE GATES OF ALASKA

"A stirring account of a remarkable journey through one of the Earth's last great wild places."

—**Robert Birkby**, author of *Mountain Madness*

"Beautifully captures the vastness of Alaska—and the determination of the human spirit."

—**Sheryl Kayne**, author of *Volunteer Vacations Across America* and *Immersion Travel USA*

"Wow! I opened the book and found myself in the heart of Alaska's wild frontier, something I can only dream of doing."

—**Kevin Runolfson**, author of *The Things You Find on the Appalachian Trail*

CROSSING THE GATES OF ALASKA

One Man, Two Dogs
600 Miles Off the Map

DAVE METZ

CITADEL PRESS
Kensington Publishing Corp.
www.kensingtonbooks.com

CITADEL PRESS BOOKS are published by
Kensington Publishing Corp.
119 West 40th Street
New York, NY 10018

All Kensington titles, imprints, and distributed lines are available at special
quantity discounts for bulk purchases for sales promotions, premiums,
fund-raising, educational, or institutional use. Special book excerpts or
customized printings can also be created to fit specific needs. For details, write
or phone the office of the Kensington special sales manager: Kensington
Publishing Corp., 119 West 40th Street, New York, NY 10018, attn: Special
Sales Department; phone 1-800-221-2647.

First printing: February 2010

10 9 8 7 6 5 4 3 2 1

Printed in the United States of America

Library of Congress Control Number: 2009937068

ISBN-13: 978-0-8065-3139-7
ISBN-10: 0-8065-3139-8

This book is dedicated to my dad.

CONTENTS

ACKNOWLEDGMENTS

This book came from the heart. I poured everything into it like it was meant to be. Writing it was as big a challenge as my adventure itself. I owe a great deal of gratitude to the people who supported me on my trek across Alaska and also to those who helped me write this book.

Thanks to Kate Epstein, my agent, who recognized the potential of my book immediately. Thanks to my editor Amy Pyle for her positive and courteous attitude, and for doing the hard work of turning my manuscript into a book. Thanks to Bob Birkby for his incredible insight on wilderness travel and his advice on my final revisions.

I'm indebted to my family and friends. Thanks to my parents, Valerie Metz and Darrel Metz, who never made monsters out of pettiness and always allowed me to come and go when I was younger. Thanks to my oldest brother Mike Metz for his limitless knowledge of skiing and hiking, and for dragging me on a backpacking trip across Oregon when I was sixteen. Thanks to my brother Rick Metz and his son Michael Metz for supporting me on my trek by supplying me with so much food. I could always count on an enormous package of food from them at every village. Thanks to my brother Steve Metz for a place to crash, and for letting me park my car in his driveway when I was away on trips more times than I could remember. Thanks to Jeff Cordell, a tireless hiker who is like our fifth brother. He believed in me from the beginning two and a half decades ago, and always supported my nomadic and impoverished lifestyle like it was a thing to behold. Most importantly, I owe great thanks to my friend Julie Firman for her endless help on my expedition and the writing of this book. Without her neither would have been possible.

A few other people who I owe some thanks are Don Hudrick for his uplifting feed back on my first draft, to Frank Hagan for giving me an old pair of telemark skis I used on the first half of my trek, and to Bob Firman and Wanda Firman for their letters of encouragement while I was on my journey.

There are a few people in Alaska who helped me and whose names I can't totally recall. I have to thank the incredible bush pilot from Kotzebue who skillfully dropped my life-saving food packages along the Noatak River, and the man ice fishing on the Hotham Inlet who selflessly gave me a thirty-inch fish to eat, and Glenn from Kiana who offered to come get me on his snowmobile if I ever needed saving.

I also must thank all the other high-spirited people of Alaska who were gracious to me on my trek and anyone who reads my story.

Using the journals I kept on my trek, I've tried to recall everything as accurately as I could. Though what seems difficult for me might not be a burden for someone else, and what is easy for me might drive someone else crazy. I've written this book almost entirely from my own point of view. I didn't want to exaggerate any of the dangers, nor play them down. I wanted people to be able to read this book so they could know what to expect if they ever decided to undertake a journey into wild Alaska.

And to Jimmy and Will. I'm not sure if they understand that I'm thanking them, but their good cheer and vitality are contagious and prop up my spirits every day of my life. I also must mention dear Jonny. His memory will never die.

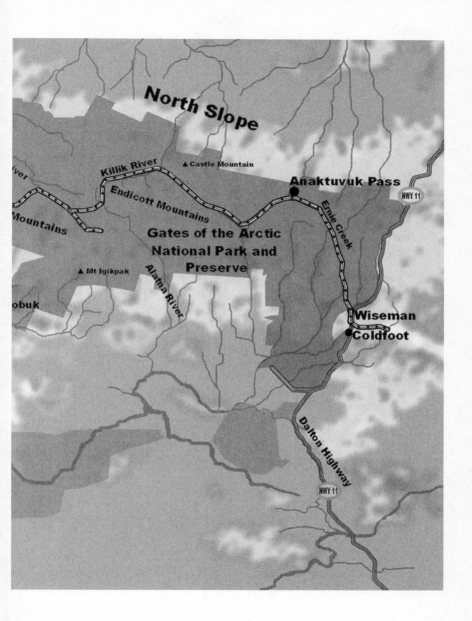

CROSSING THE GATES OF ALASKA

PROLOGUE

I'm sitting on a waist-high hummock in the middle of a barren, wind-swept pass with my two dogs in the heart of the Brooks Range. The vastness of the land makes my jaw drop and I wonder how I will walk out of here with so little food. Much of the snow that had layered this land has recently melted and left the ground saturated with a network of miniature pools and streams flowing from every indentation around. I look northeast, far down the Killik River Valley. It stretches almost straight for four days' walking time before veering north where it vanishes through jagged mountains. Then the valley spills its water onto the sprawling arctic plain.

Behind me, and flowing southward, is the Alatna River. Three hard days of hiking in that direction and I would reach the edge of the spruce forest that covers much of Alaska south of there. I might make it to the village of Alatna, a hundred miles downriver, if I were to leave now while I still have food left. Perhaps I would be able to build a log raft along the way and float out.

It's a difficult decision. I'm already raked thin from rationing a backpack filled with food and marching eight hours a day. But instead of heading south into a more forgiving land that is already teeming with fresh blossoms and green grass, I choose to stick with my original northern route. As the crow flies, I'm about eighty miles from the village of Anaktuvuk Pass. I will have to hike across treeless terrain so exposed that it feels like the wind could pick me up and carry me off and over the farthest mountains. I get the chills looking back at the harrowing passes I've already come through. They are so menacingly steep and craggy that I don't look back for long. I look forward now. I will have to move on or starve.

My body is burning itself away while I walk along such impassable ground. There are mountains to go around, gorges to cross, bogs to sidestep, oceans of brush to wade through, and miles of nagging tussocks to curse at as I waddle over them, day after day. For food there are a few lentil beans and some oats left. That's it, to hike on for about twelve more days, and that is if I hike all day every day. Emaciation will come quickly in those final few days as my broken-down body searches for more energy to fuel itself.

I left Kotzebue, Alaska, on March 26, about sixty days ago. I began by skiing out of town with the dogs pulling me, across the Hotham Inlet, and then up the Kobuk River to the village of Ambler. Then I turned up the Ambler River and skied to its headwaters. I abandoned my sleds and skis and hiked over the final pass to the Noatak River. From there I crossed over another mountain range to the Alatna River and followed it to its source. This is how I got to where I am now, and I'm miserably hungry. Most of my own food goes to my dogs, and I have not considered calling for a rescue yet. My intention is to continue east to the village of Anaktuvuk Pass, get more supplies, and hike to the town of Wiseman on the Dalton Highway. Right now, though, I grow desperate with hunger and exhaustion. The fear of starvation looms over me constantly and I am beginning to understand what a wretched death it would be.

My Airedale terriers are the long-legged type from very pure strains, and they embolden each other. They are young brothers just barely a year old. I also have an old rusty shotgun with two remaining shells. I never planned to hunt, but I never thought I would be starving, either. So when I encounter a rabbit on the lower Killik River I become excited. I unfasten the straps to my pack and let it fall to the ground where I stand. I unleash the dogs for the first time in days. Right away, they sprint off tracking the rabbit's trail down the willow-laden riverbank. They need no prompting from me because hunting is in their blood. I know the rabbit will double back on his trail repeatedly until tiring. I step back away from the willows and out onto a gravel bar to get a better view of the river's edge. The rabbit comes back through several times but I cannot get a safe shot. I'm confident the dogs will not lose the scent; they can track animals through water.

After several more passes the rabbit finally stops beside a bush, not knowing I'm near. I raise my gun swiftly until the bead on the end of the barrel lines up with the rabbit's torso, and I fire. The shot reverberates across the valley as the rabbit topples to the ground. I run to where he falls, and because I'm so hungry, rejoice over the kill. A half hour later we get another rabbit. The dogs have earned their keep today. Tonight we will eat.

The next morning I chuck my shotgun, leaving it next to some willows. With no more shells, it has become a worthless hunk of wood and steel that I cannot carry. I need to have a lighter load. I must travel faster. I can't stay here; no one ever comes here and food is scarce. I haven't seen a human being since leaving the village of Ambler about forty days ago. At least I feel some added strength now and I play a little with the dogs. Then I take out all our beans and oats, and examine them. I consolidate the packages and then burn the extra wrappers. Then I divide my portion from the dogs' and carefully put all the food away into four separate, plastic bags. We will each have only one small meal a day, but at least we will be able to eat something. On the final day I figure we will have a cup and a half of lentil beans to share between the three of us, and then all our food will be gone.

I hoist my pack onto my back, buckle my straps, and tie the dogs' leash to my chest strap so they will not run off and burn more calories than they have to. I look back towards the upper Killik River; however, I cannot see its source. I can see the pass I came over quite clearly, though. I turn back and look forward. Then I step out feeling strong, knowing that whatever happens, I will walk until I drop and am not able to get back up again. After twenty minutes I make the great sweeping turn onto Easter Creek and scan the eastern horizon with reverence, and some fear; I'm impressed by its grandeur, yet afraid that I cannot get across it. The land is enormous and so beautifully empty. The sun is already up, sitting over the starkly outlined peaks and rolling expanse of tundra that appear to be from a different, gigantic world. I walk on with deliberate and efficient steps over the tussock-filled plain and into the wild void beyond. I say to the dogs to lift their spirits, "We'll make it, pups. We'll make it."

CLOSE TO PARADISE

Drift Creek Wilderness is about as close to paradise as you can get in this world. It's a large patch of ancient rain forest in the Coast Range of Oregon, located about ten miles from the ocean. It's perpetually bathed in mist and cool air. I'm drawn there by the immensity of the trees that hide the intricate network of animal paths leading throughout the forest. I like to follow them as if I'm part of something greater than I can fully understand. Its natural antiquity draws out my most innate moods and thoughts. They are moods and thoughts that are stifled in a city, but they come to the surface when I'm in the woods and need to survive there. I cannot pin down their origin and purpose, but they make me feel light-headed and in perfect tune with my body and the world around me, like I belong in wilderness.

Enormous cedar and fir trees, with diameters up to several feet, tower like rapturous cathedrals throughout the ravines and along the ridges. Red alders flourish in places where the soil has been disturbed, and their fallen limbs make lightweight hiking sticks. I like to use them on my ascents out of the creek valley on the way home, only to toss them back on the ground when I near the end of the trail. Big leaf maples also grow on the valley floor, with more plant life sprouting from the tree surface itself. Often the mosses are so thick on these trees that you can't see the bark anywhere. Sometimes

I rest under them when it rains since their large branches offer a dry shelter, and the ground underneath is often soft with withered leaves.

Devil's club grows eight feet tall underneath the canopy where shade dominates the forest floor. The shrub was an important medicinal plant to aboriginal people, and the red berries that give the plant its distinctive character ripen into the shape of a pyramidal fist. I'm careful not to get the tiny thorns that stick out all along the stems embedded into my skin as I move past. But I usually end up with a few anyway.

In June when the salmon berries ripen to the size of Ping-Pong balls, I try to get there before the black bears eat them all. The stems of sword ferns and the leafy-green wood sorrel can be eaten as survival food in winter when other plants are scarce, though they don't have much sustenance. The ferns take a lot of effort to dig up and the wood sorrel contains an acid that will make your stomach ache if you eat too much, like eating too many green apples. In fall chanterelle mushrooms speckle the forest floor, but they are hard to notice from a distance, often mistaken for decaying orange leaves. Your eyes learn to zero in on them the longer you're there.

Some species of plants and animals in Drift Creek are so poisonous that ingesting just a few ounces will cause certain death. One example is baneberry. With its few bright red, glossy berries, it's unmistakable and virtually always unmolested by any animal, even bears, yet it looks fleshy and as palatable as the fabled fruit in the Garden of Eden. And the rough-skinned newt, which contains the same poison produced in the gonads of many puffer fish, is so deadly that you must wash your hands after you handle one. In the spring and fall after the cool rains come, hordes of amphibians become more active, especially newts. I have to be careful not to step on them as they cruise the forest floor at their somnolent pace.

Thousands of bright orange crayfish crawl along the creek bed like miniature titans, and raccoons stake out their places along the creek to feed on them. The raccoons can often be seen waddling down the bend away from you, leaving shell parts to clutter the bottom of the creek. Cutthroat trout lie in deep bubbly pockets of the creek, and Chinook salmon come charging up the currents in the fall to spawn and die. It's amazing how such a giant fish can navigate such a small creek. And when they die, their rich, rotting tissue invigorates the soil making it possible for more life to flourish.

I've spent a lot of time in Drift Creek, so I don't need to take maps or a light anymore to find my way around. Sometimes at the end of the day when darkness falls and I'm still a mile or two from the end of the trail, I can find my way by memory and sound, even when I'm not on a trail. I will walk down the ridge from the south side, cross the creek, and follow the trail to the north edge of the wilderness area. Then I return by bushwhacking down Trout Creek, slithering and twisting around the many vines and fallen logs as softly as I can. At times I will stop to climb a tall, straight tree if there is still daylight, to see where I am and to work the muscles of my back and legs. Drift Creek Wilderness is a good place to test yourself and learn how to move through a wild land. I relish the trips I take there. I used to take my dog Jonny with me when I hiked there, and we moved through the verdurous shadows like we were as light as feathers; it seemed nothing could hold us back.

I miss Jonny. He died on my shoulders while I was carrying him out of Drift Creek two years ago. Many of my memories of him have faded now like many memories do with the passing of time. But there is one memory I fight to keep so I won't forget him. We were taking our daily hike in the wooded hills behind home like we did most every day. He was ten years old and we had been almost inseparable since he was a pup. He was trotting beside me with his lanky, powerful legs while staring at me with his sharp brown eyes, not off to the side like so many dogs do. Jonny would look at your eyes without wavering and without an ounce of insecurity, like he wanted to examine your mind. Knowing dogs don't live long, I made sure to imprint that vision of him forever into my brain. It encompassed his nature, still fit at his age with that intense stare. He appeared almost to smile with that half-gaping jaw and wagging Airedale tail. I knew I had to remember him. This kind of dog comes along only once in a lifetime. There was no way I could let myself forget him.

Jonny was with me during all the years when I lived in Portland. Jonny and I were often hiking and running together in the mountains and forests. Sometimes I would ride the first couple miles of my bike workouts with him trotting beside me, before sticking him back in the yard so I could go on. We went on weeklong hikes, to local areas mainly, but we also went on a few extended journeys. We hiked for a month in western Alaska when he was two and kayaked down the Yukon River when he was three. I let him ride in a hole I hacked out of the front of my kayak with a wood saw. We took several backpacking trips to Idaho, driving across the dry country of eastern Oregon in August on our way when the nights were warm and starry. I always thought we would do the big trek together across the Gates of the Arctic National Park before he grew too old. It's a huge region that spans much of western Alaska in the Brooks Range and requires some fortitude and time to cross. We did manage to drive around Alaska for two months when he was eight. We were going to go up and live in the woods for the summer and maybe set up a base camp for future explorations. We were never able to do the big trek together, though. I was considering dropping everything that year when he was ten, to hike across the Gates of the Arctic, but then he became sick. He got better for a month, but he had an attack of pancreatic bleeding while we were hiking in Drift Creek. I think he bled internally, dying two hours later when we reached the crest of the final ridge leading out to the trailhead.

I was in shock for three days, the same way someone would be if they had lost a human companion. I couldn't eat, and I would sit staring out the window making soft sighing noises each time I took a deep breath. Jonny was with me through lonely times when I didn't have any close friends or family around me, like when I was living in a stuffy apartment working a boring, assembly-line job making computer wafers for a Korean company that treated its employees like second-class citizens. I hated going there every day because the work seemed pointless and didn't contribute to bettering the condition of wilderness or wild animals on any level, and it took up all my time, so I couldn't go hiking whenever I wanted. The big, drab building didn't have windows to look out while I worked, preventing my dreaming of far-away forests and unexplored peaks. There was just the fluorescent hissing of bright, artificial lights hanging over my head twelve hours a day. It made me feel like a forgotten slave, locked away to live out my days in the humdrum misery of an anthropocentric society. And every day I walked up a long concrete walkway with cold steel railings, like I was marching to my ill-fated doom under the hand of a draconian ruler. I marched in slowly—head slumped down, feet shuffling, almost mentally beaten—knowing this kind of life would mean certain death for me. I began experiencing panic attacks while working there. I went to work under my own free will, though, because I couldn't figure out another way to make a living.

Jonny waited inside my dreary apartment for me all day until I returned home after work. He was always happy. I don't think he knew any other way to be. His zeal and physical fervor set a significant example. I wanted to act more like Jonny: happy, carefree, and willing to jump the largest gullies in a single leap. I thought I could be like that if I went to see the remotest corners of the earth.

After a year working at the computer factory, I quit just like that. Then I moved out of my apartment to drive up to Alaska with Jonny. My coworkers all asked me what I planned to do. I made up some conventional reason like I was going back to college or that I had a new job lined up in Corvallis, but really I wanted to just tell them that I planned on living, man, living.

Jonny and I never got to make that trip to Alaska, and I was lost for a couple of months after Jonny's death. But I had friends around me this time and soon afterward I decided to get two puppies, both from the same litter so they wouldn't be lonely. I wrote a letter to the woman I got Jonny from ten years earlier, but it came back in the mail with childlike handwriting on the front that read, "This lady is dead." This made me think even more about the frailty of life: human life, animal life, and my own life. It was urgent I get on with the things that made me happy and discard most of the rest, no matter what the cost. I had to get the puppies from a different breeder. My girlfriend Julie and I drove to Doyle, California, to pick them up. I named them Jimmy and Will. They are the same type of large-bodied Airedales that Jonny was, not the shorter American Kennel Club standard type, bred down to look like a cute, shrunken knockoff of the real deal. These are tall old-style hunting dogs that are strong and exuberant, and they do not take it easy on you when they wrestle just because you are wearing your nicest clothes. You have to be ready to play with them when you step into their enclosure because they will bull into you with their entire bodies and knock you around with their heads. They think it's fun.

I walked Jimmy and Will every day, and on weekends we hiked in the mountains. I taught them to pull me on my bicycle so they could get accustomed to pulling a sled. We drove to Drift Creek and often hiked where Jonny died. And as they grew, soon I was thinking about Alaska again. Jimmy and Will would go in Jonny's place.

As a young boy I roamed the hills outside of Roseburg, Oregon. I was drawn to the cover of the oak forests and secluded little valleys of Ramp Canyon. I probably spent a third of my life there. It was an enthralling place when I was young. It had many types of animals I could watch and learn about, such as gray squirrels, deer, raccoons, gopher snakes, and tree frogs. And I always had two dogs. Wilderness and dogs seem to go together, even though dogs are not quite the same as their wild ancestor anymore, the wolf. I'm not quite the same as my wild ancestors anymore, either. It's hard for me to imagine being in wilderness without dogs; I'm never lonely with a dog.

I left Oregon heading for Alaska in late March 2007 with Jimmy and Will riding in the cargo hold of a Boeing 737. From Anchorage heading north, I gazed out the window and watched the great, white emptiness slide by, piece by piece, past my window. Alaska was still gripped in the clutches of ice and snow. It was a crystal white land to every horizon and beyond, and I was just barely beginning to grasp what I had stirred up. In Nome as the plane sat idle on the tarmac to wait out bad weather before heading up to Kotzebue, one of the pilots broadcasted that we might have to return to Anchorage. All the passengers could hear Jimmy and Will howling as if the dogs' lives depended on it. I've never been able to hear dogs howling from the plane's cargo hold before, and I was a little impressed by their voices, ratcheted up several decibels above the range of a normal domesticated mutt. Their piercing voices were one of the features bred into them over the ages for hunting, and no one can stop them when they decide to howl. Their howls are penetrating, yet deep, and will travel great distances through the woods. And their voices can pry through the metal walls of a Boeing jet with ease. I knew Jimmy and Will howled at home sometimes just to say hello, but I wondered how cold it was for them down below. I hoped the pilots could hear them so they would remember that dogs were on board. I worried for Jimmy and Will, and I did not want to return to Anchorage only to make the same flight the next day and expose them to the cold all over again. They were out of my care while I was on the plane, but once on the ground in Kotzebue, I could monitor them carefully. I could always make sure they were playful and warm. Despite their howling, I figured they would pull through with fine spirits, but it was cold outside and they made it quite clear to everyone on board that they wanted out. A half hour later we were in the air again flying for Kotzebue, just a hundred miles away where we would begin our journey across Alaska.

A LAND OF EPIC PROPORTIONS

I've had a map of Alaska for years, displayed on my wall in epic proportions. It doesn't simply display the names of towns and the length of rivers like most maps. It portrays the lowlands and the endless mountains in fine detail and vivid colors, starting with dark green at the lowest elevations where marshes, peat bogs, and woody forests lie, moving to yellow where the mountains begin to take shape, and finally golden brown where the peaks are highest. The Brooks Range is almost completely golden brown as it spans a thousand miles clear across the state horizontally like a corrugated barrier plopped down as if marking the end of the known world. To traverse the Brooks Range, you would have to follow the lay of the land and walk double that distance. The range is excessively wide and forms a subtle horseshoe shape with both east and west ends curving slightly farther north than the middle. Off the map, it's really a world that shifts dangers with the extreme change in seasons, and you would have to be nearly insane to travel there in the dead of winter when biting wind and lung-blistering cold could kill you when your back is turned, and partly a fool to endure the height of the summer mosquito season. I stared at that map a lot, dreaming about the wilds of Alaska and when I was planning my trek across the range.

Only a handful of people are known to have traversed the entire length of the Brooks Range. Most made the trek from east to west. Only a small fraction made the trek in one unbroken push, and even less did it completely on foot. Of all the reading I've done about journeys there, no one traveled the exact route I planned to take. I didn't choose my route because it had never been done before—it may have for all I know. I chose my route because it looked like one of the best ways to connect with villages where I could get food. I couldn't afford a lot of charter planes flying me in food drops. I had to mail my food to villages along the way. I also picked the town of Kotzebue, Alaska, to start; it had a fairly large airport for the size of town it was, where I wouldn't have to connect to a smaller, plane in Anchorage or Fairbanks. I could fly an Alaska Airline jet all the way from Portland, Oregon, to Kotzebue. This meant I didn't have to spend time waiting for connecting flights that would expose my dogs to cold and unfamiliar surroundings longer than necessary.

Curious, I searched the Internet to find out who had traversed the entire range. Dick Griffith had the first documented crossing from 1959 to 1979 traveling west from the village of Kaktovik to Kotzebue by foot, raft, and kayak. Roman Dial was the first person to complete the traverse in one season, traveling from Kaktovik to Kotzebue in 1986 by skis, foot, pack raft, and kayak. He made another partial traverse in 2006, incredibly traveling east from Kivalina to the Dalton Highway in just under twenty-three days. Keith Nyitray, who appeared in the April 1993 issue of *National Geographic*, made the first continuous trek of the entire range, starting from Fort McPherson in the Northwest Territories, Canada, heading west to Kotzebue. He made the journey in about ten months by dogsled, foot, snowshoe, raft, and canoe. He nearly starved to death on the Noatak River and endured a couple of months without seeing another person. I read that article at least a dozen times and often left it on my nightstand to thumb through before I went to sleep. I considered Nyitray's feat the greatest land traverse I had ever heard about. A foot traverse across the Brooks Range lacks the glamour of an expedition to the North Pole or a shot across Greenland because you can't travel nearly as far and there isn't really the danger of crossing vast reaches of ice. But the rainbow of colors on my map alone told me the rough and changing terrain could stop an army in its tracks. For a man alone, it could make him break down in despair. You're also not likely to get much notoriety when you're finished. When you're done you will have to return to the niche in society you came from and it's likely not too many people will give your accomplishment much of a glance. I didn't care too much about that. The Brooks Range was the best frontier I could find, the best place to lose myself.

There were a few more remarkable crossings of the Brooks Range. I thought all of them were nearly impossible. Never did I think I would make it across the entire range in one season, mainly because I knew I was going to have to travel farther between food drops, which meant I would have to carry a larger load and travel slower than if I could have set up a dozen or so drops. There are only a few villages in the Brooks Range where I could mail food to, so I knew my pack was going to weigh close to a hundred pounds at some points, but I went into my journey with the single goal of remaining in wilderness for a few months. I needed some sort of goal to be able to stick it out for more than a couple of weeks. I added the trek so that I would have somewhere to walk toward, a sort of end point to reach, which I didn't really care if I made it to or not. I simply wanted to reach the mountains and learn something about nature and myself. But I planned my trek out thoroughly over a thousand miles across the entire state, just in case the miles rolled by and I found myself doing better than I expected.

I prepared a long time to cross the Brooks Range and the Gates of the Arctic National Park, though most of the time I never realized specifically the long trek I would endure. From as young as ten when I learned that such a place like Alaska still existed in the world, I always had my sights set on it in some way, where rural woods were only a minute fraction of what true wilderness was supposed to be like. I wanted to be good at every aspect of moving through nature. I wanted to be able to sprint through the forest quickly and to run for long distances. I wanted to be flexible, strong, and able to climb trees like a gibbon, and most important, I wanted to develop a phantom-like sense of direction so I could never get lost.

I must have traveled to Alaska about a dozen times from the time I was eighteen until I began my trek. The land acted like a magnet on me and I couldn't stay away. My first trip was when I was eighteen. I drove up to Denali National Park with a mutual friend of my grandfather's. His plan was to drive up and learn how to become a bush pilot. My plan was to hitch a ride with him until I found a suitable place to step off the highway with my backpack and disappear into the backcountry. Well, I did that in Denali, and the reality of the land sank into me. It was mainly the immensity of Alaska and the absolute lack of people that struck me. I was instantly hooked on the place, but I wasn't mentally ready to travel the land yet. There was no place to get more food if I ran out, and no one to help me if I were to get into trouble. The first night alone I was scared, camping in grizzly bear country without any protection at all. I didn't really understand bears then, so it made my trip unnerving. I kept expecting some raging monster to rip through the wall of my tent and tear me to pieces. I didn't understand that bears weren't nearly as dangerous as I had been convinced, and that my hardwired primate brain amplified fears that were only mildly warranted, especially at night, especially alone. Satisfied that I had seen enough to realize that Alaska was the place where I wanted to come back to, I left a few days later and flew home to Oregon with my last $300 in the world. The enchantment of the last frontier had been permanently implanted within me, deeper than I could have imagined.

I conditioned myself to hike off trail, mainly because I always liked slipping through the foliage to get close to the copiousness of nature. And I always knew one day I would be going to some exotic wilderness still smoldering somewhere on the planet where humans had not yet slashed trails or roads across its fertile turf. I wanted to be ready. When I wasn't traipsing off trail in the woods somewhere, I was training fanatically: running, cycling, lifting weights, or climbing trees. I love working out. Sometimes I would lift logs in the woods when I wasn't near a weight room. I think most of the people who traversed the Brooks Range were athletic much of their lives. I can't imagine anyone just one day deciding to go for an extended trek there without having some sort of a physical fitness base and the mental strength that comes after it. Sometimes I had doubts about why I was doing all those things and spending so much time in the woods. But I never once accepted that I could do without wilderness, even when I was a child.

It wasn't until I was about thirty that my specific preparation for trekking across the Brooks Range took shape. I scanned a lot of maps over several years, always searching for the most efficient route. I pored over highly detailed maps, mile by mile, until I had a navigable route plotted out all the way across the state. I not only chose my route out of convenience, but also by picking the areas I liked the most. The route I finally mapped out for my 2007 adventure was mostly unique. I would be heading from west to east unlike most other adventurers whom I had read about who had traversed from east to west. I wouldn't be floating any major rivers, either. Adventurers who travel east to west have the time-saving luxury of floating a couple hundred miles on either the Noatak River or the Kobuk River when they are thin and aching for the finish.

I wanted to spend much of my time in the taiga forests south of the Brooks Range crest. I craved those woody areas of the globe. My plan was to start in the village of Kotzebue on the northwest coast of Alaska in late March. I had to start that time of year when the weather was brutally cold so I could ski up the Kobuk River towing a sled. I had to start when the water along the coast was still frozen so I could cross it. Skiing part of the way would seem like a more rounded adventure and a great way to get in better shape before the torturous days of hiking began to beat me down. It would be faster to ski on a major river than it would be to hike across barren woodland, especially with the dogs helping me pull my gear. I could travel critical distance early in the season before the snow melted. To cross all of Alaska on foot in one season, I most likely would have to ski, snowshoe, or dogsled part of it. I didn't want to float any rivers for a great distance. It seemed like cheating to me, not a pure on-foot adventure like I wanted.

I could have chosen the Noatak River to ski on, but it's farther north where there are no trees, and where the weather is more severe. And there aren't any villages along the Noatak once it gets away from the coast. I thought the Kobuk River would be a safer route and contain more forest cover. It would feel more like home to me while I was exploring that far-reaching land.

After the Kobuk River I planned to get more supplies in the village of Ambler, and I would then turn northeast up the Ambler River. I had to reach the headwaters of the Ambler River past all gnarled trees before the river thawed and broke apart in late April. At the headwaters I planned to begin hiking. It would be the point where I could begin traveling light and fast. Well, I hoped so anyway, but no one can ever be totally prepared for the harsh, uneven ground of Alaska.

Next I would hike over Nakmaktuak Pass to the Noatak River and cross it. Then I would head up Midas Creek and continue east on the Nigu River until I joined up with the Killik River. I would walk down the Killik for a few days and turn right onto Easter Creek, following it for several days until I hit the John River. Then I would follow the John into the village of Anaktuvuk Pass, where I was scheduled to meet Julie, my brothers Steve and Mike, my nephew Aaron, and two other friends. Then we would all hike to the village of Wiseman on the Dalton Highway together.

Trekking from Ambler to Anaktuvuk Pass was about 300 miles across some of the remotest country in the state, and the world. I could expect to be alone the entire time. I couldn't find anything specific about people hiking all the way across that region, just general information about backpacking in Alaska and about the hardcore adventurers who had traversed the entire state. When most people go backpacking or hunting in the Brooks Range, like most of Alaska's backcountry, they hire a private plane to fly them in and pick them up when they're done. The distances are just too daunting. But I wasn't going to do that. I was going to walk in from about as far away as I could get. In the Gates of the Arctic I knew I would be crossing an unknown, blurry void where I didn't know the terrain. I had to study the maps to find a way through for myself. There were no guide books and no one was going to show me the way.

The Dalton Highway would be the likely end point of my journey, but in the back of my mind I hoped somehow I would make incredible time so I could continue east toward Arctic Village. Then I would proceed to the Canadian border. But that would be an epic feat and I was pretty sure I would be a bag of bones by the time I reached Anaktuvuk Pass. I concentrated on the first half of Alaska, from Kotzebue to the Dalton Highway. I knew that distance would take at least three months.

Three months before my departure, I spent hours a day at Julie's house studying my maps, searching for the best gear on the Internet and loading food and gear into my boxes out in her garage. I got my journals ready and planned to log my miles as an estimate, following the curves of the river valleys. I had practiced using a GPS (global positioning system that uses satellites to pinpoint your location) unit and a compass before, which I would be bringing, so navigating would be more automatic when I got out there.

The first boxes I had were the largest and contained the most gear. I had to send items that I needed for coping with extreme cold and ice. One of the boxes I would send to Kotzebue had nothing but clothes. I found most of my clothes over a period of about six months. I always thought it was silly to spend a lot of money on clothes. Some high-tech gear is overrated and way overpriced. I found thick wool socks for a dollar a pair from an outdoors store in Portland. I found some expedition-weight bib pants there, too, to wear under my wind pants. I found a pile jacket, with a raised collar (critical for cold weather), from the Goodwill store in Corvallis, and several sweaters from the Salvation Army store in Roseburg for about three dollars apiece. Except for a T-shirt that I would wear in June, none of my clothes were made of cotton. They were either wool or some other synthetic fiber that wouldn't absorb too much moisture. I bought only a few items brand new specifically for this trip. The rest I scrounged up from friends, borrowed, or bought at secondhand stores. One new item was a four-season tent, and another a pair of ski boots. I knew I needed the best boots I could find to keep my toes from freezing. The toes are always the first part of the body to fail in freezing temperature. They're small and so far from the vital core of the body. I had to devote extra care to my feet. My boots were heavy-duty backcountry boots, with a thick insulated lining and a hard, outer plastic shell to keep out even the tiniest draft. Where you have to start out each morning from a tent in icy Alaska cold, you can never have boots that are too warm.

My brother Mike gave me two pairs of skis for my trip. One pair would be a backup. They were basically older style telemark skis, with a free heel so I could simulate walking. The skis were wide enough so I could manage the uneven snow surface without losing my balance, but still narrow and lightweight enough so I could make good time. Your ankles tend to bend over sideways on skis that are too thin, so you have to find the right width. On perfect flat snow I could use really narrow skis to make good time, but I would never find ideal conditions where I was going.

I had to be creative with my food since it would take up most of the weight. I packed a lot of lentil beans in bulk and stayed away from too many freeze-dried dinners. They're ludicrously expensive, plus the packaging material would weigh too much on a trek where each saved ounce was precious. I had to be able to carry a month's worth of food on my back once I started the hiking part of my journey, and the dogs had to carry about twenty-five pounds each in their packs. The main staple foods I packed were lentil beans, oats, large blocks of cheese, noodles, cocoa, coffee, powdered milk, and piles of snack food. I also packed toilet paper, matches, maps for the next leg of the journey, and mosquito repellent and sunblock on the later sections when the weather warmed up. I also packed toothpaste, dental floss, fishing line for fishing and for sewing up my clothes, and an extra shirt and hiking pants for the later sections.

As much as I stared at maps and prepared, I knew it would never be enough. The land looked immense even on my colorful wall map where instead of using two fingers, I had to use two hands to measure the distance between points. And there weren't many names of the land features, mainly wide blank spaces of drawn-in creases and folds in the mountains and varying degrees of extravagant color. I would be hiking through regions where no modern human had ever traveled and likely would come across obstacles that I would have to go around to get by, and in the process lose valuable time and energy. And there were going to be the countless miles of indestructible mounds of grass called tussocks to slow me down and frustrate me like nothing else. I knew I would face excruciating loneliness and hours of physical exertion. I planned to take a shotgun with me, but I hoped to avoid violent confrontations with large animals. I would bring it just in case so I could sleep better at night. I worried about moose or wolves attacking my dogs, and of course some of the largest bears on the planet. To prepare for them, I figured I needed to know how to get along with them and stay out of their way. Everywhere else was mine for wandering. My eyes glimmered with joy when I came upon so much wild emptiness on such a small map. I knew the more uncharted space I saw on my wall map, the more there would actually be ahead when I got on the ground. I couldn't wait.

THE NORTHWEST COAST

Fierce winds and bitter cold batter the northwest coast of Alaska
through the month of March, making life almost impossible here.
I don't quite appreciate the weather's severity until I step off the plane
and feel the arctic air scouring my body. Except for the arctic fox,
and perhaps a rare polar bear roaming in off the frozen sea, no large
animals live out in the frigid air. Even ravens haven't shown up yet.
It's far too cold.

Kotzebue is an isolated town on the tip of the Baldwin Peninsula, on the northwest coast of Alaska. It's built on a large spit of land
that juts out into Kotzebue Sound on the edge of the Chukchi Sea,
dangling at the waves' mercy. The region has a long cultural history
of being settled by the Inupiat Eskimo. I don't think Kotzebue is an
Eskimo name, but it is an Eskimo village. It's named after the Polish
explorer Otto von Kotzebue who discovered the village around 1816.
Though most of the residents are Inupiat Eskimo, I'm certain people
of other origins live here now as well, moving in from other parts of
Alaska and the lower forty-eight states, like Caucasians and perhaps
other people indigenous to Alaska like the Yupik Eskimo. Even in the
dead of winter the native people walk around without hats on and
bare-hand everything, even icy steel. If it weren't for their incredible

tolerance for wind and cold, the rest of humanity just might forsake this place. But these people have made this part of Alaska their home, despite the hardships. Like most Alaskans they have adopted snowmobiles as their primary mode of transportation and ride them around with the throttle topped out. Everywhere they go it seems to be at full speed, and the younger generation has taken to racing back and forth across the frozen ice, like it's the main activity in their lives. I wonder if they are losing touch with their culture and with wilderness by rushing their sedentary lives too much. It's ironic how sedentary people always act hastier than nomadic people. I cringe both from the cold and from the mistake of forsaking nature.

The people here don't seem to feel the bone-stabbing effects of the cold, and they can retreat into their modern houses and warm themselves. The appeal of our industrial, gadget-filled world has reached even this place—so far out on the edge of the North American continent that it seems like it could fall off into the sea and disappear. As for gadgets, I'm carrying a satellite phone with me just in case I get into trouble and want to return to the modern world myself.

When I walk off the plane in about ten-degree weather, I know Jimmy and Will must be suffering from chills, so I go inside the airport terminal and look for them. I find them sitting outside the front door of the terminal garage in their kennels. When I get to them they are distressed and shivering, so I drag their kennels inside the alcove of the rear door where it's at least ten degrees warmer and out of the wind. Then I collect all my gear off the conveyor belt and call a van to pick us up. I have a lot of winter gear, so it takes me several trips to lug it all outside where my ride will come. I feel a social phobia wakening within me, because the terminal is small and crowded with a lot of people standing around. They are patient and wait for their baggage as I weave my way through them with my gear. I feel like a novice, battered by the cold, and I never make eye contact even though I'm taller than most of them. I get the feeling these people are scrutinizing me and I begin to second-guess the journey I'm about to begin. It seems so extreme. I don't think people around here undertake adventures like this anymore. My innate restlessness and my undying urge to be on the move make me feel inferior.

My ride arrives and I load Jimmy and Will into the back of the van. The driver helps me load the kennels, but I don't let the dogs out yet. When I do they will want to run around for a while, and it will be hard to get them back in. It's better to wait a few minutes longer until I get to where I plan to camp. I have the driver take me a mile out of town where there is less noise. Even though there is only about a mile of road in the town, the driver appears mildly stressed and rushes to pick up and drop off passengers. The van passengers talk to each other quietly like they are acquaintances. I can't quite understand what they are saying, and I'm not sure if they are talking in their native language or some form of accented English that I can't decipher. An old native woman sits in the front seat on the passenger side and mumbles to the young man driving like she is a sage giving advice. She doesn't look at him, just out the front window, but the man reacts as if he understands everything. I don't know what she is saying. They all talk so softly, which is kind of a nice change when I think about it for a few minutes. There's no gaudy talk and no one aggressively controlling the conversation. There's simply the mono-tonic speech that I really don't need to understand. When we get well out of town and everyone else has exited, I have the driver let me out. Then I unload my gear and the dogs. The snow crackles beneath my feet. I let the dogs sniff around to warm up and to relieve themselves. Their breaths leave two rising columns of vapor as they thread their way over the white, glistening tundra.

I erect the tent right away, about fifty yards from the main road. It's a two-person, four-season tent made by Marmot. It's made for extreme weather, and without it I couldn't survive. The light wind that blows here constantly cuts right through me, and I'm concerned that it could increase at any time. I make sure to use several pieces of cord to tie off the middle section of the tent, to help stabilize it if the wind does kick up. I can't risk having any broken tent poles or torn fabric out here. I would have preferred to stay in a motel my first night here to adjust to the cold shock, but there were none that allowed dogs inside. I can't just leave Jimmy and Will out in this cold; they would freeze to death. Their fur isn't thick enough to withstand this kind of cold without a tent. It will be better after they acclimate, but I keep them inside the tent with me at night to keep them warm and comfortable. The first half of this trek depends on them remaining strong and healthy because they will be doing most of the pulling. They will be the main driving engines that will help me pull about 200 pounds of food and winter gear in two separate sleds. I know even before I start that my journey will not be possible without them. I could pull the sleds by myself, but it would be much slower. I have so much gear to cope with the ice and cold, that the weight I have to carry seems ridiculous. For instance, I have a snow shovel for digging out a place for my tent each day and an ice axe for chopping ice from the river to melt for drinking. I will also be getting many more clothes and large quantities of cooking fuel before I set out.

March 21, 2007

Today I move my tent closer to town and set it up underneath the bridge where it's more protected from the wind, and also so I have a shorter distance to haul my food back from the post office. Since I'm not accustomed to the cold yet, I underestimate its savagery and begin to stumble before I get close to town. It's a rude awakening how it can knock you back and put your life in peril within a few minutes' time. As I hike back toward town hauling all my gear, I get chilled and my toes start to ache. It's only out of necessity that I decide to pitch my tent under the bridge. This is as far back toward town as I can get before I get into serious trouble. I lose my ability to function properly. My toes sting and I can't get them warm no matter how fast I walk. I have to concentrate and work through the cold to set up my tent. My fingers aren't working right. I have to unfold the poles and shove them into their tent sleeves while wearing my gloves as much as possible. I take a minute when I'm not quite done to pull each of my fingers out of the finger section of my gloves and curl them up into a fist while still inside my gloves. When my fingers all come into contact with each other I clutch them together to warm them up a little, and this gives me a few more minutes of time to work before my fingers go completely numb. But once I get the tent set up, I hurry in with the dogs to warm up. Once the doors are zipped and I'm out of the icy wind, I begin to feel better.

Later in the day, because my tent is set up and I know I have a place to hurry back to for warmth, I risk walking to the grocery store. I pet the dogs as I tie them up and out of the wind. The store sits off the ground on large beams, so Jimmy and Will can lay underneath where there is dry dirt. I walk up metal-grated steps and enter through double doors, which lead me to a lobby before I enter two more doors that lead into the main store. The air inside the lobby has to be about forty degrees warmer. My glasses fog up instantly, and the warmth causes me to overheat. I yank off my balaclava and stocking cap, and I unzip my thick jacket before I enter the final doors. The store is fairly large, so as I search up and down the aisles I start to sweat. I have to stop and take off my jacket.

I buy two gallons of white gas for the stove, a loaf of cheap bread, and a gallon of milk. "Going on a camping trip," I say to the cashier, but he doesn't respond, like he doesn't hear me or care. I wouldn't want to work a full-time job here. It wouldn't allow me time to explore the wilderness around. After paying the cashier I put my jacket and hats back on before exiting the final doors. I move around the building to where the dogs are. They start sniffing my bags as I pack them up. "Come on, guys," I say. "We got to go." Then I grab the dogs, shuffle back over to my camp, and get inside the tent. I give the dogs most of the milk right away before it freezes, which it would do if I left it out overnight. It's that cold, perhaps ten below now.

March 22, 2007

I sleep in today, snuggled in my two sleeping bags like a cocoon. I remain in my sleeping bags for twelve straight hours, nearly content to wait here forever until the spring thaw arrives. I don't want to face the cold outside, or even the cold inside my tent. The thermometer hanging on the frost-covered wall of the tent reads twenty degrees and I know it must be a lot colder outside. Around one in the afternoon, the temperature on the wall of my tent where the sunlight is hitting reaches forty degrees; however, the corners are still encased in thick frost from the vapors in our breathing all night. I begin to stir in my sleeping bag and after a few minutes I sit up, brush some flaky ice crystals off my outer sleeping bag, and prepare to hike over to the post office from my frozen camp. The dogs don't move a muscle and stay curled up under their sleeping bags until I'm ready to leave the tent. Here cold weather takes on a whole new dimension. If you don't prepare for it on a trip like this, it could kill you when you aren't paying attention.

I get fully dressed, boots and all, before I go outside. Then I haul my two sleds to the post office and find that all my packages are there. There is one box filled with lentils, oats, and a few freeze-dried dinners; one box with sixty pounds of dog food; one box of assorted meals that all require adding water; one box of energy bars and snacks; and one box of warm arctic clothes. I'm grateful to get the expedition-weight bib pants. They prevent any cool drafts from reaching the skin of my lower back since they reach so far up from my waist. This also helps keep my thermal shirts tucked in and snug against my body.

I hurry around to the back of the post office where I have the dogs secured out of the wind. They stand there motionless, waiting, but when they see me coming around the corner, they start wagging their tails and jumping up and down. Jimmy likes to throw his head back and forth like a puppy. It's his way of inviting play and saying hi. Will never does this. He jumps up and down like he's on a trampoline. "Okay guys, okay guys," I say in a pleasant tone, "we're going, we're going. Don't worry." Then they jump on me and I pat them a couple of times before they calm down. I load up the boxes into my sleds, tie them down with some cord, and start towing them back to my tent. I saunter over the frozen bay along the bridge and let Jimmy and Will wrestle as we walk. They can play-fight with each other when they are standing still, walking a few miles per hour or running at a dead sprint. To them it doesn't matter where they are or what they are doing. They want to wrestle all the time, like no other dogs I've seen before.

They're handling the cold well; as long as they're moving they stay warm and exuberant. I keep them on a long rope so they can romp around without running off to chase other dogs. Their capacity for play and their vigorous nature amazes me. Nothing seems to dampen their high spirits. When they see other dogs they want to run right over to them. If they were not on leashes, they would jump on the other dogs like they had known them their entire lives. The only problem is that other dogs usually get scared and freak out over an Airedale's rough style. And if those dogs react aggressively back toward Jimmy and Will, who only want to play, they might start fighting. Airedales have a history of being used to hunt bears and mountain lions. Their lack of fear toward bears is one reason I picked them, but it could also get them into trouble. Airedales are well adapted for fighting and hunting, with huge teeth and a long muzzle that can clamp down over most other dogs' muzzles. Airedales are flexible, with lightning-fast reflexes. They are quite strong for their size and have heads and necks that look disproportionately larger than the rest of their bodies. When they rush in for an attack, they always lead with their front legs up in an attempt to knock the other dog off balance before they risk bringing in their face and mouth for biting. Airedales approach situations with little fear. They don't hesitate at all when they approach another dog or a wild animal. Wrestling with them is hard enough, and often the mere weight of their teeth and jaws will create a bruise on my arm.

Back at the bridge I unload all my supplies and put them into the tent where I can organize them in warmth. I melt snow on my stove so Jimmy and Will can drink. I have to do this at least twice a day because everything is frozen. I keep melting snow until the dogs have quenched their thirst and don't want to drink anymore. Then I pour the remainder of the water into a bottle, and during the night I stuff it inside my sleeping bag so it won't freeze and I can use it in the morning. I also put my stove in my sleeping bag; otherwise it will jam up with ice particles and not function in the morning when I'm groggy, chilled, and need to get it working quickly. At negative five to twenty degrees Fahrenheit I have no patience for a shoddy stove while I'm trying to wake up.

In the evening it gets dark around ten and we get ready to sleep. The night never gets completely dark, though. There is always some dim light giving a hint to the coming summer when for a brief period in late June, the sun will never set. Snowmobiles whiz by throughout the night. Many of these people are up at the oddest hours because they don't really have to go to work the next morning, and late in the evening is when the weather is the calmest. One of the noisy machines drives by my tent about every fifteen minutes. This is the only point where they can get to the other side of the road without having to drive on bare pavement. Here they can simply drive on the frozen water as they go under the bridge. I don't mind the people so much. If I were to get into trouble there would be someone around to go to for help.

Before going to sleep I write in my journal. I have to write with my gloves on because even inside my tent the temperature is too cold to expose my fingers for long. I wear three layers of thermal underwear, three pairs of wool socks, and a thick balaclava on my head, and a fleece hat over that. I also have on a vest and pile jacket, but still I'm a little cold. The dogs are wearing their jackets, too; the ones that my mother had made just for this trip. The dogs also nestle under an extra sleeping bag that I brought for them. I will give it to someone in a village in a few weeks along with other cold-weather gear when the temperature warms up for good. The entire floor of my tent is covered with two layers of pads to insulate us from the ice beneath. This is crucial when dealing with this kind of cold; a great amount of body heat can be lost from direct contact with ice beneath. I think it will be twenty below zero outside tonight and in the teens inside my tent. Occasionally the dogs get up during the night to change their positions, and in the process they uncover themselves. I'll wake to feel them shivering against my legs, so I have to rouse myself to cover them back up. These dogs rarely whimper, so the only way I can tell if they are cold is if their bodies are shaking. If I don't cover them back up, the cold might wear on them during the night, making the journey a little harder for them than it needs to be. I want them to be able to have fun on this trek, at least most of the time. I will need them as fresh as possible in the coming days, too, so keeping them warm, hydrated, fed, and well rested is important if I want them to pull my sleds with me. It's critical if I want to trek across Alaska.

I hope Jimmy and Will will grow strong physically and mentally from our journey. Most of the time I want them to feel free—while I watch them carefully—and to know how to maneuver across a wild landscape. I think their nature will become more animated and amiable from all the exercise and sniffing around they'll get to do. It's a locked-up sedentary life I'm hoping to eliminate from their lives, as from my own.

March 23, 2007

Today I try to light my stove outside, but it doesn't work. The cold wind extinguishes my lighter flame before I can get it to my stove to ignite the fuel. I get out my windproof matches, strike one, and put it next to the burner, but the stove doesn't ignite. I strike several matches and put them next to the burner one at a time, but still my stove doesn't ignite. I fiddle with it for about an hour before coming to the conclusion that I can't take my chances on a junky stove like this. I want to throw it down and smash it, but I put it back inside my tent instead. I walk into town to call Julie and have her order me a new stove and a windproof lighter (it's like a small blowtorch). I must have one that is designed to operate in severe cold, one that is designed to spill out liquid fuel onto the burner so I can light the fuel and allow the stove to heat up. The heat then will allow the pressurized fuel in the line to start burning as it hits the outside air.

Julie handles all the logistics back home that I can't do here. She is the woman I thought I would never find in my life. She is the anchor to which all threads of my journey are attached. Without her it would be hard for me to complete my trek. I can't depart until I have two stoves that function. To lose both my stoves or to have them break would be the end of me, because I wouldn't be able to melt snow to drink, and building fires in the brutal wind would be nearly impossible. Besides too much wind, there isn't any wood that is easily accessible. Only inside my tent can I stay warm enough to manage the arctic conditions when I'm not moving.

After warming up in the post office lobby while making my phone call, I mosey back to my camp under the bridge. There is no need to rush. I want to stay warm, but I don't want to sweat, either. Moisture next to my skin will leave me chilled to the bone. I feel the warm blood oozing through my toes so I can slow down and still retain the warmth. When I first go outside, only the first twenty minutes require some intense exertion to warm up my extremities; after that I can slow to a comfortable pace.

Knowing that tonight is going to be bitter cold again, I pull my sleeping bags out of my tent to let the condensation evaporate into the dry, arctic air. They dry well enough while the wind is blowing, even with temperatures below zero. One good thing about cold air is that it usually has low humidity, and this benefits me in a number of ways. My clothes don't retain as much moisture and my skin doesn't retain sweat for long, so I don't get very dirty. My glasses don't fog up, my sleeping bags stay fairly dry, and the inside of my tent doesn't hold as much vapor. Wood, when I start using it to build fires, will be normally dry and easy to burn.

I break down all the boxes my food arrived in and lay them on the bottom of my tent, under my pads, to insulate us even more against the frozen ground. Then I build a two-foot snow wall all around my tent and put chunks of snow on the bottom parts of my rain fly where it wavers in the wind. This should protect my tent from the wind and give me at least five more degrees of warmth inside. "Just like paradise," I say when I'm done.

I got Jonny eleven years ago with the intention of taking this journey, or something like it. He arrived by plane from Alabama, numb with loneliness from being uprooted from his family. I wish I had driven out to get him. I could have spent a few days getting to know him before I took him away from all that was familiar. He was only eleven weeks old and almost completely black, but as he grew older, the tan around his shoulders and over his legs began to stand out.

I worked several odd jobs over the years and attempted to get to quite a few wild places on earth during my years with Jonny. When I traveled north, I took Jonny with me. When I went south to tropical climates, I left Jonny home in Oregon with friends or family. I went places most people have never even heard of, like the Tama Abu Range of Sarawak on the island of Borneo and the Mackenzie Mountains in northern Canada. I had a difficult time seeing journeys through, though, because often when I would get to a place I would discover that it wasn't remote enough for me. Part of the forested habitat would be badly fragmented and all the people would be too dependent on a capitalist economy, not on their traditional mode of gathering food. I traveled to Peru three times. I kayaked both along the Amazon River outside of Iquitos and up the Los Piedras River in the Madre de Dios region to search for the Yora Indians.

I searched for the nomadic Penan Indians in Borneo, walking alone in the mountains for several weeks through pure, primordial forests that boggled my understanding of nature. Pliable vines with sharp hooks would latch on to my clothes as I tried to slide by, and hordes of leeches held firmly to my skin. I followed old signs that the Penan had been there—their overgrown trails and abandoned shelters—but I never found them. I returned the following year to hike into an even more remote region of Borneo's mountains. I was lost for three days and meandered along densely clad, jungle ridges somewhere near the headwaters of the Adang River. I had to climb high up into trees to look for ridgelines off in the distance to figure out where I was, just like I had practiced in Oregon. Sometimes I felt so disoriented that I thought my compass had to be broken.

I went to Venezuela to hike in the Guiana Highlands, hoping to find the nomadic Hoti tribe, but I barely got away from the Orinoco River before I turned back. I boated across Brazil, from Peru to the ocean, thinking about finding the Awa Guaja tribe near the end of my trip, but I got mugged in Belem by two young men. It was my boiling frustration of traveling across the Amazon jungle for two weeks in a boat loaded with obnoxious Brazilians and not getting out into the rain forest that made me so heated. Normally mild mannered, I was like a bomb waiting to go off. I drove my muggers away after I pummeled one man's jaw with my fist. They lost their nerve about robbing me and once I calmed down I lost my nerve about traveling to outlying regions of Brazil with so many hostile and unpredictable people around.

Jonny and I traveled to Alaska a number of times. I resolved to finally find and spend a long period of time roaming in a wild land, surviving on my own like humans had done for a million years before. I wanted to fish in the rivers and lakes, and collect berries in the summer, but mostly I simply wanted to hike across the unmolested land, day after day, free to go whereever I chose. Alaska seemed to be my last chance to immerse myself in wilderness, and after having spent many months in Alaska over twenty years, living there and traveling there, this was going to be my best adventure in nature yet.

TOO COLD TO WAIT

In 1980 Jimmy Carter signed into law the Alaska National Lands Conservation Act, which designated federal protection for nearly 80 million acres of public land. It's a mind-boggling amount of land, dwarfing many states and some countries. It would take me years to walk across that much land. On my trek I will travel through the Gates of the Arctic National Park, the Kobuk Valley National Park, and the Noatak National Preserve, which are all parts of this protected land. The law Carter created was controversial, as development could have been profitable, but being public land it belongs to everyone in the country, and the only way to ensure everyone gets a stake in it, including people not yet born, was to protect it. I used to believe that all of Alaska, whether protected by law or not, was still in a pristine state. I thought once I got away from Anchorage or Fairbanks and the few major highways, I would find an untarnished land everywhere I went. And when I was eighteen that seemed true, so I didn't really pay much attention to which areas were designated by law as wilderness. I figured anywhere in Alaska I went would be good. There didn't seem to be any need for wilderness protection, but I'm learning that the escalating transformation sweeping the modern world is even having its effect on Alaska.

March 25, 2007

The air temperature outside still hovers around zero degrees Fahrenheit, but during the night it gets much colder. As the morning progresses into the afternoon and the sun's rays hit my tent, little ice particles that have plastered the inside walls from my breathing during the night begin to float down like a light snow flurry. The particles that fall are crispy and dry, and they soon evaporate. There is plenty of oxygen inside my tent from the cold air, so I'm comfortable with my tent sealed up, with every vent zipped shut to keep out the cold. I run my little iso/butane stove inside to boil water, but this is dangerous. I can get away with it because I know this stove well, but I don't recommend it to anyone unless they are freezing to death and there is no other option to get warm. I'm careful not to knock it over and I operate it for only a short time; the oxygen level in my tent decreases as the toxic fumes increase. Iso/butane stoves have their advantages sometimes. They are often simpler to operate than a white gas stove, and they are often smaller. Iso/butane stoves use pressurized canisters so they don't require any priming with a pump. The mixture inside the canister is a liquid when it's under pressure, but once it hits the outside air it turns into a flammable gas. It makes for easy ignition, and you can light them even when your fingers are almost numb.

The next night is also cold and I wake up with numb toes. I'm not sure how long they have been that way. I get worried about frostbite. Since I'm already in both of my sleeping bags and under a tarp with four pairs of socks on, I'm not sure what more I can do to warm them up. I rub my feet vigorously across the floor of my tent for twenty minutes while they are in my sleeping bags, but it has no real effect. Then I take my socks off and check for any discoloration. To my relief they appear normal. I massage my bare feet with my hands and the warmth from my hands transfers to my feet. Then I run my fingers between each toe to get rid of all moisture and dirt, which also helps warm them. I find this is the most important procedure I can do to prevent frozen feet. I do it at least twice a day, once when I wake up in the morning and once before going to sleep at night.

I sit for a while fully clothed and make decaffeinated coffee with cocoa added in. I relish the steamy-warm drink and the chocolate taste here, but at home I never drink cocoa. Here I'll drink any warm beverage I have without feeling guilty. I don't worry about gaining weight or rotting my teeth; I care about eliminating my immediate discomforts. Soon, all the normal feeling returns to my feet. I can feel the warm blood surging from my feet into my toes, and I begin to feel grateful that I'm going to be fine. I also learn that sitting up helps warm my feet. Maybe this allows blood to flow into my toes more easily. I run my iso/butane stove for a couple minutes longer than I really need to just because the heat feels so good. I can't go outside until my whole body is warm. It's difficult to keep feet warm outside if you start out with cold feet. I need them to be warm once I get outside because it will take me some time to create ample body heat from exercise. And that basically is what keeps my toes warm. If I just stood still for an hour out in the cold, they would go numb. I start keeping my boots inside my outer sleeping bag at night so they will be thawed out in the morning. The number of items I must keep in my sleeping bag at night so they won't freeze up grows: my headlamp, my boots, my water bottle filled with water, my watch, and my stove. I don't mind all these things in my sleeping bag, as long as it means they will function in the morning. But I wonder if soon there won't be any room for me.

March 27, 2007

My new stove arrives, and I'm able to leave Kotzebue and those crazy snowmobiles tearing around. I pack up my food and tent to get ready to leave. It takes me a long time, and I have to get back in the tent twice to warm up my feet before I can take it down. Taking down the tent is always my final task before departing in such cold weather. Once I make the commitment to take down my tent I work fast. Then I load it up and finish lashing the sleds. As soon as everything is loaded and ready, I hurry off to get the warm blood rushing through my veins so I can warm my toes. If my toes don't get warm in thirty minutes, I have to stop, erect my tent, and get back inside to warm up. I can't risk getting frozen feet when I'm traveling alone. If the air were warmer I would probably be able to take my time and think about where I'm headed, and how dangerous the cold will be. The only reason I'm able to head out on my own at all is because I don't have time to think about it. It's too cold to sit around pondering the future. It's too cold to wait. It's too cold to think.

The way we travel is called skijoring. I think it has Scandinavian origins. I put a special harness on each dog, one that has a loop far down their back—not up toward their shoulders like cheaper harnesses—where I connect a stretchable cord from my hip belt to their harness. Jimmy and Will travel side by side. They travel in front of my skis a few yards while I travel in front of my two sleds. I also have two aluminum poles that fasten from my hip belt to my first sled, to stop it when I stop without it running up on me from behind.

I haul a heavy load and I'm a little shaky on skis; I haven't skied any this year. I used to ski every weekend years ago in the Cascade Mountains of Oregon. I got pretty good and did a few ski races, too, though backcountry skiing was my favorite. This kind of skiing is far different and it takes me a couple of hours to get accustomed to the shock cords the dogs pull with. They stretch out or snap back each time the dogs adjust their efforts. They pull strongly now since they are so fresh and fit. Each time they reach the maximum distance they can stretch the cords, I launch forward behind them as the cords snap back. The dogs haven't figured out how to keep a constant tug on their cords yet. They pull as fast and as hard as they can until their cords fully stretch out and they are forced to slow up as the tension becomes too great. Then I shoot forward as they hold their ground. The tension decreases and the dogs launch off again. "Easy guys, easy," I say, but they don't listen very well. This goes on for about fifteen minutes at the start of the first few days, but eventually the dogs learn how to anticipate the tension increase and decrease. Then they start to modify their efforts to make their pulling steadier and easier. I like to watch Will just before the sleds and I begin to shoot forward. I can almost see his mind working as his body tenses up right before the decrease in tension. He gets excited when it decreases because he loves to be able to run faster for a few strides until the tension builds back up. And he never looks back at me unless he is dead tired. A fresh animal scent on the snow in front of the dogs, or a scent carried to them by the wind, will excite them both. Then they will sprint forward like rockets, and all sense of pace and energy efficiency is forgotten. They pull like mad until they either reach the source of the scent, or it goes away. I let them run until their hearts are content at times like these, but when they want to veer off to the side I keep us on course by leaning in the opposite direction they are pulling. The snow is icy and hard, and it's difficult to keep my skis from slipping out from under me when the dogs are yanking on me. Sometimes they pull me over. The tension on their cords becomes too great for them and they realize that to decrease the tension they must get back in front of me. It's amazing how quickly they learn. And they seldom want to go back behind me. They don't want to go where they have already been. I don't blame them.

We follow snowmobile tracks four miles out onto the Baldwin Peninsula, which is a long piece of land that reaches over a hundred miles out from mainland Alaska. This time of year it looks like a flat, icy wasteland, with only an occasional shrub poking through the ice to convince me I'm on land at all. Every direction I look is level, frozen ground to the skyline. The last twenty or thirty miles of the peninsula is about ten to twenty miles wide and on a world map it looks like a skinny thumb with a fat tip protruding northwest into the dark blue sea. I plan to angle off this peninsula and head east over to the Kobuk River Delta, where I will follow the Kobuk River a hundred miles inland to the village of Ambler.

Halfway through our first day, a dog musher out on his daily training run comes up from behind. I don't have time to react so I can move off the trail to let him pass. His dogs run into us from behind, and Jimmy and Will lunge into the middle of them. As they turn they pull me over while I'm strapped to my sled and skis. I expect the man to apologize for running up on me. As I fight to get my ankles untwisted while they are still strapped to my skis, I can't see what is happening behind me. "Control your dogs," the man yells at me. I'm frustrated about having fallen over while still strapped to my gear. "Control your dogs," he yells again, which by now agitates me and sets me off. I think he expects me to apologize for being in his way.

"You ran into me," I yell back. I give him a stern look and wait for his response, but he doesn't say anything else. He manages to get his dogs past us as I hold Jimmy and Will. Then he stops about forty feet in front of us to untangle his dog lines and takes off again. Jimmy and Will don't stand still to wait for other dogs to pass like I'm sure the man is used to. Jimmy and Will are large terriers, and terriers won't stand passively to watch a dozen panting huskies gallop by. They always want to be in the thick of things, to get up close to other dogs. We follow the man's trail for a while and Jimmy and Will run hard while the fresh scent of huskies is in front of us.

We can't travel as fast as a dog sled because my sleds don't have runners like a dog sled. The entire undersurface of each of my sleds rides against the snow, and this is much slower than if it were just two thin runners sliding against the surface of the snow. On the under-surface of my sleds there are several dull, rounded fins that run the length of each sled. These help keep the sleds from sliding sideways while we are traversing side slopes. But a dog sled only works well on flat, hard-packed snow, not in the mountainous backcountry where I'm heading. Their runners will sink in deep, fresh snow, while the flat surface of my sleds will ride more on the top of the snow.

Since I injured my back before coming on this trip, my fitness suffered, so I get tired too soon and I don't want to risk re-injuring my back. I'm not really sure how I did it. I was training the dogs to get them used to pulling a sled by letting them pull me on my bicycle while I had their leashes wrapped around my waist. They tugged so hard that I think I strained my back muscles. Then the next day when I went hiking at Drift Creek, I dropped one of my shoes in the water while wading across the creek. It was January and cold outside, so I needed that shoe to be able to hike the five miles out of there. I chased that shoe down the creek for about a mile while wearing the other shoe. The wool sock on my other foot got wet from running through the creek, flopping around, smacking the bedrock like a pan-cake. I stumbled over boulders during my chase, jarring my back, but always that shoe seemed to remain just out of reach. It was a cheap sneaker and I was surprised it floated so well.

I ran right through the middle of a picnic that a young couple was having on the dry bedrock along the creek. I apologized as I ran by with my flapping sock smacking the ground. "Sorry, but I lost my shoe in the creek," I said as I ran by. They were polite and said it was okay, even with Jimmy and Will jumping on them. Once I caught up with my shoe, I waded out into waist-deep water to retrieve it before it got away again. I realized then how injured my back had become. I had to lie down for about an hour because the pain had grown too unbearable to sit up. I knew by the severity of the pain already that I was going to be laid up for several days. It was agony hiking out of there and then driving back home, but somehow I did it, hiking slowly and gritting my teeth.

I was flat on my back for the first week in severe pain wondering if I would ever be able to exercise again, not to mention trek across Alaska. But gradually I was able to do more each day and the pain began to subside. After a month I was training on my bike and lifting weights, getting ready for this journey. I rode at an easy cadence on my bicycle trainer every other day and walked down a forest trail on the alternate day so I could let Jimmy and Will run around to stay fit, which they had no problem doing. Within the last two weeks before the start of my journey I was able to increase the amount of weight I was lifting and do some good solid intervals on my bike to develop leg strength. But I never got back into the kind of shape I was in before my accident. I never missed working out for more than a few days in a row. It had always been one of the constants in my life, like dogs and wilderness.

CROSSING THE SEA ICE

When I stop for the night I have to dig out a spot for the tent with my snow shovel. The snow has a fairly hard crust, but it's too weak to support my weight. The surface below is dry and grainy, like fine, white sand. The snow is impossible to pack down. I dig almost to the tundra beneath so I can set up my tent on something solid. If I set my tent up on this grainy snow, a large depression will form under my tent whenever I sit in one place too long. You would think that after sitting in one place for a while the snow would pack together, but it doesn't. You keep sinking until you reach solid earth, so it's best to dig out the snow before you make camp and not have to worry about it later. I dig for thirty minutes. First I have to break apart the hard crust on top with my shovel, which is made of plastic and too cheap for arctic ice. I crack it within the first five minutes. "Oh, that's great," I say. I should have invested in a better one, but I can get by without it if I have to. After I break open the crust, I scoop out the grainy snow underneath. Much of the time I scoop it out with my hands that are covered with my huge arctic mittens. I put my hands together and shovel it out between my legs like a badger. I finish the job before my shovel falls apart completely, and then I set up my tent and get in for the night.

During the night I shiver for a long time. I sweated too much during the day. I think some moisture may have collected in the thermal layer that hugs my skin. I check my feet and find a spot between my toes where moisture has formed, and I wipe it dry with my fingers. I check for irregular discoloration or blistering, but I don't find any. In severe cold I can't make any mistakes. If I do I could get frostbitten toes or even die from hypothermia and frozen tissues. The warning signs of hypothermia are subtle. One is confusion, and with no one to tell me how I'm acting, I may not be able to tell I'm in trouble. The signs can appear rapidly, so I always have to pay attention to how I'm feeling and act to eliminate any body discomforts before they get worse. I'm anxious to get away from this peninsula and into the trees where I hope the wind won't be so severe and the threat of freezing to death less.

Even snuggled in my sleeping bags, I get so cold during the night that I almost panic. I cannot warm myself. I know if I have to I can light the stove to warm up the inside of my tent as a last resort, but I wouldn't be able to keep it going for long. Then I would be right back to where I am now, shivering dreadfully. I decide to curl up into a tight ball and ride out the cold. I know I can endure this cold for several hours as long as there is no wind and I remain dry. I change the thermal shirt next to my skin. I do it quickly so I won't lose any more body heat than I have to, and though I can't really detect much moisture in my shirt, I don't want to take any chances. It's astonishing how just a slight bit of moisture can make you so cold in weather like this. Changing my shirt seems to help some, and I snug down the hood of my sleeping bags and make sure they are tucked over my face so that no part of my body is open to the frigid air. Then I wait. And I shiver. I don't know how long I lie here before the sun rises, but just after I feel the first bright warmth on my tent, I stop shivering and begin to warm up again. This tent is good at trapping solar radiation and turning it into heat I can use.

Jonny and I came here almost nine years ago in the month of June. I wanted to hike across this section of Alaska and the Brooks Range like I'm attempting now, but we started too late in the year. I didn't realize how difficult it would be to hike across this kind of terrain—the tussock mounds slowed us down. We crossed the Baldwin Peninsula when there was a large network of lakes dotting the land. It was merciless, spongy ground to walk on, and mosquitoes plagued us to no end. It took twenty-seven days to hike from Kotzebue to the village of Selawik, a hundred and fifty miles away, when I thought it would only take us two weeks. We became hungry and thin toward the end, and at one point I was forced to build a log raft to float across two wide channels of seawater to reach the village of Selawik. I built it out of driftwood I found along the shores of Inland Lake, which is just an extension of the sea that has penetrated inward. I crossed the channels and walked in waist-high water for six miles towing the log raft behind me before crossing one final channel near the village. I arrived in town knowing that I would have to attempt this journey another year, and that I would have to begin in March or April when the land is still frozen hard. It's much easier to travel over. That experience made me understand how important it was to travel the low, coastal ground when it is still frozen.

March 29, 2007, seventy miles from Kiana

We finish crossing the Baldwin Peninsula and in the late afternoon arrive at the edge of the massive Hotham Inlet. I stop and gaze out over the ice while a light wind drifts across my face and stings my nose. I hesitate. "We have to cross it to reach the mainland," I say to the dogs. The mouth of the Kobuk River, which is on the other side, will lead us far into the interior of Alaska before we turn northeast toward the mountains of the Brooks Range. It's frightening skiing off onto the sea ice heading for the other side when I can't see the land ahead. It's miles across, and all I see are the white clouds floating above and the white ice below laid out before us. To go down the peninsula and around would be about 200 miles, and not really an option. I don't have the days to spare when I'm trying to cross Alaska in one season before freeze-up again in the fall. I won't have my cold-weather gear then, and I also have to return home for a job. I just hope there is land over there like the maps tell me. I take a bearing with my compass by taking what I believe is my known location on this desolate point of land, and compare it to my map. Then I find the point of land on my map where I want to reach on the other side (I can't see the land on the other side so navigating is harder) and line the arrow of my compass up appropriately. Knowing my present location and the location I want to reach tell me what compass direction I need to follow. "Just follow the little red arrow," I say. "Nothing to it." I always prefer to be able to see my next destination, which is often just a hill on the horizon. Then I can simply point the arrow to it and keep on that course even if clouds roll in and obscure it. With land being so far away, following a tiny red arrow off into the abysmal, frozen ocean alone takes nerves of steel, and I'm a bit freaked out. But it's cold and I'm chilled, so I shove off. "There must be land over there somewhere," I say to myself as I take a few more strides forward to the buried edge of the frozen sea. I stop to rest, but it's windy and cold so I don't sit down, and we don't stay long. I wonder for a minute if I should camp and begin my crossing in the morning. The weather seems to be holding right now, but by tomorrow it could be too windy and cloudy to travel, trapping me on this peninsula for days. I'm already geared up and ready to go, so instead of thinking too long and realizing the danger I'm about to face, I shove off with the dogs pulling ahead of me. I have one thing on my mind. I want to get away from the coast where the freezing wind never stops blowing.

The local people have erected tall willow branches to mark the way across, which give me some reassurance that this is a direct and safe route to the other side. The dogs start out strongly but soon they become confused about not being able to see land ahead of them. The dogs look back at me every couple of minutes for reassurance, which I've rarely seen them do before. "Good boys," I say, "hike, hike." This gives them some encouragement and they forge on. Their pulling power is outstanding and I'm sure I couldn't make this crossing in one day without them. Without the dogs, I would be able to go only one mile per hour. I know. I tried. With them pulling, we whisk along at an average of about five miles per hour.

The sky is overcast, but the clouds do not sit low enough to obscure my view of the mile just ahead of me. However, any inclement weather worries me. The wind blows into our faces as we trudge forward. I twist my neck around so I can see the outline of the landmass behind me that I'm skiing away from. It seems crazy to leave land for the emptiness of the sea ice. As I get farther from shore, it really does feel like I'm on the ocean, and the outline of the land behind becomes quite distinct from the white, flat arctic ice. Later I will find out that the distance across in the diagonal direction we are taking is twelve grueling miles, not four like I think it is. Soon I begin to wonder about the distance; it seems so far.

Will begins to tire. He always pulls harder than Jimmy in the first half of the day; he always has his shock cord stretched out farther. Now Jimmy becomes the fresher of the two and soon he takes the lead from Will. They each have their own shock cord attached to my waist belt and can pull as hard or as little as they like. I don't have them attached to the same cord because I don't want Will to have to pull Jimmy, too. Jimmy is always content to lag back while Will, who is the more aggressive of the two, seems to thrive on the exertion. Sometimes early in the day when Will is fresh, he will hunker down to put his shoulders into the effort as he tries to gain better traction on the snow.

I ski harder when the dogs slack off or tire, and I ski easier when they get excited and pull like mad. Sometimes at the beginning of the day or when they smell or see something interesting up ahead, they pull so hard and fast that I can't ski with my legs. I have to stand there using my poles to help propel us.

After two hours crossing on the sea ice, the dogs begin slowing. We need to keep moving to avoid camping on the ice where it would be dangerous. We would be exposed to the bitter wind and water would be tough to find. There isn't that much fresh snow lying on the sea ice to melt. I'm almost too cold, so I consider stopping to add more clothing. But I don't want to overheat and sweat, either, with this much exertion, so I keep moving instead.

I worry about losing visibility. Discerning the pattern of the ice surface is already difficult. It's so white, and the clouds conceal the bulk of the sun's bright rays, and in the dim light the bumps are not well defined. I hit them with my skis, and trying to travel fast causes me to waste a lot of effort trying to correct my balance. I become frantic. "Hike, hike," I yell to the dogs. They increase their pace, but it's short-lived. They are strong but can tire like pups; after all they are not even a year old. We're going as hard as we can and I'm growing fatigued as well. "Come on Jimmy, come on Will," I shout to them. They keep up the pace, but I know they will stop when they reach their limits, no matter where we are. Then I will be forced to haul the sleds by myself, or camp for the night. I'm sure the dogs are getting thirsty and they appear bewildered about moving off into a sinister, white world without any darkly outlined land in front to give them hope. I know land is over there and I try to convey to them that everything will be fine, but I often wonder. "We're okay, guys. We're okay," I say in a pleasant tone, which is hard for me to do right now because of the desperation I feel. I wonder about the cold seawater beneath the ice. The sea is perilous beneath our feet and in constant swirling motion, with a massive volume and force reaching far down into murky depths. In summertime this sea can become a monster, with waves raging through the inlet at ten feet in height. Only the frozen surface separates us from sinking into the steely darkness. What if it cracks open and swallows us up?

Halfway across we come to a small pressure ridge where the sea-ice has fractured and shifted several feet. I don't like to think about the fact that I'm miles from land on a frozen ocean, but I am. I slow down when I near the six-inch gap in the ice. The impacting ice around the gap has driven up both edges about a foot. I stop the dogs before I get to the crack by simply stopping my efforts and gliding. The dogs are tired, so when they feel more strain on their lines when I stop working, they ease up. Then I just say, "stop, stop." I look at the fissure as it snakes its way far down the ice in both directions. I don't know anything about its length, depth, or the strength of the ice around it. Snowmobiles have come through not too long ago by the looks of the tracks I'm following, so I assume the crack is safe to cross. But still, to see a haggard rift in the ocean ice gives me the creeps. I give a little quick hiss, and Will tightens his shock cord. Jimmy soon follows. Then we inch over the crack and pick up speed again. "Hike, hike," I say with some gusto in my voice. This gets the dogs trotting faster away from the rip in the ice. There is no weakening of the ice below our feet at all as we move past. There are no creaking sounds, only the freakish silence of the wide, arctic waters and the ruffled breaths from the panting dogs in front of me.

Several Eskimo say the bay ice is several feet thick, but I still don't like it. They say the bay ice is so thick that people drive trucks across without it cracking under the massive weight. I ski on and the dogs pull as we leave the ice fissure and the mainland behind us. There is no turning back now. We have come too far to get back to the side we started from in a reasonable amount of time to avoid skiing in darkness. And no way am I skiing on a frozen ocean in the dark.

In another hour I notice land in front of us. It's just a faint, thin line running far up and down the coast at first. Sometimes I think it's closer slightly to the left of the direction I'm heading, and I get the urge to change course. Several times I veer off our track only to come to my senses. I think the higher coastal banks make it look much closer that way, but it's not. It's probably a lot farther. The long, linear row of markers, however, signals that land is straight ahead and it's hard to convince myself that the marked course is correct. It takes at least another hour before I believe we have gotten any closer to land at all, but soon it becomes clear that this is the best way.

Then another hour goes by and I see a snowmobile up ahead racing along the shore. The dogs see it, too, but it's too far away for me to hear. The dogs liven up with newfound energy and run for several minutes. They now understand that land is up ahead like I had hoped and told them, not just a dreadful wasteland of wind and ice. I'm grateful that we will soon have solid ground beneath our feet, and relieved that we will be off this oceanic inlet for good.

Night is falling around ten o'clock when we come ashore utterly exhausted. I ski to some willows and pitch the tent behind them to gain at least a little protection from the wind. It has taken me about five strenuous hours of skiing to get across, and now I'm so happy I sit down for a second to pat the snowy earth. One of my most dreadfully anticipated obstacles is now behind me for good. We waste little time getting into the tent, secure from the cold and content with knowing the foundation beneath us is not an unstable mass of ice. I can sleep in peace without having to worry about the ice shifting beneath us during the night.

I begin melting snow to make dinner while the dogs doze in their own corners until their food and water are ready. They don't move an inch and wait patiently for dinner. I ask so much of them, and they never lose their amicable spirit. It has been the dogs who enabled me to cross this ice sheet, and if all goes according to plan, they will also enable me to ski up the Kobuk River in the coming weeks before it breaks apart with the warming weather.

SKIING THE KOBUK RIVER

In the morning I crawl out of my tent to look around, still relieved by my accomplishment the previous day. The dogs shoot out of the tent, too, and I rub my fingers through their fur as they dodge by to sniff around. Looking back, the edge of the Baldwin Peninsula has a high enough bank so I can just make it out. The vertical edge is bare of snow in most places, so it looks like a large brown line streaking up the coast, like someone has drawn a felt-tip marker across the middle of the white sky. The presence of that line is how I can tell the land from the sea. Everywhere else across the bay is bitter whiteness. On this side of the bay, I can see mountains twenty or thirty miles away taking shape to the north and to the south. Their distance from me, and because they are splattered with snow, makes them appear hazy and illusionary in the overcast sky. I can see on the map that those mountains will funnel in on me the farther up the Kobuk River I go, until at some points the mountains will almost butt up against the river's edge.

A man looking to be in his late fifties drives out the mouth of the Kobuk River on his snowmobile and stops by my tent to say hello. He wears so many thick, winter clothes that he looks like an astronaut. On his feet are large, white, plastic boots, also known as "bunny boots."

Draped over his legs and torso are insulated pants and a parka, and on his hands are leather mittens with furry backs that reach up to his elbows. The hood on his jacket is lined with what looks like wolverine fur. It sits back on his neck like a green pillow, and is worn over his head when the wind kicks up a few miles per hour. He wears two hats on his head: a balaclava over his entire head and a windproof cap that covers his ears over that. The only skin exposed on his body is the area around his nose, chin, and eyes, which is pink from the bitter air. He talks with such a drawl that I think he might be a Cajun from some abandoned swamp, like he has gotten used to speaking without enunciating his words. And why should he? There aren't that many people to talk to around here. He's a likable man, and by his casual mannerisms and movements I get a sense he is apparently without an ounce of ego or haste. He does everything slowly. When he moves his arm, it's slow. When he speaks, it's slow. Even the way he looks at you before he says anything is slow.

He throttles back his engine, turns off the motor, and sits on his machine in front of my camp for a minute without exhibiting any urge to say hello. He simply smiles and stares out onto the icy ocean, not to study it because he knows it well already, but to admire it I think. "Good morning," he finally says to me.

"Good morning," I say back. "Looks like you're dressed for the weather."

"Oh, yeah," he says as if the two words are an entire story. "Going out to see if I can catch some fish." He shows me a small jig that he fishes with. It's a sturdy piece of wood, but only about ten inches long. However the hook attached to it is enormous, around three inches long with a razor-sharp barb.

"What kind of fish are you after?"

"Shee fish," he says. "I'll fill up this here trailer," he says while looking back at the ten-foot-long trailer he's towing. At first I don't believe him, but he says it like he does it all the time; like catching that many fish is a guarantee. He shows me a gasoline-powered auger he uses to cut through the thick ice. The diameter of the blade is about a foot and is fastened to the end of a five-foot-long, iron shaft.

"How big do they get?" I ask, and then he holds his hands about three feet apart. "No kidding?"

"Oh, yeah," he says, like it's common knowledge around here. "I'll catch ten to twenty of them by the end of the day."

"Oh, man, that's incredible."

"I'll bring you back one when I come in," he says.

"That'd be great," I say. Then we sit making small talk for a few more minutes. He tells me that he doesn't drive too far from his cabin anymore in this deep cold. If his snowmobile breaks down he'll have to walk back before freezing to death, and he's not as fit as he used to be. He sits back on his seat for a minute, smiling like he hasn't a care in the world.

"I guess I should see if I can get a fish," he says. Then he turns the ignition and starts up the engine, gives a little wave, and idles out onto the sea before vanishing in the distance.

The Kobuk River originates a few hundred miles inland from the center of Alaska, at the foothills of the Brooks Range. The Noatak and Selawik rivers also drain into the inlet close by. They bring nutrient-rich water to the ocean, and the collision of their currents with the ocean currents makes a prime habitat for fish. And the fish get gigantic. The three major rivers gave people access to the ocean. Kotzebue's ideal location on a spit of land at the head of these three rivers made it an ideal trading post for the Eskimo of the coast, Indians of the interior, white fur traders, and explorers from across the watery horizon.

The man returns a few hours later with about fifteen fish in his trailer, the smallest one being about thirty inches long. They look like giant suckers. I'm stunned as he offers me a fish. I grab it with my gloved hands and put it in my blue, plastic sled. "Take another," he says.

"I couldn't carry another one," I say. "I have too far to go and too much to carry." He seems disappointed I don't take two fish. His hospitality is overflowing. Though he has a wife, his lack of social interaction with other people seems to make the act of sharing a prized activity, and he sits for a few minutes, perhaps hoping he can be of assistance. The fish he gives me is nearly as long as my sled. I thank the man, and after a few more minutes he sputters out onto the Kobuk and makes his way upriver to sell some of his fish to some of the few local people in the area.

I watch the man go, admiring his complete acceptance of his way of life. He doesn't squirm from the cold like I do. It doesn't appear to be a hardship for him. I get a little twinkle in my eye thinking about being like him. Eliminate the snowmobile and he's the man I always envisioned I could be, living a hardy, self-sufficient life in the core of the northern wilderness. Then I saw the fish's head off and toss it into some bushes away from camp. I cover the rest of the fish with plastic and move it away in case there are polar bears around. There probably aren't but it takes little effort so I do it anyway.

March 31, 2007

I eat breakfast early and even though it's cold outside I pack up to leave. I'm uneasy about lingering next to the wind-beaten coastline and want to keep moving inland to get away from the constant cold. I begin by skiing into the mouth of the Kobuk River. Then I follow it for several miles. It's actually just a channel of the Kobuk River called Riley Channel. The Kobuk River Delta is an impressive region of lakes, river channels, and backwater sloughs. If the terrain weren't frozen, I would never be able to cross it on foot. The land is flat for about thirty miles wide with several large river channels fanning out before dumping into the ocean. As I travel inland I can see the mountains in the distance, but they are still so far away that they never seem to grow any larger. Though I haven't sent food to Noorvik, I travel due east toward the village anyway. It's almost directly on my route, and if I get into trouble with the weather I can stop there for help.

I'm reluctant to follow the snowmobile trails at first. They often cross the river to take the most direct route, and I'm leery about skiing on top of a huge, frozen river that has a massive current beneath it. I stick to the shoreline on the left side without going too far out on the ice. But it's slow going when I'm not on a snowmobile trail. I break through the snowy crust and sink a few inches as I ski.

After several miles we take a shortcut overland where the river makes a large turn. This way is supposed to be about five miles shorter than following the river. I spend the remainder of the day skiing over several frozen lakes, which is faster than traveling on the land; their surface is smoother and harder. My sleds gain momentum over the lake ice where the wind has scraped it clean. The dogs break into a run whenever the sleds slide easily—they feel the decrease in tension on their lines—and we make great time and distance. Sometimes in the middle of a lake the ice is as clear as glass, and thin cracks penetrate several feet below me indicating the thickness. Where I can peer down into the dismal darkness, I wonder if the ice will break. Freshwater ice is weaker than seawater ice. Being able to see through the lake's surface makes me think it's weaker at those places where the snow has been blown away, but this land is frozen solid from the bitter cold and the ice never gives an inch as I slide across it. I urge the dogs to pull faster over the clear icy sections just in case. Sometimes they trot over a few feet to the side of our route, off the clear ice to find some traction on a thin layer of snow, but their lines are long enough to allow me to keep skiing straight until they get back on course. They always gravitate toward the direction I'm going. It's an uncanny sense they have, made more acute by their desire to decrease the tension in their cords. And the least amount of tension is right in front of me.

I come off the lakes and enter the northern tree line. In this region along the coast spruce trees are absent where they would exist farther inland at the same latitude. I head over low hills for several miles following a snowmobile route. A snow flurry develops, so when I come to a small ravine I set up my tent under some spruce trees. I have to dig out snow with my shovel. Then I run my stove on bare ground under the trees to melt snow to drink. It's around thirty degrees, which is warm enough for us to stay outside until the dogs have drunk their fill. Then I fill a quart container to take inside the tent with me.

An hour later to my surprise, I hear two men outside my tent. "Anyone in there?" one man asks.

"Yeah, hello," I say. "Just a moment." I put my boots on, open the door, and go outside.

"Our snow machine broke down. Do you have any water?" a man asks. The other man is lying on the trail in the snow about forty yards away. He's up on his elbow lying on his side with his feet crossed like he's relaxed, but not exhausted. They look like they've been walking for some time. I show the man my quart-size container filled with water, but it contains bits of spruce needles floating in it, so the man doesn't want it. I find it strange he doesn't want the water because of a little natural debris. I guess I've gotten used to just being able to drink any kind of water at all in this frozen world where staying warm and hydrated are far more important than cleanliness.

"I can boil you some more water," I say.

"No, that's okay, we have to keep walking," he says. "What are you doing out here? Are you surveying?" he asks.

"No, I'm skiing from Kotzebue to Ambler."

"Oh," he says with a blank face, like he isn't sure why anyone would want to do what I'm doing.

"How far is it to Noorvik?" I ask.

"It's about six miles," the man says. He looks durable and is probably an Eskimo. I imagine they were born with tolerance for the cold. Their toughness makes me feel like a wilderness novice. The men don't look that fit, but I think they will make the hike in the snow and wind without incident, just because they are used to this type of weather.

"You can stay in my tent if you don't think you can make it," I say to the man.

"That's okay, we'll be fine. We just want to keep moving so we don't get cold."

"Good luck," I say. Then the two men walk off, not minding the weather that I'm stopping to avoid. I never come across them again so I assume they make it to Noorvik.

April 1, 2007, fifty miles from Kiana

Today is April Fools' Day, but the snow and wind are no joke. Despite the weather I ski anyway, but my skis start sticking to the snow when the air temperature rises just above freezing. Balls of dry, gummy snow collect on the bottoms of my skis, forcing me to stop. I can't ski an inch until I remove all the snow from my skis, then wax them. Banging my skis together can't knock off the snow. I have to scrape much of the snow off with one of my ski poles. Stopping to wax my skis is time consuming, but I have no choice. After about an hour the wax wears off and they start sticking again, so I have to stop again. The wind and snowfall increase and by the afternoon I'm traveling in a mild blizzard, barely able to see the old snowmobile tracks through the whiteness in front of me. I'm forced to camp for the night and wait for clearer weather.

The next day the sky is still overcast and the temperature is near freezing. I trek all day and walk some in the afternoon after I become tired of waxing my skis so often. I make my way along different river channels and cross over low hills to other channels, depending on which way the snowmobile trails go. Down along the river channels the spruce trees grow rather large. Combined with the hills in the area it's difficult to catch glimpses of the mountains farther away so I can get my bearings. I use my compass and keep heading in an easterly direction assuming the local people know the most direct route to the next village. My sleds are so heavy that they may overrun me when I have to walk down steep slopes. I walk backward and lean into my sleds on the steepest sections.

Near the end of the day, I cross over through birch trees and come out on the main channel, which leads into Noorvik. The temperatures start cooling off and I'm able to resume skiing. I ski for about another hour and get within a mile of the village of Noorvik. This is the point where all the channels in the delta merge back to form one main channel. I set up camp underneath large willows. The dogs run off when I unhook them from their harnesses. They follow an animal scent into the woods—probably a moose. Moose tracks catch their interest more than any other animal around. I worry about the dogs getting caught in a trap, but since we have been exercising all day I don't think they will go far with such deep snow covering the ground, so I don't call for them or chase after them. Airedales are born to hunt. They're not like the arctic breeds, who will wander off if given the chance, but they will literally bolt full speed into the woods when they smell something. Still, I wanted Airedales again. That's what Jonny was, and I could never be content with any other breed now.

I set up my tent and unload some of my gear while I wait for the dogs. I even follow their tracks for about fifteen minutes back through the dense willow bushes and two feet of snow. I sink up to my knees following their tracks and soon realize I won't find them until they come back on their own. They return an hour later like they know what they're doing, with their mouths gaping and tails swaying. They lie down in the snow to bite out the snowballs that have collected between their toes.

With the dogs safely back I work on building a fire to cook my ten-pound fish. Building a fire in Alaska even in the winter isn't difficult. The air is so dry that the dead wood you find is almost always dry. But if there is wind, you have to find a way to protect the initial flame or else even a light wind will snuff it out. The best and easiest way to find tinder to start a fire is by breaking off some of the dead branches that grow at the base of spruce trees just above the snow. I never use live branches. It's not healthy for the tree—though spruce trees are almost indestructible—and they don't burn as well anyway. If there is a birch tree (which I can't find) nearby I will peel off a piece of dead bark for a fire starter. The resin in the bark flames up almost as good as cardboard doused in gasoline, yet it holds a flame much longer. I grab a piece of cardboard from inside my sled and lay it on the snow to keep the tinder dry. Then I shred spruce twigs in half by separating the ends with my thumb and peeling them apart. Sometimes they shred into three or four pieces, which is better for igniting the fire because they are smaller. It also exposes the inner wood, which always ignites better than bark unless the bark contains a lot of resin. I've done this so many times that I often don't realize I'm shredding twigs as I lay them down. The more time you take in laying down the twigs, the better chance your fire will flame up on the first try. And if you happen to be without a shelter at twenty below zero or so for some very unfortunate reason, you better make it count on the first try. You may be in too much trouble by the time you are ready for a second try. Fortunately for me I have a tent and it's around twenty-five degrees, so I can throw the tinder together more chaotically when I start a fire. If I don't get it going, though I'm almost sure I will, I can go inside my tent when I get cold and call it a day. If I were desperate and had lost my tent for some reason, I would prepare the tinder like I was splicing hairs with a razor before I even lit one match. Some people can light a fire with sticks. I know how but I could never do it unless I had warm, ideal conditions, so there is no way I'm going to lose my matches.

I shred about a dozen spruce twigs as I place them onto the cardboard one at a time in a little teepee shape. It takes me about three minutes. With the twigs shredded, all I need to do is hold a lighter to the twigs for a few seconds. I could put paper under the twigs, too, but I don't really need to with finely shredded twigs. They catch fire easily and flames leap up in a matter of seconds. Then I feed larger twigs into the fire as it grows, until finally it's hot enough to burn sticks and even wet logs I drag from the snow. The key to starting a fire is taking the time to prepare the first batch of twigs you plan to light. They should be small, and they have to be completely dry. And you have to arrange them so ample air can flow through each piece. After the fire is going, you can toss any kind of wood on it any way you like.

I sit cross-legged as near to the fire as I can get without burning my clothes, my mouth watering as the succulent meat drips juice into the fire with an aromatic sizzle. When I think a part of the fish has been cooked long enough, I peel away a section from the bony spine with my fingers and then plop it into my mouth. The cooked sections come off easily. Then I turn the fish while it dangles from a thin rope, just inches over the flames. I find another flaky morsel of meat and peel it away again. I give the pieces that are not quite done to the dogs. After about two hours the fish is all eaten and nothing is left except bones tossed in a scattered mess just out of reach of the dogs. I figure some other animals can benefit from those bones. There are still some specks of meat on them. I think once in a while a wild animal needs help, too. I didn't always practice that harped-about dogma, "You shouldn't feed wild animals." Except for bears. I'm pretty sure there aren't any bears awake yet, otherwise I would take the time to throw the bones in the fire, to scorch the scent right out of them. I don't really want any bears sniffing around my tent at night if I can do anything to prevent it. I don't want moose sniffing around, either, but a smelly fish doesn't attract them. And there aren't any other animals in

Alaska I would be too concerned about. Wolves and wolverines could give me some problems, but I don't think they would come close to me, or the dogs while I'm with them.

April 3, 2007, thirty-five miles from Kiana

It's about two o'clock in the morning and still dark when I wake up to the sound of a vociferous, drawn-out screech, a cross between a metallic scraping and a child's scream. It's probably a lynx. I turn on my headlamp so the animal knows I'm in my tent and hopefully won't come too close, because the dogs would freak out even more and try to bolt outside, right through the wall of my tent. I have to keep my hands on their backs to deter them. The cat circles my tent making a cry every few seconds, but this doesn't scare me. Lynx don't get that big and want to keep to themselves. The only animal I fear right now is a burly moose. I'm afraid one might walk by and become startled by my bright orange tent, then start stomping us while we are asleep inside. I think lynx cry out to flush rabbits from their hiding places or to get the rabbits to move just enough, so they can detect them with their sharp hearing. And when they voice their screech, I always wake up. I'm not sure a moose would give such a warning. I rely on each dog's ability to smell the moose, and then for them to wake up out of a sound sleep in time for me to take countermeasures. I need time to look outside before a moose gets within charging distance so I can talk the moose down or back away. But I tell myself moose are smart enough to detect us and won't get too close. I only hope so.

Jonny's sense of smell was so acute that he could detect the scent of a bear at fifty yards while sleeping soundly inside my tent with all the flaps zipped shut, if the breeze was blowing in the right direction. Once on the Yukon River he did this, waking up suddenly and then barking hysterically. His alarm gave us time to get out of the tent to see an annoyed grizzly bear coming our way. I think the bear simply wanted to walk along the open shoreline where I had pitched the tent, but we persuaded the creature to walk around through the trees away from us. We did this by simply showing ourselves to the bear and by remaining calm. I didn't want to agitate, only to urge the animal along, so I sat down with shotgun in hand, dog on leash, and waited. The bear gave some deep huffs and snorts for about five minutes before finally leaving. Though the bear would have likely walked right on by us if Jonny had not barked, I felt reassured to have him in my tent with me. Though they are only a year old, I feel just as safe with Jimmy and Will. Their fearlessness is already overly apparent, maybe too much so. But I miss the bond I had with Jonny. I miss the way he would do exactly what I needed him to do with just a slight murmur or hand signal from me, like he could read my mind.

In the morning I wake around nine thirty with the sun shining brilliantly on the wall of my tent. My body is adjusting to the strenuous work so I'm rising earlier and easier now. I have less soreness in the mornings. It's almost like when I was a teenager and felt no pain. But now I don't like to hop right out of bed and shove off skiing. I like to ease myself awake and think about things, like other adventures I want to do. I think about Julie and how we spend our mornings eating breakfast in a nice warm house, with clean coffee—Julie doesn't drink coffee—and plenty of space to move around, stretch, and wake up. Right about now, though, I'm forced to rush outside to relieve myself. The dogs always have to follow me out, and they hit everything when they exit, pulling up tent stakes and dragging out pieces of my clothing with them.

I go back inside my tent and the dogs follow me in, hitting everything as they enter. They always seem to think they need to dart through the door instead of stepping through it lightly. They also seem to think they must enter and exit at the exact same time, with both their hulking bodies trying to fit through a narrow tent opening. If it wouldn't risk damaging my tent I would think it was funny. They always exit with just a little bit more gusto than when they enter, and with a little terrier ferocity, as if they are ready to take on the new day and the world. When I used to camp with Jonny, he would rush out of the tent in the mornings growling up a storm, just in case the situation called for it.

I introduced Julie to Jonny soon after we met. He liked her immediately, like Jimmy and Will do. When she is around, Jimmy and Will won't even acknowledge my presence. Instead they dote over Julie cheerfully hoping to get attention from her. I had great admiration for Julie when I first met her, and still do. I knew she had a doctorate degree, but this didn't really intimidate me. Julie caused me to feel differently. I felt relaxed and comfortable around her. I did recognize her intelligence and her uncanny ability to infer meaning in people's half-spoken notions, though. She could make a quick-witted comment to sum up an idea I was talking about with her, and this always made me feel comfortable around her. Sometimes she would know what I was trying to say even when I wasn't quite sure yet.

April 4, 2007, eighteen miles from Kiana

Late in the afternoon I arrive at the outskirts of Kiana in good spirits after skiing the last nine miles in two hours. I slow and let the dogs play as I ski into town. After about eight days of travel, I'm right on schedule. Today is their birthday so I will let them eat as much as they want and make each of them a pot of milk from a powder mix, which they love. I brought extra milk so they will be able to eat something if they attack a porcupine and get quills in their mouth. I had to feed Jonny milk for four days once when he attacked a large porcupine along the Yukon River. Because he had quills inside his mouth, it was the only food he could ingest until I got the quills out.

A man named Glenn, a schoolteacher and trapper, stops to talk to me as I come off the frozen river to the edge of town. He is a boisterous man who speaks his mind, like he is talking over the roar of heavy machinery. He is on his way to check his traps and tells me about a lynx he caught the other day. "That's just the way it is in a 'dog eat dog' world," he says, referring to how he shot the trapped lynx in the head with a .22-caliber rifle as the lynx was crying and screaming for its life. "That lynx was screaming when he saw me coming because he knew he was done." Glenn tells me he knows the woods around here really well and rants about how he is the toughest and meanest person in town. "I'm the toughest man in town." That's what he says to me. There can't be more than twenty healthy, grown men in the entire village so it's not really that impressive. I like his friendliness, even though loud braggarts usually don't appeal to me. I can sense a jovial quality to his brash demeanor and he isn't the least intimidating to me. He was a Green Beret in the army and does not take part in pandering to get ahead. "I don't kiss anybody's ass to get ahead, like everyone else in this school." He teaches fifth graders and talks loudly at them as well, ordering them around like army privates.

I hike up the short hill to buy food from the store, then amble by the post office to get the supplies I had sent here. My youngest brother Rick and his four-year-old son Michael sent me freeze-dried meals, energy bars, and plenty of dog food. Even though I've sent myself food, it's never enough. Fortunately, Rick, Julie, my parents, my oldest brother Mike, and Julie's parents supplement my efforts. I can travel days on just a little bit of food and rely partly on my body fat to keep me going, but eventually I will have to take a rest somewhere to eat large quantities of food to rebuild my body, like here where there is a store to buy more.

The village dogs are everywhere, tied up in people's front yards like they are old, abandoned snowmobiles. They bark and growl as we pass, but this is all show. This is what happens to dogs who don't get exercised, which seems to occur in almost every remote village in Alaska. I'm not sure why these people even have dogs if they don't do anything with them. The poor animals turn into little hyper-demons, flustered with their own pent-up energy. It must be torture for them to survive a winter here attached to a six-foot rope with only a small wooden crate for shelter. Jimmy and Will used to lunge for these kinds of dogs in Kotzebue, but now they are content to walk by and ignore them. This action only appears to incite the tied dogs even more. Jimmy and Will always mark their spots in front of the dogs' yards, often just a few feet out of their frenzied reach, and then go on their way with a slight toss of their heads.

April 5, 2007, Kiana village

I walk over to Glenn's classroom to talk to him about the country ahead and to charge my camera and satellite phone batteries in the school's administration office. The school is by far the nicest and biggest building in town. The shiny, new structure sits well above the permafrost on thick cement pillars and has wide, steel-grated walkways leading to all the main entrances. I will see the exact same building in every Alaska village I come to in the next few months.

I arrive at Glenn's classroom. "Come on in," he says. "I'll print you some maps."

"That'll be great," I say. Then Glenn yells at one of his kids.

"Kerry, pick up that trash and shut the door," he says, but the girl ignores him and keeps walking out of the room. Glenn looks back at the computer and continues what he was doing. "Where are you going after here?" he asks.

"I'm going to try to ski up the Ambler River and make my way to Anaktuvuk Pass."

"That's a long way. How are you going to get over the mountains?"

"I plan on hiking over Nakmaktuak Pass."

Then Glenn prints out a map of the area and starts to study it like he is going on the journey himself. "That's going to be some sketchy stuff. It's going to get really steep here, and there will be a lot of water coming down," he says while pointing to the area on the map.

"Yeah, I know. I'll just sit and wait for a week if I have to." But I know I won't want to wait. I'll want to keep moving.

"You'll have to go up this ridge here and side-hill this section to get around these gorges," he says. Then another teacher comes in to talk with him for a minute. I slide over next to the window and look outside as they talk. After she leaves, Glenn comes back over and we finish up with the maps. "She doesn't like me. No one likes me here because I don't play politics to get ahead," he says, then looks back at the map.

"Do you have a gun?" he asks.

"Yeah."

"What kind?"

"A shotgun," I say.

"Oh, a twelve gauge?" he asks me with a hint of glee in his eyes. He likes guns.

"Yep, with shells and also some three-inch, hollow-point slugs."

"Oh, that'll do," he says. "You never know what bears will do around here. It's best to be ready for them. They'll be waking up soon." I finish charging my batteries and thank Glenn for the maps, even though I tell him twice that I have these maps already. He lets me use his phone card to call Julie back home. I talk to her for a few minutes just to see how things are going.

"You sound good," she says.

"I do?"

"Yeah, you sound like you are sure of what you are doing," she says. I don't tell her that every day I have doubts and often don't know if I can go on. But I make myself, to fulfill the commitment I made to myself before I began this journey. I know from experience that I would regret going home early.

"Really, I feel good," I say, "now that I'm getting some more food and a little rest." I don't think I ask her how her life is going back home since I'm so involved in my journey. We talk a little more, but it's not enough time to reconnect on any level. "Well, I should probably get going," I say. "I'm using this guy's calling card and I don't want to run him up a bill."

"Okay, take care of yourself," she says. "I'll miss you."

"I'll miss you, too," I say. Then we both hang up. The cold and long efforts over the past two weeks have made me catatonic toward our relationship. All I want to do is eat, rest, and nestle into a place that is warm. I feel like a blob mentally, unable to evaluate how our relationship is holding up, or if it is at all. Normally at home, I become happy with the thought of seeing her, and I think how I can brighten her day, but not now. Maybe she senses my tiredness as insensitivity toward our relationship, but I'm in a sort of survival mode. And at night when I'm sleeping, I don't have dreams about her. I usually dream about a warm place with community and some generic woman who is good to me, but no one specific.

I feel out of place in this well-kept school with my dirty clothes and my unshaven face. Everyone looks so clean and soft. I thank Glenn for his hospitality, then go over to the office to get my batteries. I walk out of the school, slip on the hard-packed snow, and almost fall down in front of the building. I have on my ski boots, and they are difficult to walk in. A young teacher and her pupils are out front learning to cross-country ski, but I don't think they see me slip. I watch them for a while and wave to them as they practice. I wonder what it would be like to live in this village and to have a reasonable income. For a moment I wish I could live here, comfortable on the edge of a great wilderness, but then it seems futile. The only people who seem to be able to live here with enough money to get by are teachers, Indians, and retired people. If I'm going to live somewhere with little money, it's going to be all the way in nature, not just lingering along the fringes hoping for the scrapings of society. After watching, I go around to the back of the school, untie the dogs, and head back down to my camp along the river.

In the evening the sky is calm, so I sit out on the embankment along the river that has been blown bare of snow. My legs stretch halfway to the bottom while resting on hard, frozen soil. The air is still, but cold, and the vapor from my breath streams out of my mouth like smoke. I gaze across the river past several miles of lowland forest toward the Waring Mountains. I can see a dozen peaks. Most have rounded summits and gentle slopes. Spruce trees fill the lower parts of the mountains and reach up into the passes that lead south to the Selawik River. I envision myself plodding through one of the passes, exploring virgin territory. I scan around me in a complete circle, amazed. Mountains are everywhere, creating an endless choice of routes I could take from here. But I will stick to my plan of heading east, toward the wild core of Alaska. I'm going to stick to the plan for once in my life.

ABORIGINAL LORE

I pull out of Kiana in the early afternoon with a backbreaking sled. I have to double-check my maps to be sure I don't head up the Squirrel River. The Kobuk River has several channels here and makes a sharp, right turn. The Squirrel River runs straight off this corner at first like the Kobuk River. If I don't pay attention I could ski straight onto the Squirrel River and travel a few miles north toward the Baird Mountains before I realize I'm going the wrong way.

I don't think I could go more than three miles a day if I didn't have any snowmobile tracks to ski on. I worry about the river breaking apart before I get to Ambler so I try to make good time. Sometimes I come across more transparent ice where I can look into the green abyss below my feet. The clarity and depth make it appear almost as if no ice lies below me at all. But I know it's several feet thick. It makes me scared anyway.

Out in the middle of the river I become even more concerned. My muscles tense up like I'm on the side of a cliff about to fall. "Oh, God, oh, God, what if I fall in?" I say in a huffed tone. I hurry to shore to gain my composure. But eventually I have to ski back out on the river to cut the next inside bend. If I travel along the shoreline all the time I will end up doubling the distance I have to go. I have to travel in a straight line from one inside bend of the river to the next as I follow the river's meandering course. Not only does that course force me to cross the river, but it also forces me to travel the longest distance possible across the river, exposing me to the middle of the river for the longest possible time. I don't like it, but the snowmobile trails go that way, too.

While following the trail cutting another bend, I worry again the ice is too weak to ski on so I stay near shore where the snow builds up into deep drifts. My skis sink in a foot on every step. We travel like this for about two hours until it becomes too difficult for the dogs to pull in the deep snow. We become tired and I decide to go back out into the middle of the river the way the snowmobiles go. I convince myself I still have several days before the river becomes too weak to support our weight. I can't afford to break through this river ice, though; it would be almost impossible for me to pull myself out. I would be dragged down by the weight of my sleds, or pulled underneath the ice by the powerful current. The Kobuk is a massive river and harbors powerful currents with tremendous volumes of water pushing anything in its path. I'm afraid my efforts against the current would be in vain. Sometimes I wait for a snowmobile to come by so I can follow its route along the river, but the farther from Kiana I go the less often these vehicles appear.

During the night I have a terrible dream. Being tired and sick, I fly home early in the season without having finished out my four months in the wild. I've had adventures in the past where I've gone home early for these reasons, only later to dread my mistake and wish I had remained. This time I'm determined not to make this same mistake. In my dream, when I return home I want to come back to Alaska to complete my adventure, but I can't. I've run out of money and have to work a dreary job again. When I wake up from my dream, I'm relieved that I'm still in the frozen arctic, facing adversity and traveling across the snowy landscape. I know that barring a severe injury to me or the dogs, I will spend four months in the Alaska wilderness, even if I'm only able to go one mile a day.

The next day the snow becomes deeper. I ski two hours longer than I plan looking for a break in the willows where I can travel through to get to the spruce trees that lay fifty yards beyond. The snow would be shallower there and offer me a more enclosed campsite. But this swath of willows is almost impenetrable and runs the edge of the river for miles. With the deep, soft powder that lays on the ground underneath the willows, it would take some time to yank all my gear through, so I decide to keep skiing forward in the direction I need to go hoping I will find an opening. In the evening, an hour before sunset, I give up and set up camp near Trinity Creek, but it's frozen solid and I can't even find it. I don't go searching for it. I find an area a few feet from the river where the willows are either buried or absent. I'm surprised to find the snow so much deeper than it was closer to the coast. I sink up to my knees when I get off my skis, then spend an hour digging out a spot for the tent. I work until dark before I finish. The nights never get pitch-black, though, so I can see well enough. Then I go down to the river, shovel away several feet of snow, and then chop enough ice to melt for drinking and cooking. I load up enough ice for tonight and the next morning. Melted snow around here still tastes horrible, so I melt river ice instead. There is still no available water anywhere since the air is consistently below freezing.

During the next day I see grizzly bear tracks in the snow, but the air is probably still too cold. I figure the bear won't stay out if there is nothing to eat. We see a fox scurrying along the ice next to shore. Jimmy gets a glimpse of the fox and becomes excited. He pulls in his harness like mad. Then Will follows. They pull for a hundred yards until they reach the spot where the fox sneaks into the woods to elude us. We continue on. Sometimes the dogs act as if they are two bodies with the same brain and interconnected senses. Sometimes when one dog reacts to an animal, the other dog will glance at him to see what he is looking at. The second dog will study the first dog's body posture and almost instantly hone in on what it is that made the first dog react. It's similar to the way an entire flock of birds will change course at what appears to be the exact same time, when really they are taking cues from each other and reacting at lightning speeds. These dogs are siblings and have always been together since birth, so their connection is almost innate.

My sleds and skis want to slide sideways down the ice that is gently sloping toward the middle of the river. I consider going over the bank to ski through the trees. It's unusual for river ice to slope down like this, toward the center of the river. I fear the ice could be weak out away from shore and I find it difficult to keep from sliding sideways. This ice is incredibly slick. It became so slick in the past few days after the snow along the bank of the river melted and then refroze as fresh ice. The three of us gain our footing on willow branches that are protruding through the ice in several places, but I worry if I miss the last of the willows, I might slide helplessly all the way out onto the river. We manage to stay along the bank, but this section makes me nervous. If I were to lose my footing, I think the dogs and I would slide forty or fifty feet. The surface of the ice appears strange out there. Its jagged and transparent appearance glistens in the sun, which makes it hard for me to study the surface features for cracks or holes. It's not white and flat like the surface I'm used to. I think it would break under our weight. I stay as close to the bank as I can while working my way into thicker willows, and after several minutes we reach an area where the river flattens out into a white surface again.

I think a dog sled race came through a couple of days before me. I find a dog bootie along the trail every mile or so. They are far smaller than my dogs' booties. I use them to protect the dogs' feet since they travel so many miles on ice. The snowmobile that was following the race for support broke down and is being towed by another one back to Kiana when three men pass me. They stop at my tent along the river. "Where you heading?" a chubby man asks me. He has a stereo and a little heater on the console of his snowmobile, which is large and new. He pulls tiny microphones out of his ears as he gets off. He's dressed completely in black; his gloves, boots, jacket, hat, they're all black and little worn.

This man isn't in a city, but his swagger and the way he chews gum seems exaggerated. "I'm skiing to Ambler," I say, not mentioning the second leg of my journey. I'm not sure they would believe it. The man in black looks at me for a moment with a grin.

"Have you seen any animals?" the other man asks.

"Just a fox," I say. They frown, hoping for something bigger I guess. I think they hunt out of season.

"I think we saw you the other day in Kiana," one man says.

"You probably did. I got more food there," I say.

"You traveled pretty far in such a short time."

"I guess so. I got caught up in a lot of soft snow that slowed me down," I say with a shrug. The chubby man climbs back onto his snowmobile while eating a piece of candy. They wish me good luck as they continue downriver.

I enter Kobuk Valley National Park and don't see many snow-mobiles anymore. A harsh wind with light snow develops, and I decide to only ski for about four hours the entire day. By the end of this time a full force storm arrives and cold wind begins to bat-ter us head-on. It blows right into our faces from the east and stings my nose and cheeks. I have no choice but to find shelter. The river has twenty-foot-high snow embankments along its edges for miles around, but I find a place to get off the river by climbing up where the snow forms a slide all the way down. I find an area away from the river underneath spruce trees where the snow is not quite as deep as the snow right along the river. I unload my sleds and carry my gear, little by little, up the deep, snowy slope, and then back into the trees. Getting to the campsite is tough. I sink into soft snow on every step and I can't really walk in it. It's more like falling forward and then pulling my legs up underneath me again. It requires trudging through snow up to my thighs.

After I pack all my gear over, I dig an area out of the snow to set up my tent. This whole process takes me about an hour and a half. After the tent is set up, we waste no time getting in with all my food and gear. I do everything inside the tent when the weather is severe like this. Once inside I feed the dogs, drink some cocoa, and eat a block of dried sausage I just picked up in Kiana. Julie sent it to me, along with other snacks and a few magazines; one was the swimsuit edition of *Sports Illustrated,* which I will burn last.

April 8, 2007, eighty-two miles from Ambler

I'm held up in my tent today. Fierce winds bomb down the river and sound like ocean waves crashing on the beach, except a bit more drawn out. It has stopped snowing for now, but the sky is still overcast; a thick layer of clouds hovers a couple of hundred feet above the river basin just waiting for me to start packing up my gear, but I'm not going anywhere today. I don't like the cold that much and I sure don't like skiing in it. It makes me feel desperate when I have to be outside working hard to make miles, when the only shelter around is the one I have to set up. Often while I'm skiing I will stop and physically check to make sure I have my tent. If I were to lose it, I would be in imminent danger of freezing to death. I don't know how effective it would be to build a snow cave, or if I could do it fast enough before my feet and hands froze. I don't want to find out, though I go over the scenario in my head in detail: how I will build it, where, with what materials, how big it will be, and what I will use for the floor and door. It's better to think through life-and-death situations before they occur. It's even better to actually go through the motions of how I would save myself, but I don't practice building snow caves on this trek. I don't have the energy. I just think about them and notice locations where I could build one as I travel. Since the snow really isn't deep enough to dig a cave from the side, I would probably try to dig a trench for my shelter. I would put spruce boughs on the bottom of the trench. Over that I would put my pads and part of my tent, I hope I could still salvage the torn remains of my tent. If I were to lose my tent I would have to use something else to keep myself off the cold snow. Then I would put more spruce branches and fabric over the top entrance to block out all the wind. It's a scenario I hope I will never have to play out, so I baby my tent preciously.

When evening arrives the wind is still howling. The trees sway and my tent shakes violently. This type of wind would be dreadful to pack up in. I don't think I will leave if it stays like this. This storm could last days, though, and I really need to get past Ambler before the river thaws out and forces me to ski through the trees every day to make distance; a near impossible chore. I prepare some lentil and sausage soup for dinner and cook it an extra few minutes to get rid of the burned spruce needles that are stuck to the bottom of the inside of my pot. I think I scooped them up with the snow. Spruce needles fall from the trees when the wind blows and new snow covers them up, so I can't see them when I collect snow to melt.

April 9, 2007

It's morning and the icy wind still whips through. It rolls off the mountains on the north side of the Kobuk River and is hurled into the valley. The wind may never stop blowing so I consider packing up today anyway. I heard a squirrel earlier, a hint of pleasant weather, but it's gone now. This wind is colder and blows harder than it did along the coast near the Hotham Inlet. The temperature must be around zero degrees Fahrenheit outside, with thirty-mile-per-hour winds. The cold air alone isn't hard to deal with, but add just a little wind, and functioning outside becomes difficult and dangerous. Fingers and toes can go numb in minutes with the icy wind blasting away.

After some time, I go outside to attempt to pack up so I can begin skiing. I take the cover off my sled and wipe away any snow that has blown inside. I unfold the aluminum poles that attach from the sled to the hip belt. Then I angle the sled so I will have a direct shot toward the river where I need to go when I leave here. I turn the sled around before I begin loading it. After about ten minutes the wind cuts me to the bone so I give up and go back inside. My fingers ache for some time afterward. I decide the air is too cold to travel today; besides, the rest day will bring back my spirits and give me added strength and time to prepare more food. Sitting here for two days makes me think about home and the people and things I miss. I worry about Julie and wonder if she will wait around for me for several months while I'm away. I call her on the satellite phone occasionally, but these calls are expensive so we really don't get to talk long. I'm usually too worn out or busy to miss home too much, but now that I have time to sit around, I do. Julie must be wondering about what I do every day.

I think about Jonny, too, and the day he died. I wonder what I could have done differently to save him, but I shake my head. I try not to dwell on his death because it makes me too sad. I want to remember the good times. I remember when Jonny attacked a porcupine while we were kayaking across Alaska. Quills were embedded all over his mouth. I tried to pull them out at first, but there was no way he was going to let me pluck them all. I had to wait until he fell asleep at night to pull them out. I would quietly position my thumb and index finger above his closed eyes. Then with one quick jerk, I would yank out a quill while he was sound asleep. Jonny would suddenly open his eyes and lift his head, wondering what had just happened. He didn't seem to know if something hurt him or if he had just awakened on his own. Then a minute later he would fall back asleep and I would yank out another. I could yank out four quills a night before he became too alert for me to continue. It took four days to remove them all, but he would have fought me with all his strength if he had been awake.

Then I think about Julie again. I was wondering what she was doing: if she was rowing on her team, riding her bike, or working too much. Mostly when I think about Julie, I wonder if she will be around when I get back, since I will be gone for so long, but there is nothing I can do about it now. I guess this is like a test for us, to see if we are committed to each other. She seems to understand how much I've dreamed about this trip, and this gives me added courage to endure the hardships to the end. Her support helps me feel invincible and gives me something comforting to look forward to when I get home. I think about her smile, her infectious cheer, her laugh, and the way she understands my half-worded conversations and mumbling voice when I'm tired. I miss the illimitable spirit she injects into me and the contentedness I get from her companionship. Why do I risk something I want less for something I want more? Maybe I'm greedy and think I can have both. Maybe we all do. Maybe thinking we can have everything is the primary, human condition. Maybe contentedness is something that must be learned. Perhaps we must practice it to perfect it. Perhaps those born in the wild have had contentedness forced upon them, because in childhood they knew no other way. Do tranquil environments nurture the serenity in children or are some children just born serene no matter what the environment? I think serenity is innate in everyone and that a chaotic environment contributes to people's hyperactivity. It makes them oblivious to their own existence. I think nature is tranquil and nurtures the innate tranquillity of humans, as well as many other species.

I start to get antsy to be moving on and don't want to stay here anymore. I'm tired of being cooped up in my small tent alone. I'm also afraid to travel when the weather is dangerously cold and when I don't know what waits ahead. The unknown is almost always unnerving. The longer I stay in one place, the more I feel the pressure to move on. Eventually this pressure will override my urge to stay. I think this, too, is part of the innate nature that humans possess, which may stem from a nomadic existence that evolved a million years ago. This feeling gets stronger when I'm alone. I begin to feel like I need to travel to where there are other people, for their companionship. I know for certain, though, that I'm not going back the way I came. I'm dead set on going forward, even if I have to wait here for two weeks. All the snowmobiles behind me take away from the wilderness feel. I want to get to the mountains where it's too rugged and far for them to travel, but I know I must wait for better weather. I know I must be patient and not do anything foolish.

In the afternoon when the air temperature is the warmest, I spend time waxing my skis and sleds to help us travel faster for when we get back on the river. It involves rubbing a stick of wax over the entire undersurface of the skis and sleds, and then smoothing out all the chunky spots with a square piece of cork material that is about four inches long. Reducing my energy expenditure or finding more food is critical when traveling on foot through such a large wilderness. It would only take a few setbacks to put me on a collision course for starvation, a collision course for death.

April 10, 2007

I wake up around eight o'clock to try to get on the trail by one o'clock. It's a slow, agonizing process getting packed up in such cold. The squirrel is squawking again. Actually, I hear two, so maybe today will be a good day. There are only slight wind gusts, nothing like yesterday. I will ski every day now until I get to Ambler, as long as the weather holds. In this kind of cold I often want to ski two days and then rest one. It takes so long to pack up that an entire day off goes a long way between travel days. Sometimes I may spend as long as four hours packing because I have to keep getting back in my tent to warm up, and then I may spend only four hours skiing. This still makes for an exhausting eight-hour day. If I take a rest day I can spend some time in the late afternoon leisurely sorting gear to make packing up a little faster for the next day when I depart.

I meet a stout woman today on the trail driving her dog team from Kobuk Village to Kiana. She seems capable and calm, and she wears a long, purple parka that looks like a thick skirt. The woman also wears a large-bladed hunting knife around her waist on the outside of her parka, which is strapped to a wide, leather belt. She could be Daniel Boone's double. She stakes down her dogs a hundred yards away and comes over to talk. "I can't get too close to dog teams with these dogs," I say as I hold Jimmy and Will, who are barking at the huskies.

"They chase dog teams, do they?" she asks.

"Yeah, I'm afraid so. If they get a chance," I say. I can barely hear her speak over Jimmy's and Will's constant barking. No amount of talking to them can stop them until they decide to stop by themselves, which they are not likely to do until the dog team leaves. "Where are you heading?" I ask loudly enough to be heard over the dogs. The noise doesn't appear to bother her and she acts as if there is no barking at all. She must be used to it.

"Down to Kiana from Kobuk," she says. "How about you?"

I smile, not knowing if I will get a negative response from her.

"I'm just heading east as far as I can for four months," I say, pointing in that direction and chuckling. It sounds like such a colossal journey when I say it out loud to someone. It almost sounds unbelievable, even to myself. "I want to try to get to Anaktuvuk Pass anyway. I'm supposed to meet my brothers there."

"Wow, that's great," she says. I appreciate her positive response. This kind of verbal support was a little lacking in my male-dominated family. I had to rely more on my stubborn nature to get things done.

"How long are you on the trail for?" I ask her.

"Just two weeks. I travel a bit faster than you, I think."

"That's true," I say.

We talk for a few more minutes. "There's a hot spring up the trail a ways," she says as she heads back over to her dogs. "It's not hard to find, and it's pretty nice after a day on the trail." Then the woman picks up the metal hook out of the snow that holds her dog team in place and takes off down the trail the way I had just come. I'm glad to meet another hardy adventurer, and I watch her until she sleds over the edge of the river and into the trees. As I watch her I wish the world had more people like her, those who aren't afraid to strike out on their own, and those who aren't afraid to take on the unknown. But I think most of us have to work too much. I think Julie works too much. It leaves us little time to take off for personal growth. I wish Julie had more time in her life to pursue the things she dreams about. I wish Julie and I could go on nature outings anytime for as long as we want. I wish we could go stay in a cabin on the Oregon coast, travel through Mexico, or take a stroll in Drift Creek, anytime, with no obligations to drag us back. I wish she were here, but I think this part of my journey would be too strenuous for her. It would be for anyone.

I travel fast and by the end of the day I come to a recreational cabin in Kobuk Valley National Park. The inside is dingy and dirty, but I welcome the relief from the wind. After I sweep the floor, I set my tent up inside for more warmth. It's nice to be able to spread all my food and gear out in a large dry area where I can reach items without having to dig through storage bags, and where there is no wind to freeze my fingers when I take off my gloves.

While camped at the park shelter, two natives from Kobuk Village pull up in their snowmobiles towing a trailer full of huskies. The natives' faces are much darker with more chiseled features than the faces of other indigenous people I've seen so far. They act introverted and aloof like they don't want much to do with me, but they do tell me they had just come from a dog sled race. "Really, how did you do?" I ask.

"Dead last," the taller man says as they begin adding gasoline to their snowmobiles from their reserve cans in the back of their trailer.

"You guys plan on staying here tonight?" I ask them because for a moment it looks like they are unloading their gear. I hope they don't want to stay in the cabin; I have all my gear and food laid out just the way I like it, and I plan on having a sort of relaxed evening in the comfort of the cabin. I really don't want anyone else around.

"No, we're heading upriver," one man finally replies after about a minute. He seems annoyed, but I'm relieved they aren't staying. It has been more than two weeks since I slept out of the snow, and I'm looking forward to doing it alone with just the dogs. Without other people inside, I will be able to sleep in my tent with the flap open, and the dogs can sleep on the cabin floor if it doesn't get too cold.

Several of their dogs jump out and one comes over to Jimmy, who is temporarily tied to a pole outside so I can organize the inside of the cabin. I was thinking the men might want to come in to warm up. The husky starts growling at Jimmy and I worry that Jimmy might injure the dog if I go inside. Jimmy stands nose to nose with the husky, waiting for a response. Will, who is inside the cabin, hears the husky growling at Jimmy and right away comes flying out through the half-open door in a rage. I know he intends to attack the other dog without hesitation, so I catch him and wrap my arms around him just before he tears into the husky. Will is strong and drags me a couple of feet. I'm tempted to let him loose since the two men with the huskies aren't doing anything to round up their dogs. If they don't care, I figure I shouldn't care if all our dogs intermingle. The only thing that stops me is I know Airedales can do serious damage really fast. After they finish fueling, the men finally load up their dogs. I walk a few feet closer to them. "You guys want a cup of tea for the road?" I ask them, but they only shake their heads a little, then take off upriver toward Kobuk Village without saying much. I wonder what they think of white people. I watch them go and then return with the dogs to the warmth of the cabin.

I'm not sure if the two men were Athabaskan Indians or Eskimo and I don't ask them. Athabaskans are the indigenous people mainly known throughout the interior, mostly below the arctic where there are river forests. They are divided into several regional bands, some of which are the Ingalik of the lower Yukon River and the Kuskokwin River, the Koyukon of the middle Yukon River and the Koyukuk River, the Gwitchin of the upper Yukon River and Porcupine River, and the Han of the upper Yukon River. Because the Athabaskans often hunted different animals from the Eskimo and used different material to build their shelters and make their clothes, they had a different culture. Their hunting rituals centered on different animals. Athabaskans probably hunted more moose than the Eskimo. Athabaskans probably took less food from the ocean, like whales and walruses, and they probably caught more migrating salmon than the Eskimo. Common to all Indians and Eskimo, though, was that they all moved around throughout the seasons going to where food was more abundant that time of year. One belief common to Athabaskans before their culture was disrupted by white culture— perhaps it still exists—was that the spirits of animals and humans were indistinguishable. I like this aboriginal lore, and by believing in it maybe I can treat wilderness and wild animals better.

Humans have done terrible things to one another over the years. For me the fate of aboriginals is intrinsically tied up with my concerns about the environment. I know that if you protect the Indians you protect the land, at least for a time. I'm always drawn to the idea of being able to live in the vast rain forest like the isolated Indians do. Perhaps only the few remaining nomadic tribes of the Amazon still understand nature on the level I want to. Maybe they are the only people on the planet who still live completely according to the evolution of their brains, which I think encourages them to move freely in wilderness. They have never had to endure a lifestyle that requires so much mundane work to keep an economy growing. I think most of us have to fight against our nature while living in this modern world. It's not permanent like wilderness, and it arose after our brains had evolved a consciousness to live in wilderness. We're not sure how to handle modernity at times, made evident by the impatience we feel in our daily lives.

THE ALLURE OF WILDERNESS

I know it's morning by the dim light seeping into my sleeping bag. I pull the hood tightly over my head to thwart the chill. Then I reposition my arctic jacket to cover my face. I keep every inch of my body covered so no cold air gets through, or else I will feel it spread down my neck and back. I have to go to the bathroom, so I throw on my thick jacket and ski boots, then go outside still half asleep. I miss the comfort of a warm, dry bathroom in the morning. The dogs rush out, too, hitting everything on the way. I keep one on a leash. If I don't they will run off together and not return for hours. I'm afraid a wolverine trap might kill them. The trap consists of a plastic bucket placed sideways in the snow with bait at the rear. Over the bucket's entrance is a heavy, steel-jawed trap, about two feet wide, which is large enough to crush a wolverine's head with one quick, smashing blow. It would kill a dog or wolf even quicker. Wolverine trappers are sometimes mindless of dogs, setting the traps right along dog sledding tracks. I found one trap a mile back along the river as I was searching for a place to camp under some spruce trees. I followed a single snowmobile track over the bank, hoping it would lead me to an isolated and comfortable camp spot. Instead I found a wicked, metal trap, set to kill. I left without getting too close. I had the dogs tied in front of me and didn't want to risk their becoming interested in the trap.

I hurry back inside my tent with the dogs, then straighten up everything they knock around. I push all my gear into a pile to lean against as I make breakfast. The dogs curl up and go back to sleep, content to rest a little longer in the warmth of the tent. I read Edward Abbey as I sip my drink and learn that he had a brother named Johnny. This makes me think of my dog Jonny. I miss him and sometimes reach out to him in the middle of the night when I'm on the trail. I find Jimmy and Will there in his place.

Before Edward Abbey died, he made it known to a close friend that he wanted to be buried in the desert, without the prying eyes of government, corporations, and society telling him how and where he could rest his dead bones. He had no desire to spend eternity in a graveyard lying next to the rotten corpses of the mindless masses of humanity; he saw some people as enemies of the natural world he loved. Abbey perhaps felt that this was the last great connection someone could make with nature—choosing which wild location to leave his remains. And when he died, a friend drove his pickup truck with Abbey's corpse, sitting on ice in the back, to a secret location in the desert and buried Abbey the way he wanted.

Over the dreary morning chill, I hear a lone snowmobile sputter by along the river's main course, not on the shortcut trail that I've taken to cut another bend in the river. It's the first snowmobile I've heard in two days. Maybe he's trapping, or maybe he's just going to the next village to visit friends or family. He has a way to go. I hear the grinding drone of the smoky machine fade into the distance. The silence returns and I can hear the soft scuffling of snowflakes fluttering onto my tent, the raven squawking in the trees, and more silence. Then I'm alone again on the land with the ice, the dogs, and wilderness. It's beautiful.

In the afternoon the sun breaks through the clouds and the temperature begins to warm. I head onto some high ground away from the Kobuk River and stop to sit on my sled and let the dogs rest. I pull my water bottle from my sled and drink several times while I look around. I take one gulp at a time because the water is always so cold that it hurts my head if I drink too much too quickly, like eating ice cream fast. I can't get enough of the view and watch for about twenty minutes, unable to avert my eyes. I stand up to see better. In every direction I look, even across the river, the land is laid out in low hills interspersed with spruce trees. The hills are about a hundred feet high with wide sprawling tops. They look like white Saharan sand dunes. I can see one after another quite clearly as they roll off each other into the distance. I can almost pick my exact route across them for about ten miles. The hills stretch away from me for at least twenty miles in every direction, and on the south side of the Kobuk River, they stretch out for about forty miles until they collide with larger mountains that spring up, encased in clean snow and ice. The mountains that rise up all have forests of spruce covering their bases, but those forests end abruptly as I scan farther up the mountains to their rigid peaks. I can see massive gaps between some of the mountain ranges that surround me where entire rivers flow through on their way to the Kobuk. I can't see the rivers themselves, except for the huge Kobuk a few miles away, but I can only see their valleys. I like the way a valley slips away behind a certain mountain until I can't see where it goes. I imagine it as a secret gateway to an undiscovered wilderness on the other side.

I'm convinced the land behind those mountains in Kobuk Valley National Park is an amazing place. I think there is more unseen wild land here than what I can see. And I can see a lot of wild land from this view. Snowmobiles sporadically travel the main route that leads to several villages along the Kobuk River, but once off that course, I think you would be completely alone. I'm tempted to spend my four months here exploring and roaming the many rivers and mountains, but I'm trying to meet my brothers in Anaktuvuk Pass on May 26, so I have to keep moving. This would be an enormous place to explore on foot. Looking on my map, there are rivers and mountains that I've never heard of in the region. Just to my north alone are several rivers such as the Kitlik, the Nikok, the Salmon, and the Tutuksuk, and mountains like the Akiak Mountains, and many others without names. And beyond those mountains and rivers are more rivers and mountains spread out across a world even more remote and wild.

The dogs and I soon start skiing and make our way off the high ground back down to the river where it straightens out again. Then we head east. This part of the river is frozen into continuous rough chunks that make for a bumpy ride, but only slow our progress slightly. The dogs are eager and pulling strongly. We come across wolf tracks the size of saucers on a back channel of the river. The tracks appear to be following moose. I can see footprints and fur-filled dung littering the snow. The dogs become more upbeat when they smell the wolves, and they want to follow their trail. I allow the dogs to pull hard since this is the way we need to go anyway. For a couple of minutes they go so fast that I can only help with the use of my poles, jamming them both into the river ice at the same time on each stroke. I bounce a little with both thighs and bend at the waist on each stroke while putting my entire torso into the effort. A rabbit runs across our path, which makes the dogs even more excited. I think about the lynx I heard a few nights ago and wonder if the animal caught anything.

Soon I see a moose, but there are no wolves. The moose stands back away from the river in the dense willows and deep snow. I don't know how a wolf could function in such deep snow while trying to kill a moose. Moose are cautious about walking onto ice. If they have any doubt at all about its strength, they avoid it completely. They will follow the edge of a three-foot-wide, icy creek for miles rather than risk getting stuck. Wolves aren't as afraid of thin ice as moose, and grizzly bears aren't afraid of ice at all. It never deters a large bear's course. Their trail will sometimes lead right across half-frozen creeks, rivers, and lakes in the month of May. They can claw their way out of any broken ice and if it keeps breaking on them, they just forge ahead without any change in course. If bears can't touch the bottom, they swim and climb onto the ice without too much effort. If the ice keeps breaking, they keep swimming and climbing until they get to where they are going. In a land where terrain is difficult everywhere, bears understand that going straight ahead and dealing with the terrain in front of them is more efficient than making detours. I will discover the bears' travel methods in the coming days by observing many of their tracks.

The next day we make our way along the river on fresh snowmobile tracks. It snowed last night and the clanging machines have left the trail layered with globs of icy snow that are like skiing on a field of golf balls. However, this is still easier than skiing on fresh snow without a trail. We cross over onto Onion Portage, where the trail leads overland all the way to the village of Ambler. The Jade Mountains jut up magnificently to the north and I keep skiing as I watch them. Five or six peaks appear, right in a row, with high passes between them. Their summits are steep and icy, with brown, craggy ridges running down their distinct corners. Except for the mountains' much lower elevation, they look like they belong in the Himalayas. Sometimes I stumble over uneven snow when I'm gawking at them and not watching the trail ahead.

We make good time, and because we get near Ambler so late in the day I decide to camp about three miles from town. I have to dig out a spot for my tent in deep snow. I use my blue, plastic sled as a shovel, since I broke my real shovel days ago. I dig nearly three feet down, which takes me more than an hour. I have to dig almost to the ground because the snow is so dry and powdery that it won't pack down. The air temperature is starting to drop as the sun recedes behind the hills, and the dogs can't wait to get in when I'm finished.

April 14, 2007, three and a half miles from Ambler

I get to Ambler by skiing downhill on a winding trail through spruce trees. The dogs pull so fast that I almost crash several times while going around sharp turns. On an extremely steep section, I have to take off my skis and walk backward as I ease the sleds down. I urge the dogs to walk next to me by pulling on their leashes to get them on my side, and then by giving them a few quick jerks when they try to go ahead of me. Getting the dogs to walk beside me was difficult the first time I tried it. They wanted to pull like I had encouraged them to do their entire lives. They have learned since then not to pull me when I'm walking down steep hills.

As the terrain flattens out I let the dogs run full on down a slight grade. They run like the wind and sense we are nearing something new. Like most people, the dogs enjoy coming to a village after time spent in the woods. Two miles from town I think I take a wrong turn and find myself standing on the edge of a garbage dump. This is a rude awakening, like the wind has been knocked out of me. The dump is as wide as a skyscraper, stinking of rotten and decaying food particles. I have to cover my nose with my balaclava. Someone has recently burned much of the trash, and the charred remains smolder with stench. The rancid smoke drifts across my face, reeking of fetid dairy products or some other organic material that used to be edible. I can't believe the noxious pit is so large for such a tiny village, and it makes me remember how much larger my own city dump is back home, sprawling across an entire hilltop. I see old refrigerators, computer parts, automotive chunks, unrecognizable scraps of steel, fenders, worn tires, frayed cable, splintered cabinets, broken kitchen chairs, hole-filled buckets, heaps of plastic wrappers, and food-packaging containers; and many other things all disposable that must be gotten rid of when people are finished with them.

I veer away from the dump through a few trees to get back on the main trail. I ski through a birch and spruce forest that starts to show a hint of warmth—I see water dripping off the branches. Gliding off the hills outside of town, we come off the trail, hit the main road, and blast into town as the dogs get a whiff of new scents. I have to snowplow to slow them down as we approach the town center doing about ten miles per hour. I move my feet far apart and then point the tips of my skis toward each other until they almost touch. Then I turn the insides of my feet down several times in a pumping motion, like I'm pumping my brakes. I stop the dogs by using this hard plowing motion, but this takes several attempts while saying to them, "Stop, stop." It's Sunday so the store is closed, but I check the sign on the door to see when it will open. Then I ski over to find the post office for the next day when I will come back to get my packages. We head to the river and make camp up a ways from the main port area along the Kobuk River.

Just downriver the Ambler River meets the Kobuk River. Following the Ambler River north will be our route into the mountains and the start of a far more difficult section of the journey. When I turn off the Kobuk River and start up the smaller Ambler River toward the Gates of the Arctic National Park, the frequent snowmobile tracks that I've been skiing on since Kotzebue will almost certainly vanish. There aren't any villages up that way, so people driving snowmobiles don't have much of a reason to go there. From Ambler to the next village of Anaktuvuk Pass is about 300 miles, and I'm almost positive I'll be on my own and breaking my own trails. My trip so far is going to look like a cakewalk compared to what I will face after I leave the village of Ambler.

The town is quiet and I don't hear many snowmobiles racing around like I did in Kiana and Kotzebue. Ambler is kind of a serene place and the more I look around the more I begin to like it here. Even though the village is the highest in elevation of any village I've encountered so far, it appears to sit in a protected trough. Heavily forested hills of spruce and birch almost totally surround the village, and along the river the forest is even denser, with large cottonwoods sprouting on the edge of the spruce forests. In the main center of the village are a store, a post office, and some sort of large native meeting hall. Away from the center of the village is a tightly knit row of houses; most are modern like in almost any city in rural Oregon. But there are also older log homes built with logs taken from the forest in the area. On the other side of the village center is a freshly painted school with a large field out front, covered with a foot of snow. And across the main road from the school is a medical clinic that also looks freshly painted. Neither the walls of the school nor the clinic have been blasted bare from the weather, like so many other dwellings in Alaska. The village is completely free of garbage, the clutter of building materials, and automotive debris. The few people I see outside are walking quietly like they are going somewhere. They don't stop and stare at me, or laugh or giggle, or gyrate their bodies while making fun of me. They simply walk by with polite smiles on their faces and continue on with their own affairs and leave me to mine. I recognize this politeness instantly. These people are not depressed, irrationally drunk, drugged, or belligerent. I think they are confidently calm and know and respect their place in the world. They appear comfortable where they live. In the other villages I've seen so far people rarely walked, and they all seemed to be traveling around like they didn't have a destination in mind. Along the Kobuk River and away from the village, there are a few new log cabins built up in the low hills among the spruce trees. They look like cabins and woods I would find near resort towns in the Cascade Mountains of Oregon. Besides the nice people and the forested terrain, these cabins in the woods are what most attract me to this place.

April 15, 2007

I'm nearly a week ahead of schedule now, but I will need to get up the Ambler River and across the Gates of the Arctic. I will have to cross over dozens of rivers, entire mountain ranges, and land as large as some states, so I'll need every extra day. I'm going to have to ration my food all the way to Anaktuvuk Pass, which means I will be eating smaller meals once I leave here. This is far better than starving toward the end of this leg of the journey.

I sleep comfortably during the night. Maybe it's the knowledge that I'm near people and food—safety. But I wake up again to the screech of a lynx prowling in the moonlight. It takes a special breed of cat to survive this far north, and they are the only cats that inhabit Alaska. Lynx are specific about the prey they pursue, almost exclusively snowshoe hares. Lynx have large feet for their size, which allows them to travel easily over deep snow, unlike bobcats with smaller feet and shorter legs. Bobcats are less picky in the food they eat, and they're more aggressive than lynx, but in this environment they could not compete against lynx.

Lynx have to be good at catching hares, and if the hare population crashes, they have to travel long distances in search of more hares. All cats have superb hearing, but lynx may have the best. They have a small tuft of hair that grows on the tips of their ears to fine-tune their hearing. I'm convinced they detect hares at night, not first by sight, but by sound. They hear a snowshoe hare move when they rip off their dreaded screech.

I grow to admire these solitary cats who hunt mainly at night, and every time I hear them I begin to root for them and hope they are finding enough to eat. I start to take comfort when I know a lynx is nearby. I'm not sure why. Perhaps when a lynx is around, it means a bear or a wolf pack isn't.

Before I leave here I'll scatter a little bit of dog food on the snow to give the lynx a meal since I intruded on its wanderings. I'm not sure if the lynx will eat it. I may have cost the animal a meal by being here, so it's the least I can do, especially since I can get more food from the store.

Mountain lions don't exist in Alaska, either. I don't think they can compete with wolves, or perhaps caribou are too fast for them to catch, and moose are too big for a single cat to kill. Wolves have stamina and can run down a caribou, but a mountain lion has to get close enough for a killing sprint. I'm not sure mountain lions can do this in Alaska. I think in regions where there are both mountain lions and wolves like the mountains of Idaho, there has to be forest cover so the mountain lions can avoid a pack of wolves either by hiding or by climbing a tree. One on one against a wolf a mountain lion would have no trouble, but where there is one wolf there is often at least another close by. I think lynx, too, tend to seek the cover of trees, since their habitat almost always overlaps wolf habitat.

April 16, 2008

I don three layers of socks and my hiking boots, then walk to the post office from my camp towing empty sleds. I stomp my feet outside on the metal-grated steps before entering. A man in his fifties greets me. "How can I help you?" he asks with a smile.

"I have some packages to pick up," I say, and then I tell him my name.

"Oh, yes," he says, like he has been expecting me. "You have quite a few boxes." Then he marks something on the paper in front of him and walks in the back. He returns several times until I have five bulky boxes sitting on the floor in the tiny post office lobby. Another man comes in but he stands and waits next to the wall without acting the least bit hurried or anxious. I turn to him and smile as I fumble with my boxes.

"I'm on a little ski trip," I say, not really wanting to tell him where I came from or where I'm going. I don't always think people understand those who undertake a long expedition; one that lasts several weeks and traverses countless miles. I feel like some people might think I'm wasting my time.

"Where did you come from?" he asks.

"From Kotzebue three weeks ago," I say bluntly, but with a smile.

"Wow, that's a good ways," he says, but I don't tell him where I'm heading. I don't tell him I'm getting ready to ski to Anaktuvuk Pass, and I sure don't tell him I'm trying to trek all the way across Alaska through the Brooks Range. Nobody would believe it. Most of my friends and family had a hard time believing it, except Julie and my childhood friend Jeff. Julie encouraged me from the start. "I'm going to try and make it all the way across the state," I said to her in the months before my departure. I expected doubt from her and for her to say something like "gosh," or "Are you sure you can go that far," like I got from other people. But she wasn't like that at all.

One of Julie's relatives wrote in an e-mail, "I can't believe someone would take that on." It made me feel stupid, but unaffected in the belief of my own abilities. No one's indecisiveness about what I was about to undertake made me hesitate in what I was going to do. My journey had been building in me for years, and I had become mentally ready for it. I knew what it would take to cross Alaska, and I was completely ready and mentally prepared to endure the suffering and the consequences. Julie's positive outlook on my trek gave me an added emotional boost that I wasn't expecting. She quickly became fully supportive of it, and would smile and say things like "okay" and "great" when I was preparing the logistics with her. Jeff, too, was quick to lend support like this. I sought him out before I left, knowing I could count on him to tell me that what I was doing was fantastic, that I wasn't going to miss anything important in the modern world. Jeff was always like that. He had a bright outlook on the most difficult circumstances, like strife and adversity were no big deal—insignificant and measly. I was drawn to him during times in my life when I began to doubt myself.

Thanks to my brother Rick, his son Michael, and Julie, I have ninety pounds of dog food to manhandle back to my camp. The dogs will need every bit. I load all my boxes into the sleds and then stop at the school on my way to charge the batteries on my satellite phone and camera like I did in Kiana. I walk into the main office and greet a lady working at her desk. "Good afternoon," I say, trying to be overly polite so she will help me. "I'm on a ski trip through the area," I say. "Do you think it would be possible to use an outlet to charge my satellite phone and camera?" Just about then a man, who I think is the principal, walks in. The woman relays my request. I think the teachers and school administrators are the ones in the village who are most accustomed to seeing travelers.

"Oh, sure, why don't you plug them in right there on the counter," he says.

"That would be great, thank you," I say, and then the principal walks out. I get up and plug the base of my phone into one outlet and the battery charger for my camera into another. I tell the lady sitting at the desk that I'll come back for them in a couple of hours. On my way out the door, three teachers, one woman and two men, come in and ask me where I'm heading. I tell them I'm trekking to Anaktuvuk Pass. The female teacher is cheerfully optimistic and thinks it's great.

The two men ask me a lot of skeptical questions like, "How are you going to get through all those mountains?" or "Do you know how far that is?" as if I had never looked on a map to study the distance and terrain, or like this was the first camping trip of my life.

"With a lot of time and patience," I answer the first question, like it's no big deal. "And yes it's quite a ways," I answer the second question. One of the men has a look of disbelief on his face, like someone shot him in the gut with a rifle. I try to explain to make it sound more believable. "I have three more months and I just want to see how far I can get before I have to go home." Being in the wilderness for four months is more my goal than actually getting across the Gates of the Arctic. Also I figure I can get a cheaper flight home from the Dalton Highway at the end of my trip than from anywhere else. Maybe I can hitchhike down to Fairbanks.

In the later afternoon after retrieving my camera and phone, I sort through my supplies back at my camp along the river. The temperature has risen to a comfortable thirty-two degrees, and with little wind I actually work outside my tent in just a sweater. I open all the boxes and stare at the contents, I eat several chocolate bars in about ten minutes and build a fire using the cardboard and packaging material that will burn. I bag up the packaging that won't burn to take to the garbage can in front of the grocery store before I leave. It will likely end up in the dump on the edge of town. Knowing this brings to light how much garbage humans create; it has to be taken somewhere, or dealt with somehow.

I feel like a rich man with so much food. I eat constantly while I'm at camp. I know I can buy more food at the store. It's important for me to eat as much as I can before I leave. The more calories I can pump into myself, and the dogs, the better off we'll be. And the more food I can carry out of Ambler, the greater my chances of making it to Anaktuvuk Pass. I have two dozen bagels, which I want to eat in the next day or two. They're bulky and take up space in my sleds. I would rather pack food like beans to take along because they are a more compact food, and though my sled will be heavier, I can load food with more calories into all the space. When I'm pulling sleds at the start of a 300-mile leg, I want to have a large amount of calories. By having a lot of food with me I will have to travel slower, but it will give me more time to think and plan my strategy as I make my way to Anaktuvuk Pass. At this point I really don't know if I can get to Anaktuvuk Pass. I don't even really know what lies ahead, except what the maps tell me. Besides, if I travel too fast, I will reach the high mountains when there is too much snow. I need much of that snow to melt before I begin hiking, but I still have to get up part of the Ambler River before it thaws out. By carrying a large load of food, I can ski up the river and be in position to wait for some of the snow to melt if I have to. If I can get through immediately I will, but if I can't at least I will have enough food to wait for some of the snow and ice to disappear.

April 17, 2007

In the morning I stare at all my supplies stacked in the vestibule of my tent. I wonder how I will get all this food into my sleds. I look outside. A Clark's nutcracker is sitting on a willow near my tent, and the first furry willow bud of spring has broken from its capsule. The hint of summer is in the air.

I have one large bag with nothing but beans in it that weighs about thirty pounds; one bag of energy bars, chocolates, and assorted snacks that weighs fifteen pounds; one miscellaneous food bag that weighs thirty pounds; one freeze-dried food bag that contains fifteen packets; and of course the ninety pounds of dog food. It seems impossible now, but I will somehow get it all loaded. I never leave behind food when I travel in the wilds of Alaska. I never know when I could be stranded somewhere for a month and need it.

I take the sleds down the bank from my campsite, and then I work several hours loading them. I make sure the sleds are aligned in the right direction upriver. Once they are loaded it will take some effort to move them around. I use every inch of space, making sure I get all my food in. With the weather warming, I leave some of my cold weather gear behind. I take my old extra sleeping bag, a sweater, one of my extra skis, and put them in a pile next to the garbage can and leave a sign that says FREE on it. I put the remainder of the items I want to leave behind in the trash can with all my garbage, more man-made refuse for the garbage dump.

After I finish packing, I change into my ski boots, and attach the dogs to the sleds. They bounce up and down, ready to go. They get impatient while I'm getting ready, and they start howling. They know we're leaving, but I don't think they know what is ahead. I lay my skis out in front of the sleds facing upriver. I plant both my ski poles in the snow on each side of me. "Stay guys, stay," I say to the dogs with a firm voice. By now, they don't pull until I tell them. Partly they don't pull until they feel me pulling on the sleds. It takes some of the strain off them. Now and then they'll test the weight of the sleds by leaning forward into their harnesses. Stepping into my last ski is the point where they could start pulling if they wanted to without me being able to stop them, like they did in the beginning couple of days, since I won't have a free foot to hold myself against the surface of the snow. But they don't pull until I'm ready. After my last ski is on and I have both poles in my hands, I lean into my waist belt and give a little hiss. "Get up," I say softly. It's the only cue they need. They crouch low to get traction, and in a second, the 200 pounds of cargo creaks forward and starts to glide. They put their entire exuberant bodies into the effort. We cruise upriver, past the frozen boat ramp, and make our way along a few homes on the side of the river, and then after about an hour we turn left onto the wild Ambler River.

Snowmobiles still travel along the Kobuk River, so I assume it's at least safe to get upriver a mile to where the Ambler River joins the Kobuk. I cross the Ambler River several times following snow-mobile tracks. The river is getting sketchy as the air warms and the snow begins to melt. Starting tomorrow, I won't likely cross the river anymore to cut bends. I can't risk falling under the ice. Perhaps higher in the mountains the water will only be a couple of feet deep and not so dangerous. I see several wolf and moose tracks crossing the river in various places and I begin to suspect that this region is going to be a wild place, and despite my mild trepidation of entering an unknown land alone, my heart beats with the thrill of adventure.

In my view wilderness is everything. Besides being the natural condition of the planet containing enough genetic biodiversity for life to exist for an almost infinite amount of time, it's much more. It's where sweeping vistas of ancient forests spread out before me, and where rows of indomitable mountains entice me to see what's on the other side. Wilderness is an endless world where I can explore any direction I choose, independent and self-sufficient, where the mechanical noises of industrialization have not yet penetrated. It's serene, clean, and vacant of too much humanity; a world of wild animals and a few hardy, earthly individuals who don't desire anything but to breathe, eat, and live.

BLAZING MY OWN TRAIL

April 18, 2007, twelve miles past Ambler

During the night as the temperature outside rises, rain begins to fall for the first time since my arrival in Alaska. A raging wind whips down the Ambler River with such force that it sounds like a freight train is going by. It shakes with each passing gust. I wake up just after having gone to bed. "What the hell," I say. My body is hot and sweaty, and I feel like I'm suffocating. I start yanking off clothes. I peel off three layers until I'm down to just one layer of thermal underwear and one pair of socks. I can wiggle my toes around unrestricted while warm blood surges through them. I feel my torso. Before starting my journey I had let myself gain ten extra pounds, knowing I would need the extra fat on my body. Now my ribs are starting to stick out. "Hmmm, I must have lost a few pounds," I say to myself.

In the morning the wind is still blowing, though not as hard as it was during the night. The outside air is above freezing. Little pools of water are forming on the river ice, and though I could probably get away with it, I don't think I will ski anymore on the river ice. I will have to go through the trees now and travel over land. This will be slow and far more difficult, but I can't risk falling through the river. I can let the dogs drink from a puddle this morning after I get out of my tent. This way I won't have to waste time melting snow or ice for them. Because of the overcast sky, I decide to stay put until it clears. My plan is to inch my way upriver while eating some of the food weight I'm carrying. Since I have plenty of food right now, traveling great distances in a day is not that critical; not yet. Then when I can finally get rid of my sleds and start hiking, I will have a lighter load and be able to travel faster once over the high pass.

The next day I stay put as well to wait out the snowy, wet conditions, brought in by the south wind. Large gaping holes have appeared in the ice today. Even along the edges, there are holes opening up. I can see the gurgling current rushing underneath. I will have to backtrack half a mile around the bend to where there is some open ground that I can ski on. But first I make a little foray along the Ambler up to where the Redstone River joins in. The entire route is heavily wooded, so skiing in the trees would be burdensome to nearly impossible. The Redstone looks too large to cross at its mouth, and I get the eerie feeling it will break if I try to cross it, so I return to camp.

April 20, 2007

About six inches of new snow falls during the night and in the morning the sky is still dark and gray, but since I have been waiting for two days I feel some pressure to get moving. I pack up a few hours later when I get a little lapse in the weather. Packing up with wet snow falling is miserable. Some of my gear is wet. I put a plastic sheet over my sleds while I shove gear into them from my tent. Then when all of my food and gear is out of the tent, I start to take it down. Once I remove the rain fly, I work fast to roll up the main body of the tent so it doesn't become too wet.

We leave in the afternoon and go back about a half mile, rounding a bend in the river. At the end of the bend where the river is at its most northern position on this stretch, I leave it and head northeast onto some open ground. I'm hoping I will be able to travel easier without having to dodge spruce trees. I sink into the deep, fresh snow and can only make a quarter mile an hour. I have to put ski skins on the bottom of my skis. A ski skin is a long piece of fabric designed to cover the entire undersurface of the ski. It has an adhesive surface on one side that causes it to stick to the ski without coming off. The other side is rough and rides against the surface of the snow. Ski skins allow me to climb hills or pull heavy loads without slipping backward. They can also help me slow down on steep descents or when the dogs are pulling me too strongly on slick river ice.

The dogs can't pull at all and it's difficult enough for them just to stay out in front of me. They have to hop through the snow because it's too soft and deep for them to walk through. I can't let them off their leashes. I'm afraid they will run back toward the river and fall through the ice, though it's probably safer than I think. The river's flatter surface attracts them, and they want to run. The river is fairly large, so if the dogs or I were to break through the surface we would probably go under, and I don't think I would be able to touch the bottom.

I break through the snowy surface on every stride, which stops my forward movement each time until I rock my body forward a couple of times to get the sleds moving again. When the first, larger sled breaks through the crust of the snow, it sits there like an anvil. To get the sled moving forward again requires lugging it over the rim of the fresh crust that is in front of it and through the tracks of my skis, which are too narrow for the sled to fit into. The front sled must be yanked through a narrow ski path, which is about two feet deep and bordered by hard, crusty snow. I can only make good time when the crust is firm enough so that I don't break through and make trenches with my skis. And I make even better time when neither the sleds nor I break through. Now, though, they fall through on every stride and we travel only one mile in three hours. It's exhausting and disheartening. I snap a ski pole in half trying to shove myself forward. I cram the broken pole under some straps on the top of my sled and get out my spare poles, which are longer than the others by three inches.

After an hour of struggle, we reach firmer snow away from the river. Still we break through the crust, but only about every twenty yards now. First the dogs fall through and stutter-step as they try to get back onto a firm crust. Then I try to avoid where they had fallen through by skiing just to the side, but often I also break through as well. Then the sleds slide in behind me, ramming into the pit I had just made with my skis. They jam into the side of the pit while coming to a complete halt. Since I try to go really fast hoping to propel the sleds out of the pit I had made with my skis, I'm often yanked to an abrupt, hard stop in the process. Then I have to rock my body again to drag the sleds forward and up onto some firm surface. The efforts are punishing for the muscles of my abdomen. In the coming days I develop a sharp pain in that area.

We turn due east again to get back on course and to attempt to cross the Redstone River. It flows south out of the northern mountains like so many of the rivers around do. When we get closer to the Redstone we reach trees and the dogs go the opposite direction several times, getting wrapped around them. The three of us are still just learning how to maneuver through trees and I think I will probably have to let at least one dog loose when I ski through them. The dogs can't read my mind, though Will will soon learn to pick the route through trees with uncanny intuition, so that I can follow him with enough room to maneuver my two sleds.

We travel just another mile by the end of the day and reach a place where we can cross the Redstone River to continue our route along the Ambler River. The river is only about forty feet wide, but it appears to be a well-cut channel through the land. This indicates that it might be deep, so I'm still a bit fearful to cross on ice like this, especially when there is fresh snow hiding every feature of the ice below.

I can't see cracks, or even the ice itself, so I can't predict its strength. I leave my gear and tie up the dogs to a spruce tree. Then I work my way onto the ice with my skis on; otherwise I will fall through the fresh snow that also covers the river if I didn't have them on. The snow on the river is firmer than the snow on the open ground where we just came from. I go onto the frozen river sideways, taking one small step at a time after jabbing my ice axe in front of me to check for hidden holes. I'm nervous at first, but then it becomes more apparent that this section is solid.

I go back to where I left my sleds and hook up the dogs. We work our way to the edge of the river. I hold them from pulling with brute force, and by walking without my skis on. They know to ease up when I go slowly. We have about thirty yards to cross to the other side. I hope the ice will support the weight of the dogs, both sleds, and me. When I get to the edge of the river I put my skis back on. Then I say in a quick tone, "Ready guys." They look back at me and see that I'm getting ready to ski. Then they turn their heads forward again while taking the slack out of their lines. "Hike, hike," I say with a louder tone as I pull on the sleds, which releases some tension from the dogs. They know by now this is their cue to pull as hard as they want. We pick up some speed and tread on the surface of the snow all the way across with the sleds being towed behind us, without any ice cracking. "Good job, pups," I say, relieved to be across the river. Now I won't have to follow it several miles up to get around it near its headwaters.

On the other side of the Redstone, I find spruce trees with shallow snow beneath them and set up my tent. The ground underneath spruce trees collects less snow than the ground underneath willow bushes. Actually, the ground beneath willow bushes collects the most snow of any type of ground that I've seen. I try to avoid it as much as possible, but there is almost always a row of willows along creeks and rivers that I must cross.

During the night I'm startled awake by the howling of wolves just across the Redstone River. I'm afraid they might come closer so I pull out my shotgun and lay it by my side. Then I put several shells in the pocket of my tent. During the day I carry the gun unloaded and keep a shell in my shirt pocket like Barney Fife. I don't want to shoot my foot while I'm hiking wearily. We can handle one or two wolves, but not an entire pack. My shotgun has no chamber and only holds one shell at a time, so after each shot I have to crack open the barrel and reload. I pick up the gun and look in the barrel to make sure it's clear. I don't care to sleep with a loaded weapon, either. I'm afraid of handling it when I'm half asleep. I chose a single-shot shotgun for its lightness compared to shotguns that have a chamber. I need the power and versatility of a shotgun, but I need it to be light enough for carrying. I purchased it at a sporting goods store for ninety-nine dollars a few years ago, and I learn to cradle and care for it like it's a precious infant. I carry a small bottle of oil, and every few days I ritually wipe the steel parts with a cotton cloth to keep away the rust and dirt, which will corrode it, pitting the inside of the barrel or even jamming the hammer and trigger. Though I like old-style simplicity, this modern weapon may save my life one day.

I wait to hear the wolves' footsteps pattering around my tent, but they never come. I think they trotted off once they realized I was a human. People around here like to shoot and trap wolves, as they do all across Alaska. The wolves have become wary of people for the most part, but if they find dogs without human protection around, they will likely follow and kill them, even large dogs like mine. Wolves often will come close to a tent during the night if they sense a dog is around. A pack of wolves will go out of its way to kill a nonresident wolf, a coyote, or a dog. This is why you don't see many coyotes in Alaska, and the lone wolves you do see are hastily on the move. Wolves kill other wolves and coyotes to fend off their competition for food, but I'm not sure if they kill dogs for the same reason. Maybe they think dogs are prey. Maybe it's their way of getting back at people, by killing man's best friend.

On a drive to northern Canada with Jonny when he was six years old, I had a close encounter with wolves. I was near the southern hills of the Mackenzie Mountains camped down a dirt road off the main highway. I had pitched my tent in the trees and during the night I heard wolves howl off in the distance. I think this is the way wolves make a plan and let each other know that someone or some possible food source is near. They always howl before they check things out.

I waited in the tent and sure enough, ten minutes after their howls had ended, I heard the patter of their paws coming through the woods, moving quickly like a trotting dog. I got a little nervous, so I opened the door of my tent to stick Jonny outside for him to see what was out there. That was his job. If he barked wholeheartedly I knew there would be danger. He only barked once. Then to my astonishment, Jonny did something I had never seen him do before. He got scared and shot back into my tent like a rocket, as if something menacing was just around the corner from my view. Well I freaked because Jonny was so afraid. Almost nothing can frighten an Airedale, so I panicked and froze for a minute. My heart was thumping and my hands were shaking—fight or flight. Then fearing something was coming, I raced out of my tent half dressed, ran the twenty yards through the woods to the road, and jumped in my truck as fast as I could. Jonny leaped into the truck before I could get in and clamored over all the extra gear on the seat. I waited for about fifteen minutes inside my truck. Then I got back out when there were no signs of the wolves dashing around in the dim moonlight. I could hear them howling far off in the distance while they moved away from us through the night. The fear that Jonny had displayed from facing wolves alone was one reason I wanted to get two dogs. They could face the threat together.

In a terrible crisis they could look to each other for support. And if something happened to me, they would at least still have each other.

The temperature during the night drops well below zero, so when I start skiing the next day the snow has a hard crust, which enables us to make fairly good time at first. We pass over bare hills. However, as the day warms the snow softens and my skis start sinking again. We soon come to Cross Creek, which is lined by a twenty-foot-wide wall of willows that I have to work through. The snow is deep and soft. I'm forced to unload my sleds and carry all my gear and food through the willows, across the creek, and out onto the other side where the terrain opens back up. The creek is buried in snow and I sink to my waist in places. I make half a dozen trips to go fifty feet in forty-five minutes. After I load the sleds back up I ski for another twenty minutes until I come to a flat spot that doesn't have any snow. I pitch my tent on the dry tussocks, which I relish as a welcome, warm change from camping on snow for so long. I let both the dogs loose this evening and they prance off together sniffing every bush they come to. I have a great field of view, and I watch them exploring in the distance for about half an hour before they return to camp.

April 22, 2007, twenty miles past Ambler

Today is a hard, slow day. I ski across dozens of areas that don't have snow anymore and where tussock mounds cover the land. I cross two large creeks and can hear water trickling under the ice, but it doesn't break. The creeks remain frozen in snow and ice long after the snow over the land melts. On the second creek I stop to suck some water dribbling over the ice, while the dogs lap up their fill. I fill up my water bottle by using my coffee cup, and then I sit to rest in the sun. The snow on these lower plains is starting to melt quickly. They're open to the sun much of the day and have fewer trees, while the snow at the base of the mountains and in the valleys remains longer, secluded under the shadows cast by peaks and denser forests. That's the type of terrain I'm heading for and I know there will be much more snow. When I leave I forget my water bottle, and I don't remember it until an hour later. I don't feel an urgency to go back for it. I travel only about two miles the entire day meandering my way where the patches of snow are the widest. I literally walk on my skis over the exposed tussocks as I cross from one snow patch to the next, yanking my sleds behind me with brute force.

I let the dogs run around loose when I get to camp again. This is an area of upland rises and a few scattered spruce trees. I feel like I'm far enough away from the Ambler River that they won't get onto it, and I don't believe wolverine traps are in the area. After they have been gone for more than an hour, I begin to worry as the round glowing sun sinks low on the horizon. The imminent dimness of night brings some trepidation. I like to be secure in my camp at this time, prepared to ride out the inherent feeling of danger that settles over me in the evening when I'm alone in the wild. There is some truth to this feeling. The air gets much colder, it's harder to see where I'm going and easier to get lost, and wolves often become more active.

Around ten o'clock I hear Jimmy howling over the low ridge to the west about half a mile away. I know by the sound of his voice that he is lost and confused about how to get back to camp. His penetrating yodel trails off at the end, not sharp, short, or evenly pitched like he would make if he were after an animal. This howl has loneliness in it; the fear of being left behind that anyone could recognize. The terrain looks the same for miles around. Worried about him wandering off in the wrong direction away from camp, I hurry to put on warm clothes and grab my shotgun in case he is confronting wolves. Then I start to run up. It takes me fifteen minutes and I fall through the snow up to my thighs every twenty yards, but I still move quickly, only stopping to listen for his howl to relocate his position and also to keep my own sense of direction. I don't want to get lost and not be able to find my tent again. I would not last the night in the cold. Then I hear Jimmy howling again. I rush on to find him standing in the snow looking languid and bewildered. He perks up once I call to him. At first I think he is injured, but he has simply worn himself out by running all over the area trying to find camp. Not wanting to get lost again, he follows me closely on the way back. We meet Will on the way, who acts like we're playing a fun game. He appears happy and goes over to sniff Jimmy. Then he shakes his head a couple of times to get Jimmy to romp around with him, but Jimmy is too tired. "Hey, Willy boy, how you doing?" I say. I think Will had made it to camp already, and finding I wasn't there, he set out to follow my tracks.

A few years ago when I was hiking through the forest in the Three Sisters Wilderness Area in Oregon, I was standing on the edge of a wide ridge that separated Horse Creek from Eugene Creek. I hadn't seen Jonny in about an hour, and I waited, gazing down the hill through the large trees in the direction I had just come from. Jonny could always follow my scent so I expected him to come from that way. I could see pretty well, because the trees were tall and they had few branches down low around their trunks. Low-growing shrubs of salal, Oregon grape, and sword ferns carpeted the ground in verdant green. Only the tall trunks of the trees spaced several feet from each other were partly obstructing my view. Then I heard Jonny's panting far off in the distance in the valley. I could hear his breathing long before I saw him. It meant he was running, trying to find me. And I knew where he was by the sound of his breath. In the forest of Oregon, I learned to locate many animals by sound alone, especially my dogs, where trees obscure vision. Sounds penetrate deeply in the forest.

Sometimes when Jonny stopped to listen for me he would stop breathing for a couple of seconds; I would detect the silence where just before I had heard his breathing. I would call to him since I knew he would be listening for me cracking branches while I was walking through the forest. He always stopped panting a few seconds when he was listening for something. After calling to him I would usually hear him start panting again, indicating he had heard me and was moving my way.

But this time I didn't yell for him. He was following my scent through the trees and I wanted to watch him work. He looked more like a phantom gliding along in the shadows than a dog. Since there was no trail, he had to crisscross the ground to keep finding my scent as he moved in a general forward course. I watched him as he entered my field of view among the firs and hemlocks. I knew he was on my trail and I wanted to see how he followed me. It was a thing of beauty. He slipped through the forest, loping over the ground through the ferns with soft, even strides, and his nose was next to the ground searching. Every twenty feet or so, he would shift direction to go back and regain my scent. He did this without hesitation. He knew at the precise point he got off my track and then at the precise point where he returned to my track. I could tell this by his sudden shift, which was free of indecisive body posturing. I watched him for ten minutes as he made his way back and forth up that slope, gaining on me. He looked so sure of himself, even when he kept darting back and forth. His zigzagging was calculated and purposeful. Only when he got to within thirty yards of me and could see me from the corner of his eye did he finally lift his head from the forest floor. Then he took a direct line toward me with his head up and tail wagging. At any distance over thirty yards, he relied more on his nose than he did on his long-range vision. "That a boy," I said to him as he came over and flopped down to rest, with his mouth open to catch his breath. He really looked like he was smiling. During times like these I became more aware of what he was capable of and what his limits were in finding me in the forest. These were the days of my life with Jonny that I miss the most, and often I get lost while thinking about them, almost like I'm there right now.

April 23, 2007, twenty-four miles past Ambler

I decide to head north up Kalurivik Creek away from the Ambler. I'm hoping that I will be able ski on it. It turns east near its source where there is a low pass that leads back over to the Ambler River—where the Ambler River starts to run north as well instead of east. I'm hoping to avoid the dense forest along the lower Ambler and some of the unstable ice that covers deeper water. Once I get to the creek, densely packed spruce trees and deep snow surround it on both sides. I ski along it for a while through the trees, then angle away from it hoping to find more open ground. My ski tips sink below a thin crust that is too hard for them to punch through. I have to stop and yank the tips back onto the surface on every step before skiing forward again. I do this for several hours until I decide to camp, demoralized and exhausted. I have to take my skis off to walk down the bank toward the creek to etch out a location for my tent. The spruce forest along the high bank makes it a shady location. I have to dig out a spot for my tent again. I don't know how I can make better time in deep, soft snow with so many trees to weave my way through. I consider traveling at night when the crust of snow will be harder.

We hear wolves again in the evening. I think they have been following us, probably just curious about the dogs. I'm hoping to see them and snap a few photos. I've been obsessed with animals as long as I can remember, so to see a wolf in the wild would be one of the highlights of my adventure.

April 24, 2007, thirty-two miles past Ambler

Upon waking and feeling stiff and groggy, I decide not to ski today. Not just because my shoulders, thighs, and abdomen are knotted with soreness, but because I feel mentally beaten to a frazzle from the hours of lugging the sleds, the repeated sinking of my skis into the snow, and the frustration of meandering through trees while yanking two sleds behind me. I realize if I rest my body, I will feel mentally stronger tomorrow. It's always that way, and I've learned never to make important decisions when my muscles are scourged with lactic acid and microscopic tears. That's one more major detriment I would have to concentrate to overcome.

I remain around camp for most of the day resting and eating. The spruce forest next to this creek is thick and the snow underneath the trees is deep. There really isn't room for a fire, so I build one on the creek ice a foot from shore where the deep snow ends. I break off dead twigs and branches from the lower parts of spruce trees to keep it going. The creek is frozen so solid that the fire doesn't sink into it that much, like it would in the snow. And when it does finally sink a few inches after an hour or two, I just slide all the embers and burning branches over with my foot in a single swipe. "Got to move the fire, pups," I say out loud. I never wear my good gear next to the fire any-way, so if my old hiking boots or cheap pants get a little scorched, I just douse them with snow and am not at all troubled by it. It's like a battle wound, something to be proud of while living in the wilderness.

Little trickles of water flow over the top of a small feeder creek that leads to Kalurivik Creek. I scoop water with my cup several times to fill up a pot with water. Then later in the day, I walk down the small, frozen creek until I come to Kalurivik Creek again. The creek makes a huge bend here, so I go back to get my skis and trek overland for about half a mile to the north to find a shorter route. I ski across a frozen lake and open ground before getting to the creek. This place looks like the high, lodge pole pine forests of the southern Oregon Cascade Mountains that I'm familiar with. But instead of the eleva-tion being 6,000 feet, here it's only around a thousand. And instead

Ten below zero in Kotzebue, Alaska.

Much warmer inside the tent.

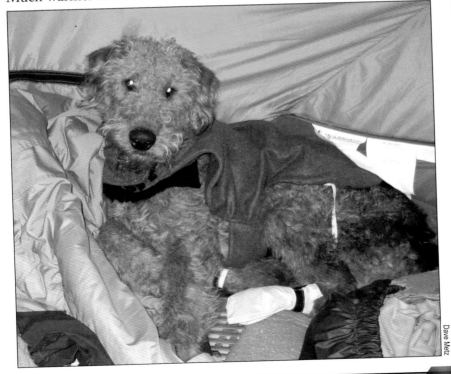

Camp along the Hotham Inlet.

Several miles of frozen sea ice.

Local man dressed for ice fishing.

Edge of the sea.

After a romp in the snow.

Chopping river ice for cooking.

A short break.

The Jade Mountains along the Kobuk River.

Waiting out a thick snowstorm.

Will napping on the tussocks.

Towing my sleds over dwindling snow.

Kalurivik Creek, my trail north.

Brush I had to ski through.

The Ambler River's headwaters in late April.

Mountains along the upper Ambler River.

Waist-deep snow in Nakmaktuak Pass.

The Noatak River in early May.

Dave Metz

A big valley where wolves roam and blend in.

Dave Metz

Caribou antlers were common.

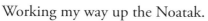

Working my way up the Noatak.

After three days of hard miles.

A pass between the Killik and Alatna rivers.

(Above) No-man's-land on Easter Creek.

(Left) An ATV track leading to Anaktuvuk Pass.

Dave Metz

Along the Anaktuvuk River.

Dave Metz

Will and me above Anaktuvuk Pass.

(Right) When you've been close to starvation, you never forget it.

(Below) A fossil of a mammoth tooth.

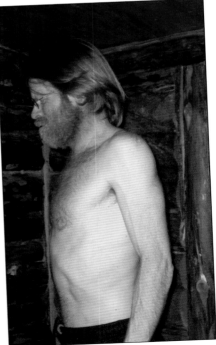

Julie Firman.

Approaching Frigid Crags and Boreal Mountain.

Frigid Crags, Boreal Mountain, the dogs, and me.

After four months, I contemplate home.

Jonny.

of the trees being lodge pole pine, here they are scraggly spruce. Satisfied this is the route I will take the next day, I head back to camp through the trees and across the lake following my tracks so I can't get lost. I'm happy to have my bearings again knowing exactly where Kalurivik Creek is and how far I will have to travel the next day to get to it before I can continue my way north.

April 25, 2007

The dogs are running loose as I ski today. They jet back and forth through the forest this morning while the crust of the snow still supports their weight. Later in the day the sun will cause the snow's surface to weaken. I catch several fleeting glimpses of them up ahead among the trees. They stop only for an instant to make sure that I'm coming. Then they dart off again to their own priorities, leaving me to hope for a glance at them now and then. As I come to the edge of the creek I see that it's still frozen. The dogs are running up and down it like it's a country road. Little snow is on it, so they are overjoyed to be running on a flat surface instead of sinking into soft snow like they have been doing for days. Deep snow still lines the shore, though, so the dogs naturally want to remain on the frozen creek. At first I call to them, fearing they will fall through the ice, but they don't come to me that well. They are young and eager to be tracking animals along the creek.

Since the dogs don't seem to be breaking through the ice, I decide to try skiing on the creek. I follow them as they disappear around a bend upstream. At first I ski cautiously next to the shore, fearful of breaking through the ice. However, after an hour my courage doubles and I believe I can make good time here. So after I catch up with the dogs, I hook myself back up to them. I make sure to put my ski skins on so I can keep the dogs from pulling me into a hole in the ice if one comes up. After an hour I become satisfied that the creek is only knee deep, so I take off my ski skins to go faster. We manage a fast pace of six miles an hour right up the center of the creek toward the mountains beyond. I'm ecstatic at our pace and the dogs are exuberant to be running on the firm surface. The creek glistens as the sun reflects off it and the mountains rise majestically on all sides as we funnel our way north into the heart of them with little effort.

I come across a set of bear tracks heading down the creek. The animal has timed emergence onto the land from winter hibernation just right, as the temperature has just warmed at least five degrees in the past few days. I suspect the bear is heading down toward the Ambler River to feed on grasses or old red berries from last year. It's amazing how those little red berries (I'm not sure what they are called) freeze in the fall and last the entire winter buried under the snow. I think they might be a vital food source for some animals in the spring. I will soon see those berries in the stomachs of ptarmigan.

I follow the bear's tracks upstream in the opposite direction of travel and marvel at the tracks' distance. The bear cuts all the bends of the creek by walking straight through the forest. After I round each corner I find tracks again coming out of the trees, straight as an arrow, not wasting any energy. Bears have what most humans used to have, but now have forgotten in the modern world, a sense of direction. Regaining that sense is not hard if you pay attention to the world around you as you move through it, with all your senses open to it, not locked up in a tin can with wheels whizzing along at break-neck speeds down a tar-plastered highway.

I travel seven or eight linear miles by the end of the day, but probably do twice that because of all the turns in the creek I have to follow. I come to a section of the creek that is free of ice as far as I can see, so I camp under spruce trees while deciding how to proceed the next day. I will probably have to ski back into the trees and the deep snow until I come to more ice on the creek. The weather is really warming up as the dogs and I head into the Schwatka Mountains. Sharp, white peaks jut up from the land on each side of us. Everywhere I look, I see picture-perfect mountains behind a swath of spruce trees.

The next day I push on toward the headwaters of Kalurivik Creek. I'm able to ski on the creek at times, but often I'm forced to go around sections that aren't frozen. I have to take off my skis on these sections and drag my sleds up a five-foot embankment. Then I have to haul them through the many willow bushes that protrude well out of the snow. Then I drop back down onto the creek where it's frozen again. Sometimes my sleds tip over sideways if I come down the bank at an angle. With all the brush, sometimes diagonally is the only way I can get down. Often I anticipate a fall, and other times I surprise myself by staying on my feet. If I believe I will take a bad fall, I will take off my skis to get down to the creek. I don't want to risk injuring my knees.

I follow a set of animal tracks. They look like small pits in a staggered pattern. They are more like the footsteps of a giant, from many giants. As I look down into the bottom of them I see the outline of a grizzly bear's rear foot. I never see the front foot track. Bears place their rear feet where their front feet step. There isn't much for them to eat up here in the mountains, so they are on a straight-shot course to areas where food is available, possibly up on a few sunny, bare slopes, or over the pass and back down to the Ambler River. Several bears have made these holes and this last one has probably made this march twenty times in its life. The bear seems to know every bend to cut and each exact time to cross the creek.

I follow on one occasion as the tracks cut back away from the main creek and follow a side channel through a dense forest. I become amazed when the course cuts back toward the main creek and then meets up with it, eliminating a large loop in the creek. The bears aren't afraid of any obstacle in their path, either. When they come to creek ice, they trudge right onto it. I can tell by their consistent track pattern that they don't even stop to ponder an alternate route. If the creek ice breaks, like I have seen from their tracks, they just keep going straight through it like nothing had happened. The bear we are following is enormous and can't be more than a day ahead of us. The dogs sniff the tracks thoroughly. They have never seen a bear before, but I get the feeling they know what the scent means.

Throughout the day after the bear tracks have veered off and the pass becomes steeper, I'm forced to cross the creek to avoid cliffs and high banks along it. I carry my gear across the creek several times, wading through the freezing water. I don't take my boots off; there's no need. They are already wet from the soggy snow, and also I can't spare the time to keep doing this several times a day. After crossing each time, I toss my gear onto the flat snow-covered bank as I come to it. I set my knees, then my bare hands, on the snow bank to get out of the water as quickly as possible (I've taken off my gloves to manipulate my gear faster). I have to wait motionless for a few seconds on the shore for my feet to stop hurting before plunging back across to get more gear. They throb from the icy water, like I had dropped a couple of bricks on them. I groan a little as the pain subsides. I can only get about ten feet in the icy water before they begin hurting again, even while wearing two pairs of wool socks and insulated ski boots. I try to wade fast, but slow enough to keep from splashing myself. The water is crystal clear, flowing with ripples over rocks and gravel. The air temperature can't be much above freezing, and I don't reflect too much on how I've grown accustomed to this hardship. I would have never waded a creek like this in winter back home. But here, out of my need to make miles, I do it like it was a summer day in Oregon.

I also come to several smaller creeks, which aren't more than three feet wide. I ski right across them without stopping to carry my gear.

I stop on the other side. Then I turn around and tug at the sleds with one fast pull using my arms, back, and legs to slide them across the water. Nothing gets very wet and this is better than stopping to carry the load across with several trips. The sleds are too heavy for me to lift up individually and carry, so I just drag them across. "The hell with it," I say.

I also come to an avalanche chute coming off the steep mountains. I drag my sleds across the rocky bottom and up the other side, again by reaching back and pulling on the poles that attach to the first sled. I have to put my entire body into it to haul them across the rocks and boulders. Because I'm only days away from abandoning my sleds, I don't care about the damage I do to them. My back muscles receive a beating from the workout, and as the days of this go by I begin to feel them getting stronger and as sinewy as finely braided cable.

As I move closer to the source of Kalurivik Creek, the mountains seem to narrow in, forming a cleft between the craggy mountains. The distance between the rock faces on each side is about a hundred yards. An intricate array of beaver dams and ponds set between these two cliffs forms a barrier. It's an unbelievable network of channels and large pools, all made by the determined rodent. Beavers' incisors grow throughout their entire life spans, so they must chew to wear them down. When beavers hear running water they want to dam it up, and they will almost never socialize with other beavers while they are outside their lodge, even with members of their immediate family. When they are outside it's all business and no play. All family interaction takes place inside the lodge. I don't see any beavers, though. They are probably still inside where there is some protection from the wind and cold. I see a couple of giant lodges built in the middle of two lakes that were formed by damming up a small creek. A foot of snow still hides the surface of the lodges, but I can tell by their mounded shape what they are.

I search each edge of the cliff faces where they come down to the water's edge, hoping to be able to skirt by the beaver dams, but I don't find a passable route. The beavers have not only dammed the entire creek across the gorge, but they have also made several dams, one after another, leading a quarter mile upstream. Some dams lead diagonally upstream. I have no choice but to drag my sleds across the snow-covered dams. I cross the first one, which is about forty feet long, without getting my feet in the water. Then I ski through a patch of spruce trees for about five minutes before coming to another set of dams. They hold back the water of several small-size lakes. I follow the edge of the first dam over toward the cliffs on my right. I take my skis off and wade a tiny outlet of water. Then I ski through wet, soft snow, littered with willow bushes. It's slower than the slowest walk. My skis sink and the tips keep running underneath willows that still have their terminal ends held down by the weight of the snow. I often have to yank my skis several times on each step to free them, or take off my sled belt and move back a few steps to go around the branches that won't break free. My sled won't slide backward because it has a steel flap with two large teeth that hang down on the back end of my sled. It digs into the snow when my sled slides back. This is a brake that I use when pulling my sleds up steep hills. When I rest, the sleds don't yank on me or pull me down the hill. The steel brake engages into the snow and holds the sleds in place. But here the brake works against me at times when I need to stop and move back a little to get my skis around the willows that won't break free from the snow. I break another ski pole while hitting branches with it to get them out of my way, so now I have two unbroken poles of different lengths. It never occurred to me that I might break two poles. Now I have to ski by holding one pole lower down from the handle, but it works well enough to continue, and in the days ahead it won't really hinder my travel much. There will be too many other hardships to make it seem significant.

I find an area where I'm able to cross another dam close to the cliff. Near the cliff face I squeeze by the remainder of the dams. After getting by, the creek flows again where the trickling water comes through the spruce forest. Then I look back once in disbelief, and leave the dams behind for good.

The land flattens out as I cross over the pass at the headwaters of Kalurivik Creek. The elevation is only a little over a thousand feet, but it seems like I'm a lot higher because of the large amount of snow still around. I start down the other side by skiing through spruce trees, and the farther down from the pass I get the farther apart the mountains on each side become. And the willow bushes seem to vanish on the other side of the pass. This makes the forest more open and possible to ski through with some speed. Since I'm heading downhill I let the dogs run free and pull the sleds by myself, like I often do when the forest is thick. While stopped for a couple of minutes to let the dogs catch up, I find a couple of leg bones from a moose. I stick them in my sled to let the dogs chew on later. They see them before I get them packed up and follow my sled like it's filled with pork chops. They're interested in my sled, for which I'm grateful. It keeps them close for a few minutes until they realize they aren't getting anything. Then they sprint off again into the trees, following each other like two little kids who are best friends. They go loping off together filled with vigor and mischievous intent.

Plenty of moose tracks lead over the pass. The moose feel safer from wolves in the deep snow and where tangled masses of willows sprout up among the spruce frees. Wolves have a hard time here and I don't see any of their tracks leading over the pass. They prefer more open ground down lower along the Ambler River where the snow isn't so deep, and where they can walk on the frozen parts of the river and on gravel bars. However, I don't think wolves would hesitate to follow a moose into deep snow if they had a chance for a kill—if the moose showed any signs of weakness. Prey animals will try to hide the slightest sign of weakness even when they are extremely sick. If they show weakness, predators like wolves will hone in on them like a band of marauding army ants. Predators become skilled at detecting the faintest frailty in their prey animals, so prey animals have to become just as good at faking good health when they are sick. Maybe humans do this, too. Perhaps we are closer to wild animals than we know. Maybe sometimes people do the opposite and fake being sick when they are healthy for sympathy. It's something that would never work in my family. If I had attempted to fake being sick, especially on a hike, I would have been laughed at, not for being weak, but because I wanted attention for something that didn't warrant attention in my family. Straight A's in school, climbing a mountain, or winning an argument over a teacher would have warranted attention among my brothers, but never being sick or pretending to be.

I come to a large lake a mile down from the pass. Will and Jimmy show up one at a time. Will approaches from behind me out of the trees from the direction I had just left, but Jimmy somehow comes from the east on the other side of the lake; from the direction we are heading. There is a gaping fissure of open water twenty feet wide and at least a mile long blocking his path from getting across to where Will and I are waiting. Jimmy looks baffled and I wonder how in the world he got over there in the first place. After a minute of looking around, he edges his feet down the side of the ice and into the water, not really sure if he will touch the bottom. It looks deep but only turns out to be a foot or two, so he stops for a while with all four feet in the water and takes a long cold drink. Will wants a drink, too, so I bend over the edge of the ice to scoop him and myself some water with my cooking pot. I drink first, straight from the pot, then give Will some. After we are done drinking, I shove the pot back into my sled and begin skiing again, heading northeast along the side of the lake. "Come on, Jimmy," I say. "Let's go." Then Jimmy hops out of the lake water and catches up with us as we ski off into the distance.

At the head of the lake I turn more eastward and ski through more spruce trees until I come to the Ambler River. We camp just across from Ulaneak Creek. What a place. This wide river valley is populated by spruce, alder, and cottonwood trees, where the air is warmer than anywhere on all my previous days. I'm a few yards north of where two creek valleys join the Ambler River at right angles—one creek on each side of the river—forming a cross on the landscape. And jagged mountains sit back towering formidably over the land like an omnipotent presence. There is a good chance that no modern human has ever come here. The Ambler flows out of some grisly peaks to the north and steep mountains flank the river's sides for several miles to the south. I seem to have come through the mountains from the west at just the right place, where there is a wide gap cleaved through the steep-walled peaks. It's like I've found a hidden corridor leading through to a hyperborean Shangri-la.

A SIGN LEFT BY SOMEONE LOST

Before getting any farther up the Ambler, I'm pelted by memories of Jonny. Watching Will brings those memories on sometimes; he reminds me more of Jonny than Jimmy in the way he acts. Most people can't even tell Jimmy and Will apart, but I can from their posture and body expressions alone. Will will look you dead in the eye, calmly yet intently, like Jonny used to do. It's like he is trying to pinpoint your mood. I think Jonny's memories now are brought on by the visions of peaks marking my course, alerting me that I'm doing something remarkable, trekking across pristine country. Sometimes I forget this journey is not only an exploration of wilderness and my own inner limits, but it's also a monument to Jonny.

Mostly when I think about Jonny, I remember the way he died. I felt like I had let him down, like I should have recognized his ailing condition in time to get him to a hospital, even though a veterinarian later told me there was nothing I could have done. I felt alone without him and responsible for his death; I should have been able to save him.

I remember how he looked at me for help when he had his attack in Drift Creek Wilderness. I didn't know what to do for him as I watched him wobble, lose control of his bowels, and a few minutes later shake and fall down. His eyes were wide open and filled with fear the entire time, but he didn't move his body or moan at all. I was afraid he was bleeding inside because his gums were as white as snow. All I could do was start carrying him out of there, while Julie carried the bulk of our gear, but something inside me told me it would be too late. He weighed seventy pounds and I carried him along with twenty pounds of gear on my back. I carried him up steep slopes shrouded by towering fir trees and carpeted by salal bushes and prehistoric-looking sword ferns, where small herds of elk hide in the shadows. When we came to waist-high logs to cross, I would either straddle them with Jonny still in my arms or set him on top of them while I clamored over, and then pick him up again and continue. I carried him for several miles without doubting I would carry him until I either got him out or he died. I owed it to him—for his constant companionship and steadfast amiability toward me. It's what I've searched for in people my entire adult life in between my travels. Maybe it's what we all search for. I never did doubt the wilderness around us, nor did I believe that the remote location was the cause of his death.

I unhitch my waist belt and sit on a dry bank to stare at the peaks ahead. Their stony sides have clean edges that cut a resplendent rift into the mountain range. They're going to fold in on me as I get closer to them, and I'm not sure if they will provide me a channel through. It doesn't matter. It is what it is and I will plod on until a wall of rock stops me, and if a gate opens through like I'm hoping, I will take it. The maps suggest a route along the river and up a narrow ridge to the arctic plains on the other side, but I won't know for sure until I get there. I wish that by completing this journey across rugged mountains, Jonny would be allowed to live again. I'll travel forward like it's true anyway.

It was several hours to the final ridge that would lead us out of Drift Creek, and I carried Jonny's limp body never really conscious of my own suffering, hiking up hills that most people couldn't do without extra weight. I thought only of Jonny and knew I would hike well beyond the limits of my strength, without doubting my commitment to him. At first I carried him in front of me in a sling I made out of my tent, but later I carried him on my shoulders, just like when he was a puppy and used to become tired on our way out of the woods from a long hike. I carried him on my shoulders in the beginning days of his life, and then a decade later, in the final hours of his life.

It took us hours to get up the hills. I stopped several times to set him on the ground to rest and to make sure Julie was coming. She looked solemn, and I partly regretted she was there to witness this. I set Jonny down where just the day before he had stopped to dig out a nest in the ground, to rest in from the running he had been doing. He liked to do that, to lay his body against the cool soil underneath.

When we reached the crest of the watershed Jonny began to have body spasms, so I set him down on the ground again. My eyes were riveted on his, and I sat with my face only a foot from his face as he gasped his last few, gaping breaths. They looked agonizing, like the terror-riddled death throws all vertebrate animals seem to experience in their final few minutes of life. I've seen this in mammals and snakes that I've tried to save after they had been run over by automobiles. I think the spasms are embedded in all vertebrate behavior, right before they die. It's an evolutionary, last-ditch effort in the struggle for life.

I don't think dying is that easy, and I believe no one wants to die. This is why animals stretch their jaws so wide several times in their final moments of life, as if they're trying to gather together every last ounce of life remaining in their bones to try to breathe a few more times in the faint hope that life will come back to them.

After Jonny finished his last spasms he stopped breathing, but I could still feel his heart beating away, growing fainter. I began mouth-to-mouth resuscitation, but his muzzle was too long and I couldn't get the air to go down his throat. I kept trying to wrap my hands around his muzzle and breathe into his mouth at the same time. The air just kept coming out the sides, and I couldn't get enough pressure to force the air down his throat and into his lungs. I was growing mad at myself and afraid for him at the same time. "It keeps coming out the damn sides," I cried, and then looked to Julie. "How do I get the air to go down his throat?" I asked her, but she was sobbing and didn't know what to do, either. Neither of us knew what to do. I tried to hold both my hands around his muzzle at the same time, but still the air came out the sides of his mouth. I couldn't get any to go down his throat. "The air keeps coming out the fucking sides," I yelled as I panicked. I couldn't believe Jonny was actually dying.

He faded so fast that it wouldn't have revived him anyway. I don't think he had enough blood left in his cells, but I kept trying. I worked on him for several minutes while Julie and I were both sobbing. I worked on him even after his heartbeat ebbed away while we were kneeling next to him in the midst of the forest. His liveliness slipped away and it grew too late. Our long string of journeys together was finished, and I had to figure out a way to carry on without him. I had very few memories of those ten years without Jonny in them in some way. I remember him so many times, sitting in the passenger seat of my truck with his head pressed up against the windshield, his eyes wide and intense, to better view the possibilities of the world around him as we made our way to the woods. It's funny how we can get so attached to our dogs, to the point where losing them is tragically sad, and continuing our lives without them seems impossible for a while.

I sat there crying while looking at him. Then I got up and walked down the forest trail with tears streaming down my face. I hadn't cried in so long and felt Jonny's death was far harder to handle than my own would have been. Jonny laid there, still and lifeless, though his vivid black and tan fur stood out against the verdant green woods and foliage that encircled us. I had to keep checking him and touching him to make sure he was really dead. His animated character was so empty that I could barely believe it was Jonny lying there on the ground. He was more like an object than a dog.

I summoned up the last bit of courage I had left and picked him up. I carried him the last mile to the trailhead, put him in the back of my truck, and covered him. Then we drove an hour home in almost total silence. Julie had her hand on my shoulder for much of the drive, but we were both too shocked to speak. I didn't bury him for two days; I couldn't come to let him go. I kept thinking he would somehow wake up and become himself again, just like always. During those two days, I went into the garage many times and lifted up Jonny's covers to make sure he was really dead. Each time I would see his distinct features, but there was no more character to him. I didn't want Julie to know that I was going into the garage to lift his covers to see if it was really him, but she must have known. I grieved terribly, like he was my brother. We had walked the wild earth for ten years together. Now I would have to walk the wilderness without him, and gather my wits to continue facing the possibilities of a beautiful and natural world.

Then I went out back and dug a hole into the soft, damp dirt two feet deep, and I made sure it was wide enough to fit Jonny's long legs into. I wrapped him up in his sleeping bag, then set him gently into the ground, to return the molecules of his body that still gyrated dynamically within him to the earth. Maybe there is more to those molecules than we know. I lifted Jonny's sleeping bag one last time to see his face and remember it with the vibrant character it used to have. I stroked the top of his muzzle twice with my first and second fingers, with my head tilted just off kilter to look at him intensely one last time. I had vivid images of him when he was alive, with his animated personality flashing through my head. His vitality lit up my mind. Then, I put the cover back over his face and buried him. "I'm so sorry, Jonny," I said. "I'm so sorry for letting you down. I wish I could have helped you. You are always in my memories, and someday our molecules will be one." I became all choked up and had to wait a couple of seconds to keep speaking. "Maybe they already are one. Farewell, little buddy." And then I patted the fresh soil into a round mound with my bare hands, so that his memory would leave a fertile vestige on the earth: a visible sign left by someone lost.

I stayed at Julie's house for a few days after Jonny's death, and I would sit often by the front window looking out at early spring. Julie came and went, doing her own thing around the house, and whenever I was sitting by the window she would touch my shoulder, like she knew what I was thinking about. I made attempts to snap out of my mournful torpor and engage her cheerily, but most of the time I really couldn't.

The plants and grasses were beginning to turn green again, and robins had returned from wherever it was they went, ready to begin another yearly cycle of life. I sat by the window for hours sometimes, sighing heavy each time my mind was overcome by memories of Jonny. I sighed hard to try to flush them away and make it so it had never happened. But I couldn't. My thoughts about Alaska and other ideas in the world had no chance of getting in. All I could do was be sad, and sigh, and dribble a tear every so often. After several days, I started taking walks and exercising again, which seemed to help ease my mind and shed some of the guilt I had over Jonny. I thought all my life I was capable of doing anything, but in the days ahead I began to realize I could never bring Jonny back. All that was left for me to do so I could be happy again was let Jonny go. So that's what I did.

Just then I stand up to go on. The dogs are pouncing around me while still in their harnesses anticipating our departure. They get just as excited each time I get ready to go, even if I have only stopped for five minutes. It's as if they forget we are already going, or maybe they just love it so much that every time is as good as the next. That's the way Jonny was. Then I say to them, "Get up guys," with a slight hiss at the end, and they lunge forward toward the impressive mountains ahead. I try not to lament or linger too much, and drop my chin and bury my mind in the struggle before us.

BREAKUP

I listen as flat rafts of ice a foot thick break off from the river's edge and float down, banging against the rocky sides. The sound is like someone off in the distance stomping on the ground or banging a drum. The ice-encased land is melting, but happening slower than I thought it would. I assumed all the snow would melt away within a week like I had seen in other places in Alaska farther south. Here in the mountains things are different. The snow and ice seem to linger on for weeks. When the midday sun hits, the snow on the sides of cliffs melts slowly and forms driblets of water that freeze solid again after the sun sinks behind the peaks. In the morning there are often long daggerlike icicles hanging off ledges of rock.

Now that I'm back down on a larger flow of water than Kalurivik Creek, I expect the terrain to be flatter and easier for a while, but I'm wrong about this. During the early afternoon, after making great progress skiing on solid river ice, I gradually have to move onto the snowy slopes to go around areas on the river where the ice has thawed. The ice on the river doesn't thaw out equally over the entire river surface like I expected. Sometimes large sections of river ice fall away into the water, where perhaps just a hundred feet away the river will be completely frozen over and unaffected by the warm air.

I arrive at a large cliff that is actually part of the side of a steep-faced mountain. It plunges all the way down to the edge of the river. I cannot cross the river here because the water is deep and swift, and I'm dumbfounded at how to proceed. From where I stand, a hundred feet up on a hill along the river, I can see part of the cliff that is closest to me and looks level enough to pass by, but I cannot see what lies beyond that. After studying all the possible routes in every direction, I see that there are no other possible routes going past this section of river. I decide to try to see what is beyond the level part of the cliff that is ahead of me, so I haul my gear down the hill in front of me and leave it along the river near the base of the cliff. Then I hike up to the part of the cliff that I could see before and cross over it. I hike about a half mile along slopes that parallel the river, until I can find a way down to the edge of the frozen river when I'm past the cliff and am able to ski along the river again. I have to go quite a ways to find a place where I will be able to go down without falling or losing the sleds. Beyond this point, far up high where I'm walking, there is no way through. The mountains become too steep. I will have to make it through this way or go back and search for a way across the river. That would take an extra day, negating all the hard work and distance I've made in the last two days. I walk back the half mile to where I left my sleds while sinking in snow.

I unload all my gear and start by making four trips up a steep, hundred-foot slope, with boulders and rocky ledges poking through the snow. I always fall through the snowy surface the deepest at places that are close to exposed rocks. It seems to be the weakest point of the snow. I learn to take a large step over that point as I come off a snowdrift and onto bare ground. Often the weak area is too wide though and I drop through the crust anyway. Sometimes I fall to my waist. It's as if the crust is made weaker by the adjoining bare rock and the heat it radiates. Will and Jimmy often jump these weak sections, but on the ones that are too large they wade across like it doesn't hinder them at all. The dogs sort of swim with their front paws to keep the front of their bodies up, while their rear legs sink down into the snow. Moving through at somewhat of a vertical angle, they usually lead the way quickly and eagerly without any prompting from me. The pair looks for some interesting smell to chase up ahead, leaving me to struggle with my own human, physical shortcomings. As they trot off up ahead and stop to look back once, they must wonder why I follow so slowly. And the cliffs and ledges around are not high enough or steep enough to be life threatening for them. I let the two brothers run loose with little concern.

Moving all my gear takes me an hour. After I get everything up the slope, I load it back into my sleds. Then I try to keep my sleds from tipping over sideways as I traverse the side of the mountain. Once I get back to the place I found to descend to the river, I take off my skis and let them slide down to the level snow below, which worries me at first; I'm afraid they will slide all the way into the river. But I have put my climbing skins on my skis to keep them from sliding that far. Climbing skins also work well when I need to slow my descent on a hill or when I need to slow my pace when the dogs are pulling too strongly along the edges of weak river ice. Without skins on, I think they are so strong that they could pull me right into dangerous sections of the river. With skins I have more stopping power against fresh dogs. Climbing skins were developed for mountaineers who wanted to climb up mountains and ski down them. With climbing skins they literally walk up the side of a snow-covered peak on their skis without sinking into the snow and without slipping backward. I'm not sure if their inventors ever thought about using them to help guard against eager terriers who would just as soon drag a person onto broken river ice while trying to find the source of some intriguing animal scent.

Next I walk down the near vertical slope backward with one of my sleds in front of me. I lean into it with my hands on the sled as I back down the deep, snowy face. A couple of times the weight of the sled nearly overruns me as I lose my footing, but I regain control each time. My feet sink about two feet into the snow, which gives me more secure footing on this steep cliff. Without the snow, I'm not sure I could get down here at all. The snow gives me a surface to make foot holes. Once down—the dogs get down easily as always—I go back for the second sled, and then repeat the process until I have all my gear past the cliff and laying on the frozen part of the river. Then I have to drag my sleds across a shallow, rocky channel to reach snow that I can ski on for a longer period of time before hitting more open water.

I start skiing forward on the river again, but after a mile I come to another cliff. This one isn't as steep as the one I just came past, and I ascend the snowy face with my ski skins on by zigzagging back and forth. Down the other side, I ski with skins on to slow my descent. I weave back and forth again until I reach the riverbed. Will takes off and runs about a half mile up the mountain chasing something. I can barely see him. He looks like a tiny spec as he moves up the mountain into a steep, icy ravine, where I don't think mountain climbers would even go. Maybe he is following a wolverine scent. Wolverines can cross right over mountain ranges undeterred by the ruggedness on their tireless pursuit for food. I worry that Will will fall into a crevasse or get engulfed by an avalanche. I see several areas where fresh snow has slid down the mountain and accumulated at the bottom, but he returns uninjured about thirty minutes later, wagging his tail and panting heavily.

I find a parklike stand of spruce trees on the level inside bend of the river and set up camp, feeling lucky to get through the day neither injured nor stuck on the other side of some impassable mountain, worrying about what to do the next day. As far as I can tell, I will be able to move forward. I've only come about two miles the entire day, but at least I have made it past a cliff that might have stopped my progress altogether.

My upper back under my right shoulder blade aches; strained from pulling the sleds repeatedly up the sheer-sided embankments. Usually there is flat terrain on the inside bends of the river, but as soon as the river turns back the other way, impassable ledges often appear. I manage to skirt around most of them through the trees, but these last two I encountered were the worst I've found so far. Since the river is too large and cold most of the time, it's easier to work my way up and around the ledges. I will be glad when I can get rid of the sleds and start hiking with only my backpack, but for now I still have too much food to carry, and there is too much snow for hiking yet.

The next day I make good time by skiing on gravel bars that are completely encased in ice, and they are pancake flat and smooth. The river is braided, and open water only flows along the edges in narrow channels. I get miles of straight, flat snow—as good as I could ever imagine, running right up the center of the river. I can see miles ahead of me where the Ambler River turns right and passes by more mammoth peaks, then disappears around the corner. Many of the peaks hold a thousand-foot wall of granite-like rock, so steep that they are uniformly gray and absent of any snow. The river seems to run straight from here, right into a mountain. It's difficult to tell that it turns right and goes by another mountain that sits just in front of it. To the left the river splits into a smaller channel and does the same thing. I can't discern a course through these mountains from this view; however, the maps tell me it's navigable. But from my view miles away, I see only an impregnable cavalcade of mountains vividly drawn across my impending horizon. It's more than a day's travel away, perhaps several days depending on how slow I go, but my view of the crisp, white row of mountains is unimpeded and fantastic. Even with all my silent fears and doubts about my treacherous traveling and working alone, I'm mesmerized by the immensity of all these mountains and the enormity of the land. I gasp and wonder why I haven't come here before. I gasp and savor at being here now.

May 1, 2007, sixty-seven miles past Ambler

I've rounded the large bend and have left the level gravel bars well behind now as I ski through the trees almost the entire day. The constant brush that is sticking up through the thinning snow torments me. I'm forced to push the brush down with my skis as I slide over them, but it's more like walking on skis, and it's slow and irritating. Then I have to yank the sleds through the brush with barbaric force. Sometimes it takes several attempts to yank my sleds two feet. The river, which is rushing through a narrow canyon, is pretty much bare of ice except on the sides. The river turns every hundred yards, so I can only ski that far before I run into a ledge along the river. I either have to cross the icy current or go back into the forest. I usually choose the trees; my feet can't take too much of the cold water, and hauling my gear across the river takes a long time.

I'm nearing the thousand-foot-steep climb that leads up to Nakmaktuak Pass and the Noatak River fifteen miles away on the other side. I will likely have to jettison my sleds and skis before I reach the climb. I don't think I can make the climb hauling sleds.

May 2, 2007, seventy-seven miles past Ambler

I spend half the day skiing through densely packed spruce trees, with willows poking through the snow. It's so slow and arduous that I think about ditching my skis and just walking, but I think I will still sink in the snow too much. I somehow find the strength to keep going. I have to push my body and jerk my sleds through thick willows and spruce trees that are growing too close together to make descent time or distance. I'm basically just keeping busy—and not really making much distance—in the hope that the snow will melt one day soon and I will be able to start hiking with some sort of speed. It's backbreaking work, and again I worry that the dogs will run off and get lost.

Once today I have to stop and wait for Jimmy for an hour, then run back to look for him after hearing him howling in the distance. I find him on the other side of a thick stand of spruce trees. I've learned to recognize when the dogs are lost by the tone and duration of their howling. Normally Will finds his way back, but once in a while he gets lost, too. Sometimes they both get lost together and follow each other around through the woods, howling from different locations far away. Sometimes I will start out for one place where they are howling, only to hear them howl from a different place by the time I think I've almost reached them. It's often better not to look for them right away, but wait until I'm sure they are lost and are going to remain in one area to wait for me.

In the afternoon I cross over the river and find river ice to ski on, but I have to wade a large, fanned-out creek delta that splits into several channels. I've gotten good at recognizing on which water crossings I have to take my skis off. Here I take them off quickly at the first channel and jump to the other side. Then I haul the one sled across the water as fast as I can—I leave the smaller, blue sled behind. Then I lug my sled across bare rocks to the next channel, and do the same. In all I cross about six braided channels of the same creek, all of which are doused by sunlight most of the day. There is little snow here and no ice covering these channels, and the water gushes through. I make camp about 200 yards farther up under spruce trees, on bare ground to my delight, where the snow has just recently melted. It's quite a warm evening with no wind and I enjoy a crackling fire with plenty of wood laying around. Except for a few puddles next to the remaining snow patches, the ground underneath the trees is dry for several hundred yards. Camping in a forest absent of snow is a welcome change, which allows me to lounge about anywhere on the ground.

The Ambler Valley here is fairly wooded by Alaska standards. It's about three or four miles wide with spruce reaching a third of the way up gentle mountains on each side. The creek I crossed is within my sight, and where it joins the Ambler, the land has been flattened out over time by sediment being carried down from mountains farther back. Much of the ice and snow left around is speckled brown with this sediment. The land around me is a nice wide oasis that could comfortably hold a hundred tents, with trees to give them shelter. Combining all the channels, the braided creek has a width of about 100 yards, still mostly edged with ice. Each braid is also lined with ice. I can also see well up the creek if I step out of the trees onto the sandy ground. It flows through a much smaller valley than the Ambler and shoots off from it at a right angle. Its gradient is also steeper than the Ambler. About half a mile upstream the gentle sloping peaks squeeze in on the creek to form an impassable gorge. But I can see beyond the gorge where higher and steeper mountains with white sides and bare, rocky ridges tower up toward the bright blue sky.

During evenings like these, when I'm warm and I can have a nice fire, I'm elated by the epic exploration I'm undertaking and the pure freedom this colossal wilderness provides. I can go anywhere from here, and I'm not bound by any of the restraints of society. The only thing that limits how long I can explore and how far I can go is the amount of food I can carry, find, or kill. I think about how Daniel Boone must have felt on his initial trek over the Cumberland Gap, or how Jim Bridger first felt when he stood along the Yellowstone River in the Rocky Mountains. Despite the moments of adversity I face, it's a lifting moment of wild grandeur that I could never get back in Oregon.

During times like these I also think about friends and life back home. Sometimes I think Julie will forget about me since I've been gone for so long. Maybe she will move or go on with her life without me. We met two plus years ago in Oregon on a blind date. She has a prominent chin, riveting blue eyes, and dark brown hair. I told her a few months later about my desire to trek in Alaska for an extended length of time in the coming years. At first she said she was not quite okay with me being gone for four months. This was the response I expected at best. I never did tell her I really wanted to stay in Alaska and live in the bush for about a year, in a cabin I was going to build with my own two hands. I was certain this would be a deal breaker because she loved being around people so much that I didn't think she would want to go or like it if I went without her. You don't see too many women (or men for that matter) living in the Alaska wilderness, so I figured she wouldn't be around long. As we continued to date, I started to believe I could make a sacrifice and continue to live in Oregon. I was certain she was happy living where she was, which was okay with me. Oregon is still a bit woodsy and I could spend parts of my summers in Alaska, or other faraway places I wanted to see yet.

I call home to her and make arrangements to have food flown in for me to pick up when I reach the Noatak River. I realize now if I don't I will have to turn around and make my way back to Ambler, or I could starve. Julie seems happy to hear me, but we can't talk for long. These short talks might actually be damaging our relationship because we don't talk enough. She gratefully arranges me a food drop. When I call her back later (we had discussed the possibility of a charter plane flying me in more food early on) she explains the plan to me. A man working for a small company out of Kotzebue will fly his tiny single-prop plane up the Noatak River to meet me. He will attempt to land on Matcharak Lake if he thinks the ice will support his plane. If he can't land, or if I can't cross the Noatak River to where the lake is, he will drop my packages from a low elevation while he flies his plane at its slowest possible speed. To me it sounds like he has done this before, so I don't worry. We coordinate a GPS location at the mouth of Nushralutak Creek where it enters the Noatak. On my map I can see plenty of level ground, so all I have to do is show up there if I can't cross the river.

I wonder if my brothers are getting excited about starting their trek in a few weeks. It's too bad Rick can't go, but he has two young children now to take care of. Mike has wanted to hike in the Gates of the Arctic National Park since he was seventeen, and I think my journey really helped him to make the decision to finally do it. I hope I can make it to Anaktuvuk Pass to meet him and Steve on May 26. It will be great to have them around and joking after having been alone for so long. Julie will be coming, too. She has made a huge sacrifice to undertake this trek, and I hope it won't be too strenuous for her.

Mike makes it a point to plan a ten-day hike every summer. One summer we went to the Bob Marshall Wilderness in Montana. One warm evening after spending the day hiking and the afternoon fishing, Steve, Mike, Jeff, Mike's army buddy Hudrick, and I were sitting around smoking cigars and drinking tequila. Jeff had his MSR stove out and was fiddling with it for about an hour trying to get it to work. He had been messing with this thing for days and had finally had enough. He got so frustrated that he stood up, threw the stove onto the ground, and started stomping it hard into the dirt over and over again, like he was killing a cobra. He was so angry. We all burst out laughing as hard as we could. We couldn't help ourselves. It was hysterical to see Jeff trying to kill a stove. After about thirty seconds, Jeff went from being mad, to laughing as hard as he could right along with us. That's the kind of camaraderie I was looking forward to when I got to Anaktuvuk Pass.

May 3, 2007, eighty-three miles past Ambler

Though I hate the waste and the fact that it means I'll leave a mark on this wilderness, today I ditch my skis, sled, thick parka, ski boots, ski skins, an extra pot, and a nice wool sweater I bought at the Salvation Army store. I have to get rid of some gear to be able to hike out of here. If I don't I won't make it. I make sure to put everything in a neat, hidden pile for a time when I might be able to come back to use the gear again. I always use inexpensive gear when I can get away with it. I have to save my money for plane tickets. Traveling frugally and simplistically makes the trek more pure to me, like wilderness. To become part of it, I must be like it—tranquil and durable enough to cross the land with only rags on my back if I have to. I would rather have it look like I've vanished without a trace when I leave here. For me this means going back to the ideals of Henry David Thoreau. The less money you spend and the longer you use something, the less damage you will be doing to the earth—and the longer I can be in wilderness before I have to work again.

I'm frustrated with dragging my sled across so much bare ground, brush, and flowing creeks, so I start hiking with my backpack, but it's so heavy that I have to take short, choppy strides, almost like a shuffle except that I lift my feet off the ground to keep from tripping over rocks. As I travel through a rugged canyon I have to hike out of the creek bed and into the trees several times to go around cliffs. I often yell profanities into the silent sky as I force my way. For several hours I alternate between busting through walls of brush and walking partly on deep snow. My pack keeps getting caught on snags. I struggle not to lose my balance while trying to work my way through. The dogs look concerned and I fear I'm at my breaking point. I sit down with my head in my hands almost sobbing.

I'm alone in this remote, wild place in the hinterland of the planet, and getting out of here will take me a month of brutal effort. Will comes over and puts his head next to my face, then doesn't move. I think he tries to understand what is wrong with me, or maybe he already knows. As I look at him out of the corner of my eye I realize that his spirit cannot be broken by any hardship that I can endure. Jimmy, and especially Will, seem to thrive on this trek, day in and day out. They grow more animated and stronger each day. They become my inspiration.

I suspect any other normal person would call it quits here, and either head back downriver or call for a plane, but not me. I know this is leading to something greater than it looks, and I try to keep my composure. The dogs are weary, too, but content, and they look to me for reassurance. I pull myself together after a few minutes, thinking to myself that whenever this trek becomes too much for me, I can leave any time and start home, or I can set up my tent and stay put for a couple of weeks. No one is forcing me to do this. Knowing this, I stand up, gather my thoughts, and decide I need a serious change in course to get through the brush, trees, and deep snow. I turn to my right and hike down to the creek out of all the brush and trees, cross it, and reach the other side. It's a roomy, open place to camp, which is actually the very edge of the northern tree line that winds its way across North America. My brother Mike told me that it was Bob Marshall who said the reason trees don't grow any farther north was because they hadn't had enough time to become established yet after the last ice age, not because it was too windy and cold for them to grow this far north like everyone thought.

Once I stop for the day I feel much better. I always feel better at the end of the day after the difficult work is done, but since today was extra difficult and tedious, the contrast is stronger. I relax at camp in the evening sun and watch the dogs trot off and up one of the slopes to dig for rodents. They follow each other, being sure to sniff every hole and dig some at the ones that have a fresh scent. I don't know where they get their energy, but it brightens my spirits to see the ability they have at moving across this terrain. It inspires me to keep moving.

There will be a steep climb tomorrow up and toward the pass. I can see the slope from here. It looks like a difficult route, and I've never heard or read about anybody hiking it before. If I didn't have maps and by looking around me, I would believe this was an impossible route. Except for that narrow thousand-foot strip of tundra that I hope to climb, there are nothing but cliff-faced mountains and gorges in front of me. I've never seen so many cliffs and steep mountains with snowmelt rushing off their flanks. Far more barren, rocky landscape exists here than wooded valleys, like no other place I've been before, and it has taken me weeks to get here. The trouble, if I acknowledge it as trouble, was worth it.

NAKMAKTUAK PASS

May 5, 2007, ninety-five miles past Ambler

I hike hard and steady up the long, steep slope out of the serenity of the Ambler River basin. I creep upward with my heavy load and stop to bend over now and then to relieve some of the strain on my shoulders. A ptarmigan flies off making a series of guttural squawks— about thirty in ten seconds while retreating from me. This bird is the first one I've seen and I watch it land in the distance. These grouse-like birds don't like to fly that far and have to beat their wings really fast, so they have strong pectoral muscles. Ptarmigans fly low to the ground and don't catch the air currents to soar aloft like raptors and some other birds. They don't need to because their food is all over the tundra and they don't migrate.

I turn around and stare at the canyon behind me from where I've just come. The higher I go the deeper and steeper the valley looks. I trudge on and keep my breathing even, making sure not to exert too much effort. It's better to hike that way when you have a long way to go. Hiking with too many vigorous efforts is less efficient than hiking steady. You can travel farther in a day with less energy. I crest a mountain, which is actually the beginning of a high, vast plateau that seems to stretch forever northward. I have to pick my way across an unstable rocky slide near the top, but it isn't too bad. I stay off the snow because it forms the beginning of a long chute, that falls a thousand feet. I can't risk slipping on it so I step along the edge, up and around where there is solid rock. I reach the top of the climb, believing I have an easy shot to the Noatak River now.

I think the worst is behind me, but I couldn't be more wrong. I come over a rise to find myself on the upland plateau. I wince and take a deep breath knowing I have to cross it. The land appears grimly desolate, with rocks and boulders strewn upon the surface and wind-scoured mountains posed to devour me from both sides. My course runs dead north into the arctic like a gigantic trench—an abyssal canyon hemmed in on both sides by sheer, icy peaks that appear to be from either a prehistoric time or another world where mega-therian mammals or beastly aliens reign. It's an eerie place, so exposed that there is nowhere to take shelter except in my dwarfed tent that buckles in the wind. The idea that I'm exploring such a wild region doesn't really dawn on me. I begin to feel desperate to get moving through this cyclopean corridor of ice and rock toward the Noatak River and out of these mountains. But it's a grueling stretch and will take several days.

The north side of Nakmaktuak Pass is treacherous and cold during the first part of May. Deep ravines and craggy cliffs lacerate the terrain. The ground is plagued by snowy sections, that are often a hundred yards wide and about three feet deep. I sink up to my thighs every ten steps or so. There isn't enough snow to ski on and too much snow to walk on easily. The only thing keeping me going is that I know I will get a food drop and a chance to rest when I reach the Noatak River, about twelve linear miles from here.

The direction through the pass parallels the upper Ambler River. This deep gorge with nearly vertical faces on each side runs through this region for several miles. Then it turns to the right ninety degrees and cuts across my course as it leads up the sides of the mountains.

I have to somehow find a route across it to continue on my course toward the Noatak River.

I spend the first day on this plateau hiking and breaking through thigh-high snowy sections where the crust is too weak to support my weight. Sometimes I walk delicately with short, calculated steps, but still I break through to my thighs and curse at the dull gray sky. Each time when I break through, it surprises me and I fall with a thud. I never seem ready when it happens, even though it occurs many times and I know it's coming again soon. Sometimes I land so fast that I nearly jam my knee. Once I break through the surface crust, there is nothing to hold my weight except airy powder that is too dry to be compacted. Each time I fall through, I have to haul myself back to the surface while carrying a load that weighs at least sixty pounds (my pack is so heavy because I carry a seven-pound winter tent, a six-pound shotgun, shells, and some remaining winter gear). Then I have to stand and start walking again. It's only a minute or so before I break through again. I try to go around some of these snowy sections, but often this takes more time and energy because these snowy sections usually are quite long, like giant fingers clutching the land. Eventually I have to face another one and cross it. The only way is to become a posthole maker, and I'll make hundreds of holes in the snow by the time I'm through this place.

I learn to look for a hint of grass that peeks through the snow, where the snow is the shallowest and offers the easiest path. I'm sure to fall through in these places on every step, but at least I know that it won't be as deep as the sections without grass. I learn to read the snow, too. The glossy, smooth-looking areas of snow have the strongest crust and will support my weight for a longer period of time than the sections that are often right next to them and have a rougher-looking crust. I think the weaker snow is what's left after the sun has melted the stronger surface crust. The difference in the two types of snow is difficult to recognize at first, but I learn how to do it by watching Will walk ahead of me. At first I can't figure out why he walks such a meandering path across the snow, like he is drunk or crazy. Then I realize he is staying on the smooth-looking surfaces to avoid breaking through the snow. Sure enough, these are the only areas that support my weight, and when they run out I fall into the snow up to my thighs.

Sometimes I have to walk forty yards wading up to my thighs before I can reach bare ground or find hard crust to walk on. Sometimes after I fall through, it takes me several minutes to be able to yank my legs loose to take even one step. These are the worst moments. I fret terribly and curse like a drunken sailor. I never think about abandoning my wilderness trek, I just accept that I will have to endure very extreme hiking, like nothing I've ever done before.

I worry for the dogs. I can't maneuver this region with them leashed to me so I have to let them roam free. Several times they approach the edge of the Ambler River Gorge. I shout at the top of my lungs to call them back, but they don't respond very well. To lose footing and slide off the snowy rim of the canyon would mean a plunge of more than a hundred feet down an eighty-degree precipice. Sometimes the dogs sprint off right toward the canyon's edge, and after several times I realize they won't fall. But still, they get closer than I would like. I worry for Will the most. He always gets the closest. Many snow-filled gullies slope down toward the rim of the canyon, and their gradients increase the closer to the rim you get. If we were to walk too close and start falling, getting out would be nearly impossible. Once you get far enough down them, and if you don't realize the danger ahead of time, you will slide right over and plummet to certain death.

One time I yell to Will at the top of my lungs when he walks out onto one of these small gullies. "Will, come here," I yell. "Will, come back, come back." I shout this several times until he somehow listens to me and recognizes the danger. He turns and walks out of the gully as calmly as he walked into it. I become relieved and wonder if he would have fallen if I weren't there to warn him. When I come to these gullies, I make sure to walk far up and away from them, so that if I slip and fall down I will be able to stop myself well before getting to the edge of the precipice. When I cross these gullies I also know from many previous observations that the dogs can cling to incredibly steep slopes and still climb back out. These dogs have remarkable balance and climbing abilities. But I would not be able to save them if they were to get stuck on such a steep slope. I'm desperate to get through this merciless section and have to concentrate on keeping myself safe. The dogs will have to take care of themselves. At this point, I'm so demoralized and tired that I cannot watch after them very well.

Few plants grow on this plateau, mainly lichens and short grasses that grow in sunken areas where they are sheltered from much of the wind. I know if a storm front rolls in, I could be tent-bound for days in high-velocity winds and bitter cold. I never linger here and hurry my pace as much as I can, but it's backbreaking work and the first day I hike only two miles as the crow flies. I travel in a zigzag pattern trying to dodge some of the aggravating snowdrifts. They fill every depressed piece of land around and occupy about half the total land area.

During the first night on this barren, wind-blasted plateau, I set up camp on the only level piece of ground that doesn't have snow on it. I don't want to dig out a spot in the snow if I don't have to. It's a lot of work. This campsite, however, is only fifty yards from the edge of the canyon, which gives me the chills. I keep the dogs leashed while we are at camp, and during the night I bring them in. Because I'm so afraid for them falling, I tie their leashes to my arms. We rest warmly even with savage wind gusts knocking the tent around. The wind rocks the tent like a passing locomotive and I worry about breaking a tent pole, or the fabric tearing apart. I can do nothing during the night but wait out the wind-driven tempest, knowing that if my tent goes, there will be little hope we can survive a night.

There are a hundred ways to die up here, but most of the time I'm calm, and even light-hearted. I know I have to be vigilant and plan ahead at all times. I have to move across the land while always thinking about my safety. I could fall off a cliff, freeze to death, fall into a snowy hole, be hit by falling rocks, break through ice, lose my tent, get too exhausted to continue, starve, or become dehydrated. By far and away my worst fear, however, is that I might climb into an impassable gorge and not be able to get back out. All these dangers are made twice as deadly by traveling without another person. There would be no one around with opposable thumbs to help save me if I were to need saving. I wish I had someone here to help me. I could freeze my fingers in an hour and there would be no other person to help set up my tent. There would be no one to haul me out of a ravine if I were to get trapped.

I leave my wet boots outside in the vestibule of my tent overnight and in the morning they are frozen solid, like bricks. It takes me an hour to get them thawed out enough to put my feet into. I put the boots next to the dogs to use their body heat. They don't seem to mind as long as I put my jacket over the boots first. When they curl up to sleep some more, I slide the boots over so that they are up against their bodies. Then later, I bend the boots back and forth, trying to break some of the ice. Finally I put on two pairs of wool socks and stick my feet in, lace them up, and hope for the best. I can see the sun peeking through the mountains, so I hope it will be a sunny day and that my feet won't get too cold.

The second day crossing the pass is more difficult than the first. Again we only manage two or three miles. The snowdrift crossings continue like a bad dream until we reach the place I had feared while looking at the map the previous day. It's where the Ambler River gorge turns right and cleaves the valley in half, creating a formidable obstacle that I will have to figure out how to cross. The Ambler River, which is the size of a creek now—but still has a mega-size gorge to contain it—comes up the valley from the south before cutting across my course. I'm traveling on the east side of the Ambler before it turns in front of me, and there was no way I could have crossed it earlier. The river was even deeper then. It cuts across my route in front of me like a lacerated wound. Then it extends high up into the steep, jagged mountains to the east. There doesn't appear to be a way to cross up there, either, and I can't waste the energy to walk all the way up there when I'm pretty sure it would be for nothing. I have to find a way across where I am.

When I come to the edge of the canyon, I scan the rim for a safe way down. I see a forty-yard-wide section that extends all the way to the bottom. I study the other side to find a feasible way up before I go down. Nowhere does the climb out on the other side look easy, and only two routes out even look possible. Everywhere, the canyon walls are almost vertical and the rocks splinter into friable, icy shards. I feel despondent, but I know I have to get across this chasm somehow. I have to get across here or turn back for Ambler, which is at least a three-week slog back, and I don't know if I have enough food to make it. I don't know if I could face that, but it would be better than falling to my death with no one here to find me and with no one to take care of the dogs.

I head down slowly, keeping my pack balanced so it won't topple me over and cause me to somersault down the steep slope. If this slope still had snow on it, I'm sure I wouldn't be able to get down without falling. I wouldn't even try. When I reach the bottom I look for a way across the ten-foot-wide channel, which is frozen over with ice and snow except for a slushy creek flowing over the top of it. The channel is made up of a bottom layer of water, then hard ice on top of that, and then snow on top of that with water slicing a thin fissure over the surface. These types of creeks are dangerous to cross. I can't tell anything about the depth underneath the surface water. I never know if I will be able to wade the water on the surface without breaking through the ice layer underneath. I watch Will. He is excited about exploring new ground as usual. He crosses at the narrowest point with Jimmy following him. I hone in on that spot and follow them. I make it across with only wet feet—normal for a day's hike around here. Wet feet go with the territory and rubber boots are too heavy and cumbersome to hike in, so I wear leather hiking boots. On most days my feet are soaked the entire day. Only when I take off my boots inside the tent do I get to dry my feet out and warm up.

I pick a route up the other side that doesn't have snow for the first fifty feet. At first I climb without any problems. Then I turn and walk along horizontally to go around a steep cliff that looms above me. I come to a snowy section, rising abruptly into the same rocky cliff. I try to cross it at the flattest section so I can keep going and make my way around the cliff to go up at another place. But just below this flat snowy section is a sheer drop of about fifty feet. One fall and I could slide over the edge. I take a few baby steps onto the snow to see how it feels, but immediately my body starts to tense up as I see the drop. I can't see over the edge and have to assume it's straight down. I turn around before I freeze up completely, then walk back down to search for another way up, not wanting to risk a fall. The dogs have already gone across this dangerous section. They walked assuredly across it like they would on any snowy surface. I don't know if they understood the danger or didn't see it as dangerous. I think if they were to fall, they would be seriously injured. Sometimes I think they are more like Dall sheep than dogs by the way they can climb.

I search downstream by trying to walk the ice that covers the creek. I have to walk along cliffs that reach straight down beneath the surface of the water. There is no bank whatsoever to walk on. It looks deep even at the edge. The walls of the cliffs appear brittle as I try to take small steps along the edge ice, but the ice here is thin. I find some whiter ice in the middle that looks thicker. I walk on this hoping that just around the corner there will be a piece of solid ground I can dive for if the ice breaks, but I turn the corner to see even more cliffs and more deep water with thinly crusted ice over it. I'm pretty sure the water is over my head, which causes me to tense up again. Fearing I'm about to fall through the ice, I hesitate for a second and almost panic. Then I pivot around and make a hasty retreat back across the ice, hoping it will not break and send me falling in over my head with a full pack on my back. Luckily I make it back without falling through, just creaking ice. Then I look for another route. I start feeling uneasy about getting out of this canyon. I don't want to get trapped in here.

This canyon is just the first huge obstacle of many blocking my route to Anaktuvuk Pass. First I have to get out of this precipitous canyon, then spend days walking forward in waist-deep snow drifts to reach the Noatak River, only to be still a hundred miles in the middle of this empty mountain range. I talk aloud to myself, which helps settle my nerves. Deep within my gut I know this journey is within my capabilities, so I don't freak out. I'm not religious, but I say a few prayers out loud, reverting subconsciously to my Catholic school upbringing just in case. In the course of several days, I say around a dozen "Our Fathers" and a dozen "Hail Marys," all because I don't know what else I can do. It helps soothe my mind. This makes me think about how people revert to religion when times are hard—after they have exhausted all the alternatives they know. But there are always alternatives, and I try to tell myself this as I venture over the land, wide eyed and afraid.

The only other possible way out of this canyon looked too difficult from the rim I had descended from. It starts out as a rocky slope
for the first fifty feet from the bottom, then reaches a snowy incline
that gradually gets steeper until it reaches a ten-foot-high, vertical
wall at the top. This way really is my last chance. I must get up it.
I try to relax as I climb until I reach the snow, not fully committing
myself to the climb yet. As I ascend onto the snow, the slope becomes
steeper and I must dig the toes of my boots in several times on each
step to make a foothold that will support my weight and the weight
of my pack. I don't have ropes or even an ice axe anymore to stop me
if I were to fall.

When I reach the vertical section, I look back down one time to
decide if a fall would cause me serious injury. Gauging the distance
correctly to the bottom is important so I know if I will die or not.
I look down and study the drop, and since the bottom tapers off into
a sixty-degree slide, I don't think I would die if I were to fall. But
I might get injured, which could be disastrous enough this far from
help. "I got to do it," I say out loud to psych myself up. "This is the
only way." I shake my hands to loosen them up. Then without looking down again, I dig toeholds one after another without stopping.
"Our father who art in heaven, hallowed be thy name," I start saying almost unknowingly as I climb. "Thy kingdom come, thy will be
done. Please let me get out of here." I jam the toe of my boot into the
snow several times to form each step, which I can never get more than
a couple of inches deep. They're just barely large enough to get the toe
of my boot in. After digging about ten steps with my boot tips, my
quadriceps and calves grow fatigued, but the fear of falling keeps me
going. I reach the lip at the top. I know my steps have to be perfect,
but also made quickly. If just one were to give way, I would plunge
down fifty feet smashing into the rocks at the bottom. To make it
over this snowy ledge is a difficult challenge. In better circumstances

I probably wouldn't attempt this climb without ropes and a climbing partner. I have to change the angle of my body from vertical to about sixty degrees while still digging toeholds with my feet down at the vertical angle. I keep going without stopping, and after about fifteen minutes I dig my bare hands into the snow like claws to hold my weight so I can lift both legs up and over the ledge. This is the most dangerous part of the climb. Both my feet will be free at the same time for a couple of seconds, with only my fingers rammed into the snow to hold my entire weight. And the fall from here would be the farthest and steepest one possible of the entire climb. Only my arms will keep me from falling.

When I have my hands positioned into the snow securely, with all my fingers dug in, I lift both legs over carefully all the while gasping for air. First I have to pull my body up a few inches, then hold my entire body weight and the weight of my pack on the palm of my hands while my fingers are still dug into the snow to keep me from slipping back. I'm sure I couldn't perform this maneuver unless my life depended on it. I hoist my feet all the way up over the rim until they are just inches below my hands, then I jam both boots into the snow again to secure myself. I still have to push on for another thirty yards until the ledge reaches bare ground and levels off some. I'm still afraid to stand up. I might slip, so I keep my hands on the snow in front of me to act as multipronged hooks that will arrest me if I start to fall. My hands must be freezing, but with the fear surging through my body, I don't perceive the pain. I push my body as hard as I can because I don't think my muscles will hold up much longer. Just standing in place causes great fatigue. Only when I'm twenty feet away from the edge I had just come over do I stop digging toeholds, stand up, and start walking. My legs quiver from fatigue and will soon fail, but I cannot sit down to rest or I will slide down and over the edge. After a few more steps, I reach the bare ground and fall onto it, relieved to be out of the gorge and out of danger.

The dogs come down from over the top and lick my face. They easily went up diagonally away from my route, which wasn't quite as steep as the place I went up. Their way was too dangerous for me; the drop below at the top of the diagonal was steeper and farther. I watched them going up while trying not to lose my concentration, but there would have been nothing I could have done at that point to help them. I was too worried about myself. They went up in single file without batting an eye, with Will bringing up the rear. His rear foot slipped back once causing him to slide a few inches, but the other three feet easily took up his weight. I think since they are nimble and without packs (I'm carrying them since now they're empty), a fall for them wouldn't have been a problem.

I sit on the dry ground for a few minutes to enjoy the feeling of being out of danger. "Good boys," I say to the dogs in a friendly high-pitched tone like I'm talking to a baby. "You guys can really climb."

The next day the snowdrift crossings continue. I still break through every ten feet and go around those I can. Sometimes I climb partway up on the mountains where bare slopes lead, hoping to get around some snow. Normally it's better to slog straight across snowdrifts. Climbing can take just as much time.

More creeks cut across my path. One that I have to cross is a hundred-foot-wide trench with several feet of snow piled into it, with a stream of water somewhere in the middle concealed underneath. I follow Will for about twenty minutes as we wade into the deep snow, which gets wetter as we get closer to the center of the creek bed. Will stops about twenty yards short before making his crossing. This worries me; he rarely stops to wait for me. I assume he is unsure of the hidden danger or that he doesn't care so much for the deep slush he has run into. I don't want to wade back and find a different route. It all looks the same anyway, so I trudge forward hoping to cross right where Will has stopped. I take the lead from the dogs, patting their sturdy rib cages as I slide by while they stand waiting for me to go ahead. "What's wrong you guys? You doing okay?" I say to them. They're in single file waiting, up to their chests in snow with Jimmy in the rear. But once I take a step past them they follow instantly at my pace, without making any extra body movements and without making any sounds. They're content for me to show them the way.

Soon I find myself up to my waist in soft snow—it's more slush than snow and not too pleasant. I feel solid ground beneath my feet so I wade haplessly on through the waist-high mush for about forty feet, nearly squealing from the dreadful wet cold, and the uncertain topography beneath my feet. I can't use my hands in the slushy snow. Only the surface directly under my feet will support any weight. I have to be careful not to lose my balance and tip over into the deep slush. I might not be able to stand back up quite so easily with my heavy pack. The cold starts to hurt my legs, especially around my shins, but I keep my concentration so I won't fall. After a couple of minutes of wading, the slush becomes shallower and I get onto some creek rocks near the other side to warm my feet back up. Just getting them out of the snow and water is enough to get them to stop throbbing. The dogs hop and walk out of the slush, and once they get on the rocks beside me, dash off over the rim of the creek bed to go exploring.

This routine of crossing slush-filled creeks, snowdrifts, and barren rock continues the same way for two more days until I reach Nushralutak Creek, which will lead us down to the Noatak River. Here the snow begins to dwindle as we decrease in elevation. I feel some security again when I see the Noatak Valley approaching and the steepness of the mountains around me decreasing. Some ptarmigan and dry grass appear—life. On the final night before reaching the

Noatak River, I camp well below the snow line, where the tundra is dry and forms a soft bed. My apprehension subsides now that I'm out of the harrowing pass, and for the time, out of danger. Only now does it dawn on me what I've just done. I spent the past twenty-one days crossing the Schwatka Mountains in late April, and I'm pretty sure I won't do it again, at least not this time of year.

FALLING IN THE ICY RIVER

May 9, 2007, 120 miles past Ambler, 160 miles from Anaktuvuk Pass
I start out hiking, and according to my maps I have only four miles to go to reach the Noatak River. Finding my route here in the arctic is not that hard. I only take a GPS reading to be sure of my position. I often can watch the next pass I have to take or the next mountain I have to go around for days before I get there, so this gives me plenty of time to study and plan my route ahead. Also, few trees block my view, and there aren't any at all on this side of Nakmaktuak Pass, unless you count willow bushes. It's just wide-open tundra. Finding my way would be more difficult if the land was flatter and didn't have mountains to serve as navigational landmarks.

I near the Noatak River after some easy hiking and watch a grizzly bear as I come off the final hillocks to the river plain. The bear is lumbering along the edge of a frozen lake. Lakes here stay frozen long after the snow on the ground has all melted. I'm about a hundred feet higher, so I get a good view of the bear. I sit down on a hummock for about twenty minutes to watch where it goes. I can see for miles across vast expanses of arctic tundra. The bear lumbers along the edge ice to the other end of the lake and never stops walking. Then the animal crosses some grassy ground to Nushralutak Creek and somehow disappears into the distant landscape.

After the bear is gone, I get up and continue my way down to the Noatak, crossing where the bear walked minutes before. This is the first bear I've seen on this trek, and I'm not quite sure how the bears react in this region. I walk cautiously with the dogs close by, my shotgun easily accessible and my shotgun slugs in my pants pocket. I never like hiking with a loaded gun. I'm more likely to trip and shoot myself than to be mauled by a bear. I talk with a pleasant tone, yet loudly enough to be heard when I pass through some head-high willows. The bear will probably smell me long before it hears me, though, especially since the wind is blowing in the animal's direction. I never see the bear again, but I figure it knows I'm in the area and that it is probably content to keep a distance from the dogs and me.

When I reach the river, I'm anxious to cross right away since my feet are already wet and I can't envision myself crossing in the morning when it's colder outside and my muscles are sore. I can dry out in the evening, and in the morning I'll have the pleasure of starting the day with dry boots. I want to cross over to Matcharak Lake, which is big enough for a plane to land on and bring me supplies. If I can't make it to this lake, the plane will have to drop my packages from the air. The ground is too uneven to land on. If I don't get this food drop, I'm certain I will run out of food long before reaching Anaktuvuk Pass, and I'm not sure what I will do then, or which way I will go to walk out before I starve. But for now I worry about getting across the river. Great slabs of ice are jammed up in various heaps up and down the river, making it appear bitterly cold. I look across the river and the ice. I feel the chill it produces, and the air coming off it makes me shiver. I feel apprehensive about another barrier confronting me. I'm never sure if I can get by them. And out here in this timeless, empty void, I have to get by all of them to get out of here. Not only do I have to hike a hundred miles, but also I have to keep confronting impasses that rattle my confidence. I have to believe I can do anything and not mentally break down.

To rid the apprehensiveness I feel, I decide to toughen up and cross right away so I can eliminate another barrier and start with a more tranquil mind in the morning. I don't take off my pack. I think I can manage the thigh-deep current even though the water is icy cold. I hold my hand in the water and it starts to ache right away. I pull it out and put my glove back on before the frigid wind makes it worse. I walk downriver about a hundred yards to where there are dry gravel bars extending several feet out off each side of the river. I pause for a moment and figure since I've crossed many cold creeks and rivers in the lower United States, this one will be the same. I unfasten my waist belt in case I fall in the water. Then I start wading somewhat fast to hurry on across before my feet hurt.

I think I can just waltz right across the Noatak River, like all the other rivers I've encountered, then be on my merry way north. My intuition warns me to be careful, though, so I stop wading and scan the river for a minute, thinking about my options. I don't really have many. "What the hell?" I say as I look at the dogs who are getting ready to cross, too. They can sense when I'm getting ready to cross a river like this and will fall in line behind me without a single sound from me. I figure I should keep wading fast to avoid being in the river longer than necessary. I have about fifty yards to go to reach another level gravel bar on the other side. It looks flat the entire way. No problem, I think. It starts out ankle deep, then knee deep. Just keep going I tell myself, and soon it will level off and start getting shallow again. Right about then a problem appears. My feet begin sliding like I'm on a sheet of ice going down a hill. "Damn it!" I say. I am on a sheet of ice. The bottom of the river is covered with it and I'm being swept downriver by the current. In a mild panic, I try to step back toward the shore, but when I start to step off my foot slips and the river whirls me around 180 degrees like a big buffoon. I plunge into the frigid water over my head while landing sideways.

Lifting my body up out on the open tundra after a fall had always been a feat of superstrength, but it took some time. I don't know how I get to my feet within seconds after falling in the river. But before I know it, I'm up again on two feet, though my back is facing down-river and my feet are still sliding along with the current at about a mile per hour. I'm afraid to move my feet because this might cause me to lose balance and fall again. For a moment I stand there sliding, too paralyzed to do anything. The cold water on my chest took my breath away, and I moan a little, too faint to be heard. I don't move a muscle for what seems a long time, but it's really only a few seconds. I'm simply waiting for another fall that I think is sure to come. Will is already bobbing up and down on his toes back for shore. In those few seconds of sliding, my mind goes through the procedure I believe I will have to do in order to get out of the river. I will slide out of my pack, let myself slip back down into the icy current, and begin sort of half swimming and half floundering toward shore while towing my pack with one hand as it lies submerged in the water. I have to make sure to keep hold of my pack at all times, no matter what happens. If I lose my gear here, I'll probably lose my life. I get ready. I'm sure I will slip and fall in again at any moment.

Right about when I'm sure I'll fall again, my feet slide onto a rough surface and I gain a bit of traction on some pebbles. I'm able to take a half step toward shore in that same second. Then I take two more steps, which gets me out of the worst of the current and onto a better gravel surface. I keep walking for about half a minute until I'm out of the water completely. Then I call to the dogs as I walk onto dry land dripping from head to toe, "Pups, we're camping right here tonight." I go up over the bank, set up my tent, and build a fire to dry out my wet clothes before the sun goes down. We will have to find a different place to cross upriver.

I was hoping to avoid this sort of incident ever since leaving Kotzebue and had done pretty well. I had a few close calls, like crossing thawing rivers and hearing them crack beneath my skis, and skirting cliffs along the edge of rivers and creeks where the water beneath the ice was fairly deep. With a journey of this amount of time spent crossing rivers and traveling along them, it seemed inevitable that I would fall in at least once. I'm fortunate to get away without being too cold. It gives me a clearer outlook on the way I travel and live. All is not as it seems. There is a place and time for moving quickly without much forethought, where intuitive thinking is more important than slow, logical planning. However, getting ready to cross a frozen river in northern Alaska in early May isn't one of them. I came out of that river thankful. I'm thankful that the air temperature is around thirty-five degrees and not ten below zero like it was when I began my trek six weeks earlier. I'm thankful the mishap is over and I only lost my comfort. I'm thankful the dogs got out with only a brisk bath. They didn't seem to mind. In all, I got off easy, and I don't fret much for falling in the water. Quite the contrary, I look more forward to the days ahead when the plane will drop my food from the air and I'll be able to feast again.

Building a fire is easy and I get one roaring in just a few minutes. The dry arctic air in this part of Alaska leaves the dead willow bushes dry and brittle. I only have to gather them up from the base of bushes, throw them into a pile, and ignite small tinder underneath. It takes about two minutes.

As I warm up by the fire, a fox trots by down to the river's edge and jumps onto an ice raft that is the first in a long line of ice rafts reaching almost all the way across the river, but they're too tipsy for me to walk on. The fox jumps from one to the next like it's something the animal does every day. When it comes to the last raft, there is a ten-foot gap of deep water keeping it from the other side. The fox doesn't even break stride, but simply leaps out as far as possible off the last raft, lands with a splash just a foot from the other shore, jumps out of the water, and runs up the bank. I shake my head as it disappears. If only it were that easy for me, I would be across already and on my way.

May 10, 2007

In the morning I call home to Julie and tell her about falling in the river and to make sure the plane is coming to drop off my supplies. She is good at organizing things back home that help me on my trek. "Hey, Julie, how are things?" I ask her.

"Great, how are you?" she asks, drawing out the word "are."

"I'm fine. I just wanted to call and check on the food drop."

"He should be there tomorrow."

"Oh, great," I say. "I don't think I could make it out of here if he didn't show up," I say bluntly, and there is a long pause on the other end of the line that is not the normal satellite phone delay (later she tells me this comment made her worry). Sometimes I forget that the adventures I do in my life make my friends and family worry. I forget that what challenge in the wild would make someone else cringe only invigorates me. I become used to the risks and I speak frankly about the danger. I want to make sure the drop happens, too, so I have to be clear to Julie how much I need it. It would take me weeks to hike out of here, if I didn't starve first.

At this point on my journey I have almost no food left, so it's a small gamble I'm taking by relying on an airplane and a pilot to save my life. Julie and I talk for only about five minutes, and these short conversations always make me feel like I say good-bye too soon, without getting to find out what is going on with her life. There are critical things about my journey that have to be discussed before we can make small talk, before we can have the idle talk that helps bind relationships together. But I can't relax and work on binding our relationship when details about my journey need to be hashed out. The threat of something happening to me keeps me sharp eyed and unable to make pleasant small talk, until Julie and I agree on a time for the plane to arrive and before the phone cuts out on us, like it sometimes does.

"How is your rowing?" I ask.

"Great. I rowed with the 'A' boat yesterday for the first time."

"Really, you must be getting good."

"Oh, I'm not sure about that," she says, but I know how strong of a rower she is.

"I think the coaches know what a natural you are," I say.

"I don't know."

"Oh, I know. You're good at it."

"Maybe," she says, and then we talk just a little more. It's important I don't let my phone battery run down too much. I call Julie frequently on this trek and I want to be able to keep calling her on a regular basis, as well as my parents occasionally. Even though I have a spare battery I still need to keep the calls short because I still have a long way to go to Anaktuvuk Pass. I need to be able to call in an emergency if one ever comes up, and once I run down my main battery I won't be able to call home to chat anymore. I'll feel even more alone and vulnerable.

"I wish we could talk more," I say.

"I know—me, too."

"Take care of yourself," I say, and then hang up. These short conversations always leave me missing home even more, but I never let it get me down. I just put all those longings aside, knowing that they will be realized at the end of my trek. I'm better at doing that now that I'm older. I'm better at enduring hardships to finish a journey so that I can discover incredible rewards, like getting in shape and seeing wilderness that people don't get to see.

I realize how worn out I've become. Today is my first rest day in more than ten days and I hobble around camp stiff and sore. I saunter down to the river and throw in my fishing line with a silver lure attached to it, but the cold wind makes my hands hurt after a couple of minutes, so I quit. I'm not getting any bites anyway. In these arctic rivers, you either get bites right away or none at all. Fishing longer is pointless. I'm not sure what causes this exactly. Perhaps when the water is high, the current becomes too turbulent and cloudy. These conditions are tougher for fish to feed and makes it hard for them to find your lure. When the waters recede and the fish start congregating in slack currents there should be plenty of them. The calmer waters make it easier for the fish to feed and they should be voracious. With no one else around to fish them out, I should catch one right away.

I end up sitting by the fire most of the day making biscuits. I have an entire box left. I use the lid of my cooking pot for a pan and put it on the fire. These biscuits don't require any oil to cook. I simply sprinkle dry biscuit mix over each one. Then I put them in the pan until they rise a little, but I don't wait for them to cook all the way. I'm too hungry. I eat about a dozen of them, one after another until I'm stuffed. I wouldn't eat like this if I thought a plane filled with food wasn't coming. I give the dogs a couple of biscuits, too, which they bolt down without chewing.

I have plenty of time to rest and clear my mind from the stress of traveling over such cold and jagged mountains. I've become irritable from the constant desperation to make distance. I need to let that feeling go and travel only when I feel well, but often I have to make miles when I don't want to go. I don't want to carry a murderous load across such irregular ground. I dread having to put it on my back.

I don't want to stay, either. Being this far away from any town—about a hundred straight miles—means my food will run out if I linger too long. I'm sort of in a pinch, one that has plagued nomadic people in the arctic for centuries. I don't want to stay, but I don't want to go, either. The comfort of the familiar and the drive to be on the move to find more food are always two opposing forces in a nomad's life. To know when to follow each one is the key to survival. And there is little room for error.

Ice blocks the size of pickup trucks lay in the Noatak River. Once in a while one will collide into another or break apart sounding like someone is working nearby throwing blocks of cement into the bed of a truck. The sound makes me think of people, which I'm starting to miss. I know no one is nearby, though. Sometimes I forget this and I talk to myself instead. "Oh, that's just ice breaking off," I say. "It sure is loud." I look out at the river. Sometimes I ask myself questions aloud because there is no one else here to listen, and the process of going over a human conversation settles me. The dogs really don't understand me so I pretend that someone will answer my questions. "How am I going to get across that river?" I ask myself loudly. Then I always answer my own questions after I think about the problem for a moment. "I'll just walk upriver until I find a place to cross, no problem. If I have to, I'll tie some rope to my pack and swim the thing." It's as if I begin thinking out loud, and my urge to tell someone my thoughts escalates within me. Then I start saying what I'm thinking as if I were talking to another person to replace the verbal support I would normally get from a travel partner.

I never really gave enough merit to the verbal communication and the idle chitchat that takes place within a small group of people. When you're trying to survive in the wild it packs a mighty punch. The American Indians must have known this. Mountain men of the American West must have learned this. Ishi, the last surviving member of the Yahi Tribe in California, must have known this. I'm being forced to understand this importance, too. Besides providing some facts you can't answer yourself, the sound of another voice gives you hope. Another voice can tell you that you're still alive and will never die. And when you've been alone in the wild for a long time, you will believe it. I think it's inevitable that you start talking to yourself when you're alone like this. The verbal communication humans have evolved with from living in groups becomes so missed that soon you're forced to talk to yourself to fill the voiceless vacuum. Back home I'm usually not a loud person, but here in this fathomless wilderness the ability to survive alone relies heavily on my ability to convince myself that I'm invincible. Talking boisterously can help do this. I have to make myself believe that I own this land. I learn to talk like thunder and walk like a giant. If you just pretend you know what you're doing, maybe you will start to believe it, and saying things out loud helps you believe something. This is half the battle of beating adversity even against incredible odds.

This valley is about five to ten miles wide and pancake flat, interspersed with dry dead grasses left from the previous year. There are gullies here and there with sodden sides and very little rock. It's much wider and flatter than anywhere on the Ambler River, and the openness of the place makes it seem brighter, like it's held under bright lights. This feeling lifts my spirits. The ground is completely dry except for a few areas where snow has recently melted. If it weren't so cold, and if there weren't any snow-covered mountains off in the distance, it would almost look like an African savannah. The ground looks so warm and inviting I often lie on it and roll around. When I do, Jimmy and Will always want to jump on me to play. "You crazy dogs," I say. I think it was my struggle for weeks over ice and snow that attracts me to this dry earth. Even though the air is cold, the dry soil makes me think it's much warmer. Very little snow is on the valley floor; there's only ice along the river. The edges of the valley rise up very gently at first. I could walk a mile heading up a mountain from where the flat plane ends to where a forty-five-degree slope begins. This gentleness in terrain also eases my trepidation. The land doesn't appear at all menacing. But if I were to hike high enough, snow would appear on the mountains, like the mountains I just crossed. Except for the Noatak Valley, crossing mountain passes in this region has been harder than any other place I've hiked before. The sides of creeks are usually the sides of steep mountains, and they are often hard to get by.

By late afternoon my boots dry out for the most part, as well as the three pairs of wool socks I was wearing when I fell in the river. I will put at least one pair of socks in my sleeping bag overnight to dry them out all the way. I unload the contents of my pack to see how much food I have left. I'm hoping for something I missed, but I find nothing extra. My pack doesn't contain much. My seven-pound tent takes up most of the space now, but I will tie it to the outside along with my shotgun once I fill it back up with food. (If I were smart I would have a lighter weight tent flown in now since the weather is warmer than when I started.) I also carry a set of rain gear, gloves, thermal underwear, a vest, a stocking hat and a ball cap, a small digital camera, a satellite phone that weighs about a pound, my journal, and a paperback book with pages missing because I've been using them for toilet paper and then burning them after I've read them. I have a toothbrush but no toothpaste left, a two-inch-long comb, a small pocketknife, fishing line, four or five lures but no fishing pole, a few lighters and windproof matches, a three-foot-long sleeping pad, a lightweight sleeping bag, extra glasses, a pair of sunglasses, maps, a GPS unit, lip balm for my fair skin, a few shotgun shells, a plastic spoon with the handle broken in half, a plastic cup, a small cooking pot, coffee, lentils, and biscuit mix.

I have no water bottle—I lost it somewhere. I don't have much more worth mentioning.

An icy wind blows all day, enough to make a thin film of ice over all pools of water that thawed out in the previous week. While making my biscuits and basking in the warmth of the fire, I often lie down and let some of the wind blow over the top of me. During these couple of days of cold, I cut dry grass with my pocketknife and stuff it into a couple of cloth bags and put them in my sleeping bag at night for some added insulation, since I got rid of one of my two sleeping bags at Ambler and some clothes on the other side of Nakmaktuak Pass. It's colder here than I thought it would be.

The next day around noon, as I'm out for a walk to loosen my muscles, the bush plane arrives with my load of food from Kotzebue. The plane appears from over the peaks just to the southeast and catches me off guard. I don't hear him sooner because of the cold wind blowing. I run as hard as I can back to my orange tent so I won't miss the plane, but my legs feel rubbery. The pilot buzzes my tent once before I get back, and then a second time just as I arrive. I wave to him while gasping for breath as he flies only fifty feet above the ground. He must wonder what I'm doing all alone here and why anyone would attempt such a feat in an enormous, untrammeled land. Then the pilot turns the plane and flies way downwind to give himself plenty of time to judge where he will drop the food packages. As he gets farther away I lose the sound of his engine, though I can still see the plane well enough. The infinite spread of the land in the valley combined with the clear arctic sky make distances deceiving. The plane is farther away than I think, and since it looks nothing like the features of the landscape, I can still pick it out against the wild backdrop. It seems to flutter right up against peaks that are well over ten miles away, like a large winged dot slipping ever so slightly across the pinnacled heights. The distance from me to the plane can't be much more than a mile, but because I can see so far in the clear sky, the plane looks like it's flying into the side of one of the mountains. The pilot turns the plane, and after a two-second delay, the roar of the engine resonates back to me quite clearly like it just restarted. He banks the plane back around in a wide arc and then straightens out its trajectory, flying into the wind while throttling down his engine to slow his speed. Then he makes a slow approach back toward my tent while I stand watching. The speed and power have been so reduced that the engine sounds like a low-thumping purr. The speed of the headwind keeps the plane aloft.

He drops the first two boxes within a hundred feet of my tent. They are all well wrapped in cardboard and a lot of duct tape, which is how I would have wrapped them. They bounce and roll like they are landing on the moon, just at a faster speed. He then circles back around and drops off two more boxes, placing them even closer to my tent. One splits open a little and a few pellets of dog food sprinkle out onto the tundra, but I watch where they scatter so I can collect every bit later. The pilot makes a final pass and drops the remaining box. Then he tilts the plane's wings back and forth to indicate he is finished. I wave knowing I can eat my fill tonight and continue my journey without having to worry about starving to death for a while.

The plane soars off over Matcharak Lake. Then it turns and starts back down the Noatak River for home, flying low over the land. I lose the sound of his engine long before I see the plane disappear over the mountains. I watch for some time, but then, too, the sight of the plane fades into the arctic air. I feel some loneliness when the plane is out of sight, and I look down and scratch the dirt with my boots, savoring the thought of human contact. This is part of the journey I suppose—becoming content with my own thoughts along with the physical challenges I endure. I realize I'm on my own again in this large wilderness, far away from any civilization and any human salvation.

In the afternoon I feed the dogs as much as they can eat. I have more food than the three of us can carry right now, and this will give us a chance to put on fat reserves and rebuild depleted muscle, but we can't add that much weight in such a short time. All I can hope to do is restore a little glycogen in my muscles. I eat half a pound of chocolate and six bagels right away, which go down like empty air. My gut is limitless, and for dinner I eat a gallon of noodles and melted cheese, and another six bagels and more chocolate later in the evening. It's nice to have food whenever you want it. We often take this luxury for granted in America, where even small amounts of food can be overkill for our sedentary existence. But when you exercise all day, the amount of food required to sustain you may increase fivefold, so someone who could get by with 1,500 calories a day when not exercising now would require nearly 8,000 calories. And that is a heaping pile of food indeed. It's almost inconceivable for some people to believe another human could eat that much and still remain as thin as a rail.

To come up with enough food, and to be able to hike 200 miles on what you can carry, is a huge challenge. It's my greatest obstacle to overcome, worse than the loneliness and the bitter cold. If I absolutely have to, I could endure walking for a week without any food, or if I choose the alternative of sitting in one place waiting for help to arrive, I could last thirty days on the same amount of fat reserves and other body tissues. Often the most important question to ask yourself in a wilderness survival situation is, should I hike out or should I stay put? I could last longer if I stay put, but on the upper Noatak River there isn't going to be anyone coming along soon. "It's too remote," I say to myself while allowing my eyes to sweep the horizon. Spellbound, I say, "It's so far out there, man, crazy." Walking out would be my only choice unless I was sure someone was coming for me. But no one would be coming, and I knew this from the start. This isn't like hiking in Oregon where loping hikers wearing nylon shorts come by every hour. This is true wilderness and I'm on my own, just like I wanted, so I will have to be moving on.

NOATAK, THE FORGONE FRONTIER

May 11, 2007

I leave camp today with a tremendous load on my back. I have so much food stuffed into my backpack that several pieces of gear have to be tied on the outside. My tent is strapped on one side of my pack, and my tarps and pad, with a saw rolled up inside them, is strapped on the other side. On the top, outside of my pack, is fastened my wind pants and parka, and my shotgun is on top of them. My pack is so heavy that I can't lift it off the ground with my arms. I strap it on while I sit on the ground. Then I strain with the muscles of my abdomen to get over onto all fours. I have to be careful not to injure or pull a muscle. Next I bring my knees up toward my chest one at a time so my feet are flat on the ground, then push off the ground with both arms, helping my legs press up to get to the standing position. I push with both arms while beginning to press with my legs, until my arms can't reach the ground anymore and my torso has begun to straighten out. Then only my legs are left pressing my body up until I'm standing. Only my legs are strong enough to lift this monstrous load off the ground.

I've loaded the dogs' packs with food, and they each carry about twenty-five pounds. Their loads don't dampen their high spirits any. They act like they don't wear them at all, except they walk a little slower and bump into things a lot as they brush up against them with the sides of their packs sticking out away from their bodies. They never think to adjust for their added girth; they walk like they always do. I don't have the heart to tell them that they won't be able to run around like they're used to.

I like to dawdle in the mornings, enjoying the moments while preparing to leave. I drink coffee, make oatmeal, write, and think about the days gone by, the days ahead, and about my life and friends back home. I read a novel I brought along with me, *The Invisible Man* by H. G. Wells. I wonder why the main character chooses to remain around people when he can't be seen—to hear their voices? Why doesn't he go live in a country cottage by himself? He seeks human companionship I suppose, even though he can't reveal to anyone that he's invisible. He must wear a disguise in society, and it must be a good one. He hides his invisibility to be accepted among people. I'm not sure why the people in the town begin to fear the invisible man so much. He hasn't done anything to hurt them yet. I wonder if his invisibility causes him to go crazy. I wonder if some people's introversions cause them to retreat farther into themselves, away from society and toward nature, or if extroverted people are just unaware of their own existence. I think the invisible man was an extrovert made invisible, and his inability to be seen turns him into an insane killer. Sometimes I think we are all born serene and mainly introverted, but our lack of connection with nature forces us to become too aggressive. Modernity harbors too many chaotic distractions from what is relevant to our daily lives, and these distractions cause stress.

I miss home, but I won't leave Alaska early unless my life or the dogs' lives are in jeopardy. Alaska is like my second home and the wilderness here is second to none in the entire world. I relish surviving as I travel the land. There is no trail to follow or town nearby with a nice grocery store to buy food from. I do most of my cooking and writing inside my tent, but when the weather warms up I will do it sitting next to a fire, soaking up the meditative glow of the flames under the northern sky and peaks. I wonder how anyone can really enjoy life if they're not comfortable in uncomfortable circumstances, like in the wild. If I can enjoy myself here, where life is hard yet beautiful, I can enjoy myself at home even more. I remember the play entitled *Curse of the Starving Class,* saying aloud how I think the line goes. "You have to sleep on a board once in a while to bring yourself back to reality." You have to endure a little hardship to knock the ego and pride out of yourself. While surviving in wilderness there is no place for them. They only get in the way while you are trying to stay alive.

We come to the Ipnelivik River at about six o'clock in the evening and cross it without any problems. This small tributary of the Noatak harbors water that is only up to my shins. I think it will be much deeper when more snow higher up melts. Then we come to a mile stretch of tundra with about a foot and a half of water on it. Ice is already forming over the surface from the cold wind. It's clear, thin ice that crumples when I step on it. The only way through is to walk in this water, because it extends far over to the base of the mountains and originates from the river. Also, looking for another route would take too much time. I would have to walk a couple of miles up this tributary to the base of the peaks and attempt to cut back over along some higher ground. I would rather stay as close to the Noatak in case the tussock mounds become too difficult. I might be able to find level shores within the river channel to hike on.

The dogs see a small herd of caribou and begin to chase them before I can deter them or get leashes on them. I figured with their heavy packs they wouldn't run off. They sprint away with their full packs bouncing on their backs like purses. The caribou have a huge advantage over dogs, and wolves, too, in terrain like this. I think they prefer it when wolves are around. Their legs are long enough so their bodies don't drag in the water as they run. Wolves have long legs, too, like many mammals in Alaska, but their bodies are more likely to splash the surface of the water and slow them down. I watch the caribou trot off at about twenty miles per hour and stop to look back at the dogs. Jimmy and Will keep trudging on after them through the water, and when they get close to the caribou, the caribou trot off again. The dogs have no chance of getting close to them, and I can only watch in frustration so if they drop a pack, I'll know where it is. I can't afford to lose any food, not even dog food. I think wolves kill their prey mostly on ground that is more flat and solid. This wet terrain enables moose and caribou to survive the pursuit of a wolf pack. With flat, open ground that doesn't dampen their running ability, I think a healthy pack can run down most any land mammal (except maybe a pronghorn) if they can keep it in view, since a caribou would probably outpace a wolf at first. If wolves don't abandon a chase, and the terrain is flat, they should be able to come back on the caribou. But the ground is almost never flat for very long.

After the dogs return a half hour later, their packs are soaking wet and Jimmy's pack is nearly falling off. I get infuriated and scold them. I have to bend over while standing in a foot of freezing water with my toes going numb, trying to put his pack back on, and they don't hold still for that long. They squirm whenever I attempt to adjust their straps, and I can't take off my own heavy pack. There's nowhere dry to lay it; there's nothing but water and submerged grass all around. And it starts raining, with the wind blowing it sideways. The wind, rain, water, and cold air feel like it could cripple me, both physically and mentally. My toes hurt and I want to cry. Once I get Jimmy's pack back on and leash them up, we slosh briskly through another mile of water. I walk like an iron-faced man trying to keep it together. We make camp on the first dry ground we come to, behind a clump of bushes to block part of the wind.

May 12, 2007, 155 miles from Anaktuvuk Pass

In the morning I try to pack up early, but I have to stop often to put my hands in my jacket to warm them up. I can't believe it's still so cold. I wear gloves as much as possible, but I have to take them off for tasks that require dexterity, like tying things. Winter still seems to clutch this region. "When the hell is it gonna warm up?" I say as I squint into the wind. I look up to examine the snow-clad peaks that still surround me, and then I reflect on where I am.

Getting across the Noatak is proving to be a challenge. Everywhere I look there is a deep channel that is chest high with a current. It's not that wide of a channel, perhaps just twenty feet across, but it persists everywhere I check in the river. I will have to head upriver until the river splits apart or sprawls out flat onto gravel bars and try to cross there. This means that I won't head north to the Nigu River up Midas Creek. Instead, I will try to cross over the pass at the source of Portage Creek, which leads over to the upper Alatna River.

These unpredictable sheets of ice continue to cover the bottom of the river, and ice lines the river's edge as well, in giant, monolithic slabs. Just envisioning myself wading the cold river is unnerving. I don't want to fall in again.

The cold air freezes the surface of the Noatak into new, thin layers, and the current causes them to crumple and break as they move downriver. It's quite a sight to see, as long, thin sheets of river ice crumble and fold in upon themselves as they hit thicker slabs of winter ice that haven't begun to melt yet. The collisions make loud grumbling noises, which echo across the valley like thunder, and the dogs look on, intrigued with the noise. They can't quite pinpoint where the sound originates. I think they half expect a huge animal to pop out of the river and run by them so they can chase it. They sit next to me with their eyes riveted on the river without making a peep, waiting for something to happen. I know they are aching to chase something. To them, a loud, unexplainable noise means something to chase.

I decide to rest for the day and spend some time sorting out and drying the dog food that got wet. It's important not to let it spoil. I pick out wet pieces with my fingers meticulously and set them aside into a pile on some plastic. I make sure to feed the dogs the wet pieces first. We will need every morsel of food, even the wet ones. I've been feeding them twice a day since the food drop to build up their strength and body mass for a hard push to the village of Anaktuvuk Pass, over a hundred miles away, but I'm running behind and don't know if I will make it there as scheduled to meet my brothers. Mike is going to harass me if I don't make it in time. He loves hard hiking so much that I think he wants me to be there so we can all enjoy it together. Steve will probably cut me a little slack. He's not as outspoken as Mike and will usually be the one who goes the extra mile when we others have given up. He does it because the rest of us either can't or won't.

On a backpacking trip in Glacier Peak Wilderness about six years ago with Mike, Steve, and a few other friends, Steve and I decided to hike the last twenty-four miles in one day. We had to work on Monday and wanted to get home on a Saturday so we could rest. It turned out to be a difficult hike for me. When we reached the trailhead my feet were too sore, and though I could have walked farther if my life depended on it or if I were alone, I left it to Steve to hike the last three miles to get the car. We were hiking an eight-day loop and had left it at a different trailhead. Originally, we had decided I would be the one to hike the three extra miles, but when I got there I said, "You're going to have to go get the car. I don't think I can hike anymore." Steve refused at first like he always does, but seeing I wasn't going, he finally stood up and took off down the road for the car. He always had naturally thick legs, and though he usually walked slower, they seemed to be able to take more punishment than the rest of ours. He has this unbendable demeanor, too—stoic and lighthearted with a tinge of retaliation in his voice. At the end of our twenty-four-mile day, it remained the same as it was at the beginning, when mine was starting to unravel. This mental strength is gold and I hope I have some of that for this long four-month trek. I think I'll need it.

Six miles a day seems to be about as far as I can go with this heavy pack on my back, especially since I have to fumble my way over tussock mounds without slipping and falling over. Soon I will have to lighten the load to travel faster. My friend Jeff is going to meet me as well. He's a good friend of our entire family who used to come over and eat all our food when we were in high school. I haven't seen him in over a year. We used to hike in the Cascade Mountains when we were in our late teens. I don't want to miss the comradeship and good cheer that will encircle the group through the long grueling days, but especially in the evenings when we will joke about every conceivable topic in the world while drinking tequila and smoking cigars. Mike has made it a tradition to bring alcohol and cigars on all our hiking trips, and I'm looking forward to introducing Julie to it. I don't think she has ever smoked a cigar. I hope my brothers don't make her cry with their rough, sarcastic humor. She jokingly told me she might. I wonder if she minds experiencing a brand of social interaction different from her polite decorum. Maybe it will be better for me not to worry about her and let her interact with my brothers however she likes. She is strong willed and can handle my brothers. Maybe it's my weakness to worry about her manners or my brothers' lack of manners. Sometimes I think I'm too crude for her to like me, too absentminded at times, and always talking about adventure, instead of teaching myself to focus more on her interests.

During these days I let the dogs walk without a leash, but sometimes they lag way behind digging for rodents in the dry hillocks. The marmots have come out and they make their burrows in dry mounds that sit above the wet tundra. It's exhausting for me to keep the dogs moving, and I often have to go back and stop them from digging so we can move forward across the land.

Jimmy falls into a small slough with his pack on and can't get out of the cold water. I have to run 200 yards back following his frightful howl. When I get to him, his front legs are propped up on the side of the slough, but he can't get the rest of himself out with his pack on. I reach down and grab the scruff of his neck and pull him up. "You crazy dog," I say. Then he shakes himself off like nothing happened.

Another time he comes running back without his pack. I have to walk back and look for it. Now I don't put anything in their packs that I can't do without. Scolding them really doesn't do any good. I've tried. They're hunting dogs to the core and nothing is going to stop them from sniffing, tracking, digging, chasing, and hunting no matter what. But when they both come running back without their packs, I realize I'm going to have to keep them leashed permanently. I find one pack right away, but I spend an hour searching for the other next to a hill where I last saw them digging. I think about leaving the pack behind, but it has twenty pounds of dog food in it. I envision difficult times ahead, and something in my gut tells me I have to find it if I want to make it out of here—if I want the three of us to make it out of here. We are like one unit and food for the dogs is like food for me. Leaving a dog behind is not an option. I would probably let myself starve first. I owe them that much for them being here.

The pack ends up being right next to where the first one was. I miss it the first time I walk by because it's laying in a depression behind a bush. It's funny how things can seem to vanish out on the wide-open tundra even when there are no trees around.

I shoot a ptarmigan today. I feel bad about it, but it helps keep the dogs from becoming too skinny. I know that I should take advantage of the food source while I can. I may be starving later and not be able to find anything at all to eat. I only wound the bird, so it flies off and lands a hundred yards away. I don't take my eyes off that place. I want to save my shells, so I run across the tundra, sneak up, and then leap onto it. Later that evening I pluck the feathers and throw the entire bird on a fire without gutting it. I eat the breast, which is dark and has most of the meat, and the drumsticks, which aren't nearly as meaty. I give the rest to the dogs. They eat everything, even the bones, which are quite delicate and flimsy. The dogs crunch them up with their teeth. To feed the dogs other times, I put the scraps in a pot of lentils. The hot broth helps to keep them well hydrated and makes them feel more satiated. They sleep better when they are full and well hydrated, and they recover faster. And if they are healthy, then this is one less thing I have to worry about.

Scores of ptarmigan appear along the Noatak Valley, pairing up in early May to begin the courting season. The male is larger than the female and will keep his white appearance even after the snow melts. The female will lose the white appearance and turn brown so that she can blend into the surrounding tundra. The male's white color serves to draw attention to himself out on the brown tundra so the female can stay hidden. When I come upon a pair, the male will usually fly off first in full view, only to land on a white patch of snow fifty feet or so away. Then he will hide on the patch of snow while the female stays where she is, hoping she will go unnoticed. Sometimes she will fly off if I get too close. Other times the male will fly back in full view to divert my attention again. The male can become bold to protect the female, and he is the one often sacrificed to save his family after the babies hatch in June. When the male is alone, he will almost always look for a white patch of snow for camouflage. But when he and the female are with the nest, he will sit in full view, and the female will blend into the brown tundra. This is a great strategy to help their off-spring survive. I think many males are killed and eaten by predators;

I see many places where white ptarmigan feathers are left laying on the tundra. Or perhaps the males were fighting.

May 13, 2007

I'm camped near the mouth of Ipnelivik River with light wind and a feathery snow falling. My fingers get cold when I go outside, but at least the ground doesn't have snow on it. All the snow that falls disintegrates when it lands.

Geese fly over by the hundreds, in massive, V-shaped waves that appear about every ten minutes. Sometimes several formations will pass overhead at once, containing hundreds of birds squawking at each other as they make their way westward. I'm not sure if they are heading for the coast or if they are making their way farther north, but I never see any stop along this stretch of the Noatak River. They forgo the opportunity to feed and rest for possibly better country farther on. There are large lakes and enormous stretches of tundra grasses all around. Even though it looks like a great place for them to spend the summer, they pass it by.

May 14, 2007

I walk through knee-high tussock mounds for several hours. The water between each mound is mostly frozen, so when I step between the tussocks I often slip and lose my footing. Twice I fall with my heavy pack on. I try to maneuver around icy sections, but it all ends up being the same. I reach the Igning River late in the afternoon and cross it, hardly getting my feet wet. It's another small, shallow tributary of the Noatak and also flows in from the south side, the side I've been walking on since I arrived at the Noatak.

I cross through tall willows on the other side of the river and set up my camp on the edge of them so that I can see over the tundra on the other side. Then I let Will loose to run around. He takes off, and

I see him twenty minutes later a mile away running full out along the side of a mountain. He looks like a dot and runs horizontally around the mountain. I watch him for about a half hour until he disappears around the other side. Seeing him run is incredible. He runs so fast for so long. I recognize him by the way he gallops and by the way he keeps his head next to the ground like he is tracking an animal. He returns about thirty minutes later following his exact same route instead of running straight down to camp. When he gets back he flops down panting. I tie him up and give him a pot of water from the river. Then I let Jimmy loose and he runs off, too, but he doesn't stay gone as long.

May 15, 2007, 142 miles from Anaktuvuk Pass

I wake to the first warm morning of the trip. I go outside without shivering and without my hands aching from the cold. Small birds are singing, and robins are here, too, just like in Oregon on a mild, wintry day. There is no wind, and the sun that brightens the land makes me warm, giving me hope.

I spread the contents of my tent outside on the ground to air them out. I take my time packing up, resting in between tasks to look at the scenery. I stroll through the willows to the river, holding the branches back so they won't whip back into my face. I have the dogs tied up, but their collars are loose enough that they can yank out of them if they have to. I creep out quietly from the willows when I reach the edge of the river and scan every direction before I leave the cover. This is when you are likely to run into a bear, early in the morning when you have been quiet all night and your scent isn't so scattered over every-thing. A bear usually will smell you and avoid your camp, but once in a while they slip up and miss your scent as they waddle down from the upper part of the river. They're not expecting to see people here. This time it's all clear. I wash the pan from breakfast and sit on the bank to stare up the Igning River. Mountains flank it on both sides as it meanders its way south to its source. You could spend several weeks up there exploring all the side creeks and the headwaters of the river and still not see everything. Then you could walk two days to the next tributary and explore it as well. There are so many small rivers like this, remote and untouched by human presence. If you have never seen a place like this before, it would be hard to envision. I can see the Igning River for about a mile or two. It's lost in the distance and obscured by willows and gravel bars until I can only see a river flood plain. The valley gets narrower farther up, and makes an easy right turn passing along the edge of three or four snowy mountains right in a row. Between each mountain is a depression where a rugged pass goes through, to where I wouldn't know unless I studied the map. I can see perhaps fifteen miles up the valley to where it curves behind more white mountains near its headwaters and disappears. I think later in the year when most of the snow is gone, you could hike across that divide to the headwaters of the next river on the other side and make your way south.

After I get packed up, I put the packs on the dogs and leash them to me. I don't want them running off so much anymore, and they need to conserve some of their energy; they need to use their energy to move us forward across the landscape.

As I'm leaving camp from the Igning River, a pack of silvery wolves appears out of nowhere off the tundra. The dogs start barking right away, which alerts me from my daydreaming. I'm deep in thought and looking at the ground as I walk. When I first glance at the wolves I think they're caribou, but within a second I realize several wolves are trotting up the draw toward me. They're walling me in on one side. They move calmly up the hill to where I'm standing, and I perceive their power. The wild creatures fan out, and for a few moments I'm at their mercy. They move silently without rushing and look at one another every minute or so for some sort of cue: whether to attack us, study us, or trot off I suppose. I think they are after the dogs. I hurry to yank out my shotgun, which is strapped under the flap on the top of my backpack. The wolves are so close they could tear into us in the couple of seconds when I have to look down and away from them to get my gun off my pack. Thankfully they stop just thirty yards in front of us. The dogs are going berserk, barking and lunging fiercely toward the wolves. I can barely hold the two Airedales. Unnerved by the crazed dogs, the wolves are rock steady and stand their ground silently, like nothing can frighten or harm them. If I didn't have my gun, and if they choose to rush in, they could kill us anytime. They are large, like the build of a sinewy St. Bernard but much quicker and smarter. If the dogs were to get loose, they would probably run right into the middle of them away from my protection. I wouldn't likely be able to reach them in time if the pack were to lead them away from me. These larger-boned Airedales probably stand the best chance of most dogs against a wolf, but still, they are not as powerful as wolves. So I'm lucky the dogs are leashed up today. All their running off in the previous days turned out to be a good thing because I was compelled to leash them up today. An old man in Fairbanks told me about an Airedale he knew who fought against a wolf once. "He was holding his own pretty good for a while," he said casually. "He was nearly as quick and agile as the wolf, moving around, keeping his feet."

"He lived?" I asked, interested in what the man would say next.

"No, then he died. The wolf killed him," he said nonchalantly.

"Oh," I said. "That's too bad."

"You see, Airedales are fearless and very tough dogs, but wolves are, well, they're like professionals. They kill for a living. Dogs don't have a chance, one on one," he said. "Not even Airedales."

If Jimmy and Will get away from me, they will likely be killed by the nine wolves converging in on them. I hold their leashes with all my strength and move around to grab Will's head to take some of his leverage away and block his view in order to calm him down. He's always feistier than Jimmy, though Jimmy is bigger by five pounds and probably stronger. Jimmy feeds off Will's aggression, so if I can calm Will down, Jimmy will calm down on his own. And Will would never relent against these wolves until they killed him. That is the nature of an Airedale terrier.

After studying us for a couple of minutes, the wolves all turn one after another and spread out like a platoon on patrol as they trot off effortlessly toward the Igning River. I can see them a couple hundred yards away as they pause to inspect my previous camp. Then they wade across the Igning River and trot upstream toward the pass. I watch them as they drift off into the distant landscape—silver dots at first, and then I can't see them at all. They know where they are going and don't hurry their pace to get there.

Natural selection helps lead to the increased viability of a species in nature. Domesticated animals, like dogs but not wild wolves, breed without many of the intricate pressures that are found in a natural environment. In the long term, can their progeny continue to exist if they do not diffuse back into the natural environment? Will they have to be let loose from human manipulation? Perhaps it's inevitable if their lineage is to survive. Can the human line continue to exist without evolving in the wild, or has our parting from nature already started our evolutionary demise? By destroying nature, will we destroy ourselves?

Wolves over dogs is a prime example of how nature breeds superior life. I couldn't imagine a hundred-pound dog running down and killing a caribou, but a wolf can. Perhaps a domesticated dog could do it if he were raised in the wild, right alongside the wolf. I don't know for sure. Maybe being raised in a certain environment plays a larger part in shaping an animal's ability than we realize. Maybe there is no special gene needed for killing a caribou at all. Or perhaps the dog still has it but never gets to fully develop its function during his lifetime because he never has to. Or perhaps if the dog remains domesticated too long, his lineage will lose critical genes that enable him to survive in the wild.

Sometimes I think I could survive out in the Alaska wilderness, now that my mind and body are growing accustomed to the wilderness itself and the physical exertion. I could never have made this journey for one week, let alone four months, when I was twenty. I have practiced being in the wild for the past twenty years of my life. Not totally of course. Our laws about attaining food keep me working some job to support the infrastructure of a society that often ranks wilderness as less important than the economy, or even a caffè latte. Nature is subtle in ways and might eventually reveal how imposing it is and how minuscule the human species really is. But we still might not understand its importance even as our numbers decline. We still might not comprehend the idea that most people lose touch with nature more and more as the days go by. I want to go the other direction, away from many ideologies of an industrial-driven society, back to where we belong: right alongside the wolf and the bear in the wild, or partly so anyway, to where the majority of my day is spent directly obtaining my own food, or at least getting it on a local level. Our ancestors evolved to be in the wild a million years ago, and today we likely still retain the same physical and genetic stock they had; we still possess the same hardwired brain to survive in the wild as they did. I think that by stifling these thoughts and by living a sedentary life away from nature, we create a huge gamut of problems for ourselves, like depression in some individuals, hostility in others, and the inability to survive after a natural calamity because we don't know the first thing about finding food in nature. Though I feel my efforts will never be enough to make me as competent at surviving in the wilderness as, say, a wild wolf or a Penan man of Borneo, I can at least strive to go back that way to better myself—to the core of our evolution and the purpose of our existence. If a day comes when there is no wilderness left, then we as a species will perhaps evolve into a less effective organism. If wilderness vanishes then we will likely follow.

At home in Oregon, I will go into the small wilderness areas, often the same place where Jonny died. I will walk in with only a sheet of plastic, the clothes on my back, and some bread, and spend three days wandering under the canopy of trees. I feel alive there, and with more practice I can in time become aware of the feelings that are hidden in the recesses of my brain. Even in small bits of wilderness for just a few days, I can actually learn something. I can get fitter and churn up my primal thoughts needed to cope with feeling comfortable in wilderness. I don't like the destruction of vast frontier wilderness, and being connected to the natural world at least on a modest level is required for us to be able to extract food from it on a sustainable level. A connection to nature will keep us alive.

LUCKY SIX GORGE

May 16, 2007, 136 miles from Anaktuvuk Pass

I walk over ground marked by tussock mounds, waist-high brush, and half-frozen puddles of water all over the place. I cut back and forth way too much searching for better ground, but the terrain is terrible everywhere I look. I make it to the mouth of Portage Creek, which leads up to the pass I need to take to continue over to the Alatna River and on with my trek. The problem is that I'm still on the wrong side of the Noatak River trying to find a way across. I camp next to tall willow bushes, and Jimmy finds the lower leg bone of a caribou. He chews it up piece by piece and eats the whole thing while I look for a way across. He devours every single bit of bone and cartilage, as well as the black, keratinous hoof.

May 17, 2007, 130 miles from Anaktuvuk Pass

I spend the entire day searching for a way across the Noatak, but the river rose six more inches during the night and decreased my chances for crossing. I think about crossing, but I'm afraid I will slip and fall in the water. I slither into the cold current several times without my gear. I'm up to my waist before I'm even a quarter of the way across. This discourages me, but I make several more attempts as I hike upriver along the gravel and willows. Each time I turn a corner I start to think this will be the place I get across. I figure eventually the river will contain a wide gravel bottom where the channel flattens out all the way across, but it never does.

I follow its twisting course, resting every half hour to study the water from a perched point on the riverbank. Sometimes I drop my pack and walk back and forth along sandy sections looking for a thread of land or an unlikely ridge underwater that winds all the way across, but they all sputter out into the hazy depths off shore. I toss rocks into the current while thinking and to see if they make a sound of hitting other rocks. A few places have platforms of ice lodged in the middle of the river with a swift current sweeping around them. If only I could hop my way from platform to platform until I reach the other side, but they never line up just right and there is never enough of them, In other places the river is a deep, green slough well over my head and about ninety feet across. In other spots most of the river flows over the top of ice, ice that used to be the top of the river, but with the snow melting all around the rushing water has etched a new course over the top of what used to be surface ice. I consider tying a rope to my pack and swimming to the other side, towing my pack after me, but the water is bone-cracking cold. I think about making a raft by cutting off a large section of river ice with my saw, but soon set that idea aside as well.

Soon I give up and leave the river channel. It meanders so much that I walk twice the distance I would on the tundra. I move away from the river about a quarter of a mile and hike a straight line between the row of peaks on my right and the riverbed on my left. I can't really tell if there is a crossing point from this far away. I don't plan on moving back to the river to check for a while unless a section of the river looks extra promising. I look for gravel wedges that have carved the river in half or where the river has split into several channels, but I don't see anything worth checking. I decide to keep hiking toward the Noatak River headwaters. I can at least hike up for a day or two to look for an easier way across, but by that time I will need to make an urgent attempt at crossing, even if it means swimming. If I don't I will fall behind schedule and risk running out of food in the final days of this leg of my trek.

May 19, 2007, 125 miles from Anaktuvuk Pass

I hike for several hours to reach Twelve-Mile Creek, but I'm still on the wrong side of the river. I spend an hour trying to cross, but the river is dangerous here. Deep, swift channels divide thick walls of ice that have formed on the sides. At first I think I might be able to cross after I wade a shallow section that puts me on an island of ice in the middle of the river. I attempt to continue across but the other side of the island has an abrupt edge against a dark, green, swirling channel, which I estimate to be at least chest deep. The current flows about twenty yards directly into an ice-walled cut bank. I fear I could get pushed up against it if I were to slip and fall into the churning water. I'm desperate to get across, though, so I begin rushing, but then I think about falling into the river again and about being swept under or pinned against the ice. I stop just short of taking a step into the deep channel. I notice chunks of ice the size of garbage cans breaking off from the edge I'm standing on—unstable ice. I retreat while coaxing the dogs to follow. They sense the danger and I don't think they want anything to do with crossing here, so they follow right behind me.

We get back to the side we had come from and start hiking upriver again. I have to go up to high ground to make it around a cliff next to the river. I hike 200 feet up the side of a mountain until the slopes aren't so steep. Then I continue forward with violent efforts straight up the mountain now and then when I have to go around a rocky outcrop. After about an hour once around the cliff I hike back down to the river. Then we traverse a mile-long section of level, wet ground, where many streams have turned into wide torrents of water. We wade dozens of them for over an hour, some up to my thighs. They never seem to end. I'm actually crossing an alluvial fan of a side river that feeds into the Noatak. The water has risen so high from snowmelt that even tussocks are submerged. It's like walking across a low-level lake.

After this mile section, I veer over to the edge of the Noatak again to see what it looks like. The closer I get the more I realize something I haven't seen before. When I crash through the last of the brush and I'm standing next to the river, my spirits skyrocket with the sudden hope of crossing. The river has ice all the way across. This is the only place where I've seen river ice extending all the way across the Noatak. I put my pack down and fasten the dogs to a bush. There is a gaping hole on the river right near where I lay my pack, and the entire river's volume is gushing through this hole, being forced down under the ice and causing powerful whirlpools. I have to go downriver about twenty yards until I'm sure the ice is solid, where it has not been weakened from being too close to the edge of the colliding water. I stay away from this ice that has the full force of the river pummeling into it, where it's most likely to collapse.

I discover some ice that is dark blue to white all the way across. I've learned this is the safest ice. This ice has cracks, but ironically, it's safer to walk along the cracks. They're formed when the thinner parts next to it sink down a few inches into the river. The thickest ice remains where the crack has formed, and the cracked ice often runs along a slight ridge of stronger and thicker ice, at least in these smaller mountain rivers. Sometimes these ridges will lay over the top of sandbars or shallow water.

I walk carefully along a crack until I get past the flow of the current. A month ago I would have never walked on ice like this, but back then I didn't understand which ice was thin and which ice was thick enough to support my weight. Satisfied that this is a safe way across, I go back for my pack and the dogs. I rush because the day is warm and this section of ice will surely be gone soon, perhaps within a day. After having searched for a way across for days, I don't want to wait one second more and risk losing my chance to cross over the river to get myself back on course.

We hurry across this time, following the exact footprints that I had just made. I scrutinize the crack while I follow it as it meanders past the last of my footprints and then on toward the other side. I study it for weakness. Then I scurry across feeling that being quick is imperative. When this ice bridge is gone, the river will continue to rise in the coming days as the snow from higher up keeps melting. The longer I wait, the farther up this river I will have to hike to get across.

We reach the other side safely, and I become elated while standing on the tundra. Before I rejoice, I look around to make sure I'm all the way across and not just on a large island. "Good job, puppies," I say. "We've made it across. I can't believe it." Small victories like this bring fleeting jubilation, but it's often beaten out of me by the hours of arduous hiking each day. I try not to take for granted that I'm alive, healthy, and still have the strength to get myself out of here.

The river makes a ninety-degree left-hand turn, which shows up even on the largest scaled maps. It's possible to hike up the hill some and cut part of the turn, which we do. From the top I see a moose feeding in the swampy brush on the other side. The animal watches me as I walk past but doesn't move. This one looks pretty relaxed, like this is a safe location. I wonder how the moose got here and what pass was used. Surely the weather will get too cold to spend the winter. At first I think it might have come over Gull Pass, but soon I will find out that it's far too treacherous for moose to travel through.

Wolves have a real tough time pursuing moose in water, lakes, bogs, or brush. Moose have such long powerful legs that they can easily plow through this type of terrain, outdistancing wolves. Or they can stand their ground, stomping an unlucky wolf who gets too close. Wolves can't mount a good attack off such marshy terrain. I continue to walk, keeping a steady course so I won't spook the moose. Their bodies are deceptively agile and powerful. Their long legs may look clumsy at first, but when they run the purpose of these long legs is apparent as they pass over the tallest brush. I come across a wolf kill up higher on the tundra. They didn't leave much, except a lot of fur and bone fragments scattered all around. Nothing is left for the dogs to eat.

As I round the corner I can see the mouth of the Tupik River. It's a feasible route south back across the mountains leading to the Reed River. The valley is filled with a good amount of snow, which I'm not too comfortable about, but it's also fairly wide and flat. I could possibly take that way out if I become desperate enough to leave here to get more food, but for now I pass it by.

Instead of going back downriver to cross over a shorter pass up Portage Creek, I push upriver hoping to cross Gull Pass over to the Alatna River. From there I will go south instead of north. Then I'll head east again on the Kutuk River before reaching the John River and up to Anaktuvuk Pass. The Noatak River keeps getting smaller as I head up, and soon it shrinks into a large winding creek. Its source is even farther up, flowing out of high, snowy mountains. Normally I find a large gap much lower than the mountains it passes through. But the source of the Noatak looks different. The land is heaved up in a long series of barren plateaus, with the creek rising up with it. There is no cleft to squeeze through. If I wanted to cross over that pass I would have to climb much higher than I'm used to doing.

If you want to get out of the Noatak Valley before you starve to death or winter comes, you better have a good plan. Only a few passes that lead out from here are navigable on foot, and I have yet to find one of them. The jagged whiteness is formidable, and the distances and endurance required to walk across this land are incredible. To cross one of these passes isn't merely going up and past one peak and then descending back down. These passes all contain a series of peaks, with the route getting steeper and higher until you reach the apex in the middle and start the long descent toward the river valley on the other side. The far middle of the pass isn't normally visible when the crossing begins, so you really don't know for sure how steep it gets until you are way in there and committed to the crossing. I look at the contour lines on my maps, but I can still never be sure. The closer together the contour lines the steeper the terrain.

Gull Pass is rightly named. A small species of gull lives here this time of year, lingering around the water's edge and soaring on the wind gusts. They are hardy-looking birds and fly like nothing can knock them out of the sky. If you are a bird, crossing Gull Pass gives you an easy shot north to the Arctic Ocean or south toward the land of spruce and alders where the air temperature is probably ten degrees warmer. I suspect they routinely fly over this pass, and I in no way believe I can get through it because a bird can, but I've already committed myself to trying. To get through would be a great shortcut and save me many days in travel time. If I don't make it through, I'll be a week behind schedule and a week short on food. I could starve if I have to turn back.

Lucky Six Creek is the name of the creek leading up to Gull Pass from the Noatak River. It meets the Noatak River at a right angle, close to where the Noatak River makes a right turn south and begins its terraced rise toward the headwaters. I will soon discover that Lucky Six Creek is wrongly named, unless the one who named it means you have to be lucky indeed to get through in one piece.

I finish out the day's hike and pitch my tent at the mouth of Lucky Six Creek on firm, yet soft ground covered with level soil and short grasses. The ground isn't wet at all, but the creek is a full-forced torrent, and when I go to dip my pan for water I'm careful not to slip. I keep the dogs on a leash when they drink from it, fearing they will wade into the water to drink like they always do and be swept away. It's that torrential. I hold their leashes so they have to drink from the edge, but the water is so chocolate brown and fast that even this scares me. I watch the dogs as they drink and keep their leashes tight so they can't step into it.

The soft, dry ground makes a great mattress for the night, and I get one of the best night's sleep on the entire trek. There isn't any snow in this vicinity. We are on the north side of the Noatak River, which seems to receive much more direct sunlight and is not shaded by mountains. The peaks across from me are completely white at this elevation. Gull Pass is more than 3,500 feet and higher than any other pass I will face on this trek. That elevation feels like 10,000 feet, and here in the arctic the only plants growing that high are a few lichens.

By now I've detoured off my originally planned route up Midas Creek by over fifty miles. I don't even have proper maps of this region. I only have maps with a scale of 1:250,000. I might as well be using a road map. Putting a latitude and longitude reading on these maps is possible, but the scale is so large that I could be so far off that it isn't worth the trouble. Taking a GPS reading gives me two numbers. One is the latitude, which runs horizontally on the map, the other is the longitude, which runs vertically. All I have to do is follow the two lines on the map until they intersect and that is my location. On my large-scale maps, that intersection might be the size of a football stadium, and when I'm traversing the sides of cliffs, I need to know exactly which cliff I'm on, so crossing Gull Pass without knowing exactly how steep it is could be a problem with vague maps. I have maps of the upper Alatna River on the other side of Gull Pass, about thirty miles away, so I figure all I need to do is get through the pass, make it to the Alatna River, take a left and walk upriver for a couple of days until my exact location shows up again on my more detailed maps. But to not have very detailed maps of the most rugged section is asking for trouble. I could spend an eternity hiking in there only to find out I can't get through. Then I'll be forced to come back out while trying to remember the exact way I got in there. It's a big gamble. I make a call home to Julie to discuss my dilemma. I ask her to look up my route on the 1:63,000-scale maps, which I think is the best scale for navigating through the Brooks Range. A scale any smaller than that and you would have to carry a lot of maps. You don't really get much better detail anyway. "Hi, Julie," I say. She's happy to hear from me and asks me where I am.

"What's your location, Dave?"

"Where you at?" I say jokingly. It's our running joke.

"You can just say, where are you, or where am I. You don't need to add 'at,'" she explains to me to play along.

"I like to say 'Where am I at?' That's how they say it in Roseburg." I giggle for a second, amused at my own simplemindedness. "I finally made it across the Noatak," I say.

"That's great news," she says, and I tell her about crossing on the ice. I ask her to look at the maps and tell me if the terrain is too steep to get through Gull Pass.

"I might try to hike through Gull Pass," I say.

"Hold on a minute," she says, and boots up her computer and opens a program that contains all the maps of Alaska in two different scales. Then she studies the tightness of the contour lines through Gull Pass. "I don't know, Dave."

"What does it look like?"

"I think I'd go back," she says.

"Really. I don't think I can handle going all the way back," I say. At this point I've come so far that I don't want to turn around. I want to somehow turn this detour into a shortcut. I discuss the route over Gull Pass a little longer.

"Yeah, I think I would go back if I were you," she says. Julie knows how much trouble I had crossing the ravines in Nakmaktuak Pass. She had studied the detailed maps of that area, too, so she can compare those maps with the region through Gull Pass. To her Gull Pass looks much worse.

"I don't think I can go back. It's too far," I say, a little demoralized. "It's days back."

"I know," she says. "But it looks steep and you might have to turn around anyway."

I want to turn my gamble into a win somehow. Even though my odds of getting through have just gotten worse, I decide to try getting through anyway. "I'm going to try and make it over Gull Pass," I say adamantly. Once I make up my mind, Julie doesn't try to persuade me otherwise. She's good about accepting someone's decision. And after a few more minutes we say good-bye.

"Be careful and keep me posted," she says.

"I will. I'll call when I make it through."

The next morning I see several Dall sheep moving down from the entrance to the pass, but I'm not sure if they came from the other side of the pass. It's about six linear miles to the top. They appear to be grazing, sunning themselves, and perhaps trying to reach water. At first I think their presence is a good indicator that it's possible for me to make it through the pass because they could. Soon I will realize it's better not to hike where Dall sheep go. They go there for a good reason. They are the only large animals that can possibly go there over the rugged cliffs and near vertical drops. At first I don't know this and head up, feeling like I'm hiking on the slopes of the Alps. I walk over short-cropped grasses and bare dirt, like some domestic sheep have been grazing. Immediately, though, the creek turns into a crumbly looking gorge, with vertical sides that reach all the way down to the creek bottom. I travel a few hundred feet above the creek on a wide, horizontal ribbon of passable slopes. They're steep, but not as steep as the cliffs below and above me where the cliffs of the creek gorge drop away and the cliffs of the mountain peaks loom to the heavens. The hiking gets more difficult the farther back toward Gull Pass I go. I should turn back right away, but I'm steadfast about getting through to the Alatna River on the other side. If I don't get through I will have to spend another two days going back to Portage Creek.

I soon come to a smaller creek flowing through a high-sided ravine, which cuts across my path on its way down to Lucky Six Creek. I'm at least a hundred feet up from the water of the creek, so I have to find a way down this ravine and up the other side. Going down isn't too bad, but the other side is nearly vertical. At least it's covered with grass and brash. This not only stabilizes the soil but also gives me something to hold on to as I climb. I use the brush to haul myself up sodden ledges, which were formed naturally over the years by the soil giving way on such a steep face as the trickling water cuts down into the earth. The brush provides me something to hold on to in case I fall, and I don't think I could make the climb without it.

I lead the dogs behind me on their leashes because I'm afraid they might run off and fall over the crumbling edges. The climb is backbreaking work and I sweat profusely, with perspiration dripping off my nose and creating a film over my glasses. I haul myself up on ledges, literally climbing by pulling on brush. Then I pause and urge the dogs up as I tug on their leashes. This is hard for them, but they are strong enough to scramble up each ledge with a full pack. They have grown into amazing athletes, and their strength amazes me. Several times Jimmy's pack slides off his back, and I have to go down and get it several feet below. After about a twenty-minute climb, I reach the top and sit down to rest with some disbelief about how much effort is needed to hike through this place. I fear we will encounter more of these near impassable ravines and I'm not sure if I'm prepared for them. I'm not sure if I want to take the risk to cross them or expend this amount of energy to get through.

I get up and continue hiking anyway hoping the terrain will somehow get easier. After about thirty minutes I come to another ravine, which is worse than the first one. And it's too deep and steep to cross. The ravine is made mostly of loose pieces of tiny rubble and doesn't have any vegetation on the opposite slope. I watch the slopes long enough to see small landslides of grainy gravel falling into piles at the bottom. I can see faint sheep trails leading up and crossways, and I wonder how on earth the sheep can climb on that without falling to their deaths. The slopes are almost vertical, and the ravine originates out of some cliff-faced peaks above, so going up and around is impossible. I decide to go down to where the ravine enters Lucky Six Creek Gorge at a right angle. It's really the only possible route, and I don't expect to be able to get through, but I try it anyway. I'm driven on by a subtle fear: to get through this pass and over to the Alatna River where I believe the terrain will be more forgiving. I'm also driven by the fear of running out of food.

I follow the rim of this ravine down to Lucky Six Creek. A thin, sloping strip of land, no more than ten feet wide anywhere, and at times just a foot or two wide, leads down the final fifty-foot drop into Lucky Six Creek. It's the only way through in this immense gorge. This knife-edge ridge is angled just gently enough for me to get down the ridge between the two creeks, and there are obvious signs that sheep use it as the only route to the bottom. On each side of the knife-edge ridge are cliffs so brittle and vertical that not even Dall sheep can climb on them without falling.

I start down and get scared about falling. I tense up and have to stop to get my fears in check. I have to stay cautious, but I can't let my muscles freeze up in the most critical sections of the route or I could fall. I have to be able to keep moving. After a minute and a few deep breaths I get the courage to continue down. I try to keep the gentler sections of the ridge just below me and steer away from sections that lead above exposed cliffs, but there is really little room to maneuver and it appears there is only one way to go. At times I move along just inches from the edge of a sheer drop. I make sure to lean my body inward with my hands on the rocky slope while I pass, so if I lose my balance I will be more likely to fall inward against the few feet of slope, not away from it. I ease up to stop the dogs before the dangerous areas so that they will heel and walk slowly behind me.

After a few minutes I make it down and regain my composure. I plan to walk up Lucky Six Creek Gorge until I find a way to the opposite slopes of Lucky Six Creek. As I reach the creek I startle several Dall sheep who run upstream and disappear. When I get into the creek bed and look around the corner, I see nothing but collapsing cliffs and boulders, so I don't know where they have possibly gone. Dall sheep are amazing climbers and must have miraculously gone up somewhere, but I never see them again.

I have to slide down an eight-foot ledge to reach the edge of the creek. I do this with some care after sliding my pack down on a rope first. I toss the dogs' packs down and hope I can get back up if I have to return this way. I help the dogs by catching them partly as they begin to jump down. Then I walk up the creek, right next to the sides. They are a hundred feet high, composed of loose dirt and rock, and look like they routinely collapse. I hurry past all the unstable sections, being sure not to touch and dislodge any large stacks of boulders or gritty slabs of rock. It all looks unstable, though. At times I'm just inches from the crumbling walls and would be smashed if the walls were to fall in on me. Knowing my chance of surviving diminishes the longer I lag along these cliffs makes me move faster. After several minutes of this I come to a place where I can climb out the other side. I know I have to get out of this creek bed soon because hiking in it for any great length of time is too risky, and I'm almost sure to come to an impassable ledge or be smashed by falling rocks.

The route out is another steep slope covered with soil and grass, and luckily it has hardly any rocks. As the dogs and I climb, we come to several sections where water dripping down from melting snow higher up has frozen into hard, slick mounds. We have to go around several of these and make sure our footing is not on ice but on soil. If I were to slip and fall over, the slope is steep enough for me to tumble all the way to the bottom. In about twenty minutes, I reach the top and gaze back down at the chasm. The slopes on this side of Lucky Creek gorge are even steeper, but I continue on a while longer hoping that somehow a safe route through the gorge will unfold in front of me, like magic. I'm almost sure I won't find one, though, but I hike for about half an hour longer until coming to my senses. It's better to go back the way I came and walk a few extra days back to Portage Creek than to fall into a shivery abyss and die. At this point, being alive anywhere but here is far more agreeable to me, even if it involves hiking across tussock mounds and water, as long as there are no chances for me to fall into a gorge.

I hike back to the mouth of Lucky Six Creek on this side the entire way. There is more snow on this side, but I can't face crossing back through that crumbly gorge again. I cross two side ravines with snow at the bottom. They are not as unstable as the two on the other side of Lucky Six Creek, but they are still steep. I have to wade through slushy snow to cross them, making sure a dropoff isn't hidden below in the snow. This takes some probing with my foot in several locations while my other foot supports the weight of my body. All around is nothing but a plunging ravine with near vertical sides. A tiny creek flows down this narrow ravine, but its route is still basically plummeting down the side of the cliff-like slope on the side of Lucky Six Creek gorge. The snow at the bottom of this side creek looks flat, but it could simply be covering the edge of a treacherous drop, so I have to make sure the snow will support my weight before I step onto it.

After another two hours, I leave the gorge in one piece. I'm relieved when the slopes level off and I can see a straight line back to the banks of the Noatak River again, without any cross ravines in my path. I reach the Noatak and start hiking back down, knowing that I could have been seriously hurt. It was like walking into a death trap. The farther in there I got the steeper the sides became and the farther it was to get out. Now when I see signs that Dall sheep have come through, I don't go that way unless I see signs (their droppings, tracks, or hair snagged on brush) of moose and caribou as well. Once I'm well clear of the sight of Lucky Six Creek, I set up camp. I don't want to think about that place again, so I make sure I can't see it, either.

I know I'm way behind schedule now and worry about my food supply running out in the days ahead, so the next day, because I'm so anxious to get back on schedule and on my way over these mountains to the Alatna River, I put in the longest day of the trek out of sheer will. I hike back to the mouth of Portage Creek in one day instead of the two it had taken me to get to Lucky Six Creek. We travel fifteen linear miles in eight continuous hours with no rest, except to lean over for a few seconds occasionally and to take a couple of sit-down breaks. As I walk, the dogs stutter step over the tussock mounds to keep up with me. This hike makes even them tired. My feet are sore before we reach camp and the dogs are worn out, too. Near the end of the day they start walking with their heads down.

Just when Portage Creek comes into full view and I get ready to find a campsite, we come over a little rise in the land and encounter a grizzly. The bear is just out of charging distance and feeding on roots and plants right in our path. The grizzly doesn't see us at first, and the dogs' view of the bear is still blocked by the rise of land. The wind is blowing from the side so that neither the bear nor the dogs detect each other's scent—lucky for me. I take my pack off and get the dogs ready in case I have to let them loose so they can defend themselves. I also pull out my shotgun and take a three-inch-hollow point slug out of my pocket. If necessary, I will have to hit the bear dead center in the head. And since I have a breechloader, I will only get one chance. My chances might be better if I were to just curl up in a ball and not do anything at all, or if I were to throw a rock at the bear. At least a rock wouldn't make the animal so angry and desperate to defend itself. And when grizzlies decide to defend themselves, they don't run away like most other animals on the planet. Grizzlies rush and plow into humans like a locomotive, intent on disabling completely.

I try to get ready before the bear notices me. My plan for a bear attack is to hold the dogs until the last few feet of a charge, then release the dogs at the instant before I think the bear will be upon me. The dogs at this point might charge for the bear. Airedales might be the only dog breed that will do this, and the two of them might incite each other into going full out in their efforts. Then I will use my gun if I have to and still can. I know that bears normally won't give people any trouble, so I'm counting on this one running off. "Nice little bear," I say under my trembling breath. I can't stop my hands from shaking, and I know the bear will pick up on this. "Settle down. Settle down," I mumble to myself.

After I'm ready with gun in hand and after I've taken the packs off the dogs, I give a soft, pleasant hoot and keep my head tilted down to not look aggressive. The bear brings a massive, square head up, sniffing the air and looking my way for a few seconds trying to figure out what I am. Grizzly eyes become fixed upon me and its body turns motionless. I feel the intensity of a stare and worry for a second, hoping the bear won't charge, but thinking it just might. Then the creature turns to look slowly around, and in another second sprints off in the other direction away from me toward a thicket along a tiny stream. There the grizzly stops, a hulking, brown body becoming so camouflaged that I can't see the bear at all anymore. I know the grizzly is in there just sitting because I don't see it come out from the other side. The bushes are not that big, but the animal blends in like a chameleon. I'm too exhausted to hike much farther, so I allow about a hundred yards' leeway, as I pass, talking softly and never looking toward harm's way. Then I camp at the mouth of Portage Creek, just a quarter mile from the bear's thicket. I can see the thicket from my camp, but I never see the bear come out. I don't worry, though. I know it won't bother us. After seeing the bear's obvious fear, I feel badly for the animal. Also my orange tent is visible, so I know our camp won't be disturbed. I sit out in the warm evening looking up at the thicket every so often while cooking lentils over the fire, but I never see the bear again.

May 23, 2007, 125 miles from Anaktuvuk Pass

We start up Portage Creek, hiking on the tundra about thirty yards away from the creek. There is no gorge like on Lucky Six Creek. The creek bed lays out flat and the slopes of the mountains around me start out at the edge of the creek in a gentle concave shape, and higher up they never really get so steep that the soil can slide away. I'm overjoyed, but I keep my fingers crossed anyway about being able to get through the final pass at the top of the divide, which is still a few miles away. Even after studying the maps, I still never know quite what to expect when crossing through these mountain passes. Sometimes small mountain streams create gaping gorges, with walls that are impossible to get by. They don't always show up on the topographical maps. The cliffs aren't high enough to affect more than one or two contour lines on a map at most, but they can still be high enough to be an impassable barrier.

The dogs are looking a bit thin, and I will be out of dog food in a couple of days. Then they will have to start eating my food. They do well enough on lentil beans, and I still have enough to last them for a couple of weeks. I fed Jonny lentil beans for two weeks when I ran out of dog food on our monthlong hike across the Baldwin Peninsula nine years earlier. Lentil beans are a great food for hiking. They are such a small, compact bean that they take little time to cook, and they're inexpensive. You carry them as dry weight, so you don't have to carry any added weight in moisture. Lentils also contain a lot of calories.

I make the ten-mile crossing over the mountain pass to the Alatna River in one grueling day. The ground is firm most of the way, and there isn't too much brush until I reach the Alatna River side of the pass. I find signs that moose and caribou went up through here; I find their droppings, broken brush, and tracks. This reassures me that the pass is navigable for me, since I think I can climb as well as they can. Moose and caribou must learn these routes from their parents and never forget them. Knowing which route to travel through is certainly vital for their survival.

The creek doesn't have ice, and the water is only ankle deep, so where the mountains reach the creek and form a cliff, I take a few steps at the edge of the creek to get by. At the crest of the divide we walk by two lakes, still mostly frozen over except near the southern edge where two ducks are paddling around. I take a break and snap off a couple of photos. Looking east toward the Alatna Valley where I'm heading, I can see that it's quite a bit lower than the Noatak Valley. I can't see the river, though. It sits so low on the landscape that the convex curve of the descent in front of me blocks my full view. Dark-colored cliffs exist up high and well away from the creek. They're not crumbly rocks made out of compacted, yellowish clay like on Gull Pass. Instead, these cliffs are made up of large chunks of solid, gray rock, which don't appear to break apart. I keep looking for Dall sheep, but I think they might prefer the softer rocks instead of these hard, unbreakable slabs that don't allow even the most modest trail to be formed. This terrain above me might be more suited for mountain goats, and I scan the cliffs for them as I walk along, but I'm not sure if they inhabit this region. Far across the Alatna River, the peaks are dark gray there as well. This gives the entire river valley a dark and gloomy appearance. I feel like I'm entering a new wilderness on this side of the pass, far different from the illuminated Noatak Valley where bright yellow grasses make up the sides of many of the peaks.

As we descend we enter into high brush, which may be the worst of the trip so far. I first attempt to hike through it, but it offers me no mercy. The boughs are thick and so convoluted that I can't just slide by them. I have to walk over the tops of most of them, and getting the dogs through is brutal work. The creek leading down to the Alatna River, which has no name on the map, is frozen over, and I make my way out of the brush by somersaulting down an embankment to reach the water. Well, really I roll over the tops of impenetrable brush like I used to do when my brothers and I played in my neighbor's hedge when we were kids. I drop off the last compacted row of twisted brush with an amazing acrobatic roll, making sure to land on my feet. The weight of my pack almost smashes me to the creek bottom. The brush is so thick that it extends well away from the creek's edge. I fell down the last couple of feet of empty air, plopping right smack into the ankle-high water, well away from the edge of the creek. "How about that," I say to the dogs while feeling a little proud of my maneuver and happy to have the Alatna in view. They don't seem to care, though, and are already sniffing the creek bed for signs of animals to chase.

After a few yards, I can walk on top of the creek, thankful to be out of the tangled mass of brush. Though I've grown sick of ice, I'm glad to find the creek is frozen over most of the way—it lays in an area that is blocked from the sun most of the day. The ice on the creek is white and thick, leading me three miles down to the Alatna River. Unlike Portage Creek, this creek is encased almost completely in a sheet of ice, with only foot-wide gaps here and there where the water rushes through. But I step across most of them with only a slight jump. For the dogs, it's no effort at all.

Once near the river I cut the corner to the left by walking across level ground that is relatively void of brush. It looks like the river floodplain. This kind of ground often doesn't contain the nasty tussocks or pliable brush like the higher ground. I have to cross through a fifty-foot swath of tall willows to reach the edge of the Alatna, but I'm mostly able to slide by each bush without getting my backpack too snagged on them. Once in a while, I have to lean a little hard to snap off a branch that latches onto my pack, but I'm used to this by now. Sometimes my shotgun gets hung up. I like to lay it horizontally on the top of my pack while I hike, but on messy brushy sections, I'll tie it on vertically to the center, on the outside of the back of my pack. This way the barrel doesn't get caught as much. I rarely have to do this, though, and usually I can power my way through the short swaths of brush.

Once I reach the edge of the river, I find a flat, open area to set up camp, sheltered from what little wind there is by the tall willows. The Alatna River feels like a lush, inviting place compared to previous areas I've been to so far on this trek. I'm near the edge of the spruce forest, which stretches downriver, south from here. Although there is still ice along the edge of the river, the air feels much warmer and raises my spirits.

From this point there are only two conceivable routes for me to follow. One leads south down the Alatna River through boreal forests to the village of Alatna—civilization. It's about eighty miles and well within the reach of food and safety. About half-way the Alatna River meanders by the Arrigetch Peaks, which to the Eskimo means "fingers of the hand extended." One of the first white people thought to explore these peaks was legendary adventurer Bob Marshall back in the early 1900s. They're some of the most menacing stretch of peaks in the Brooks Range and look like giant, pointy knuckles of granite slabs, with sharp ridges tapering off their faces. Bob Marshall fought hard for the preservation of vast, frontier-type wilderness like the Brooks Range.

Bob Marshall, raised in New York in a comfortable household, was well educated. He was drawn to Alaska to explore one of the last unknown parts of America, like Lewis and Clark. He clung to his spirit of wild adventure and made several expeditions into the Brooks Range in his short life. He was a strong advocate of not only social equality and wilderness preservation, but also a tireless campaigner for the rights of the poor. He believed they should have the right to visit wilderness as much as anyone else.

Bob Marshall explored various regions between my position and what is now the Dalton Highway. Besides the Arrigetch Peaks, he forged a route up the North Fork of the Koyukuk River over a hundred miles to my east, which is over a week's hike from Wiseman if you have detailed maps. He traveled up the Hunt Fork of the John River, where I hope to stumble upon in about two weeks if everything goes according to plan. Marshall traveled these areas when there were no maps, which to me seems impossible. One travel method he and his companion used was to start from a well-known village of the time, like Bettles or Wiseman, and head up one of the main rivers like the Alatna, the John, or the North Fork of the Koyukuk, with a boat filled with supplies. Once the river became too small for boat travel they started hiking, and Bob Marshall could hike like no other human on the planet. He was a ruthless marcher, often covering thirty miles in one day, or climbing some out-of-the-way peak just for the exhilaration. His method of out-and-back was practical at the time when they didn't know the lay of the land, didn't have any maps, and didn't know how far they could go. When he became low on food, he and his partner could head back the way they came. But they got out there in the wilderness so incredibly far with the gear and knowledge they had at the time. It still makes me shudder to think about it.

I'm about fifty linear miles farther out than Bob Marshall ever traveled, and soon I will be about seventy. If it weren't for the accuracy of maps and my satellite phone, I would never be here on my own. Without maps I don't think I would be able to find my way through this rugged region before my food ran out.

In 1935, along with Aldo Leopold and others, Marshall helped form the Wilderness Society. During his life he was instrumental in forming protection for vast tracts of wilderness across the United States. He died presumably of a heart attack just shy of thirty-nine, and it wasn't until decades after his death that his dream of protecting the Brooks Range came true with the creation of the Gates of the Arctic National Park. It remains virtually as wild now as it was when Bob Marshall first explored here.

I would feel confident heading south from here because I could probably float part of the river if I were to become weak and tired. I could fish in the river as I made my way out of the wild heading downhill for home. It would be well within my abilities, comfortable and pleasant. But it would mean the end of my journey, because at that point I would be so far south that heading east would be insurmountable with so many large rivers to cross and miles of forests and lowland bogs to trudge through. This way south was meant to be a last chance to abort my trek before committing to a more northern, desolate route. And if I head south, it means no coming back to this point to continue on again. It would be too far to get back here and continue east in one season after I were to get more supplies.

I don't head south, though. Maybe I'm a fool, or just plainly addicted to this out-and-out expedition. It's as close to a real exploration I'll ever get. I'm steadfast on going forward toward Anaktuvuk Pass. This means I have to head up the Alatna River, farther into the obscure gut of wild Alaska where few people have ever gone. By taking this course, I have to travel due north for several days to go around the western end of the Endicott Mountains before heading eastward along their northern rim. Crossing directly over them would be impractical; from what I can see, they're mostly cliff faced, with many of the passes between peaks being gouged-out clefts. Going around would be far quicker and safer, and I would be more assured of getting through. Trekking north also means if anything goes wrong, there won't be any rivers to float down to escape. They all go the wrong way, north into the Arctic Ocean 300 miles over the other side of the range. I'll be traveling by the seat of my pants, praying for the miles to unfold steadily as I traipse across the land. I'll be hoping for nothing to go wrong.

I'm hoping not to starve and to find some scant morsel to eat along the way, even if it's just the marrow of some rotten caribou bone—anything to help. A rabbit darts through my camp, which makes me think even more about food. I've burned many calories in the past two days and I actually feel thinner than I did three days earlier. This worries me, and I realize how fast my body can deteriorate with such long efforts and not enough to eat. I've probably burned nearly 20,000 calories in the past two days and haven't taken in close to that. This kind of lopsided energy exchange can't go on for long. Sometime soon I will somehow have to eat more.

The dogs go crazy tugging on their leashes to get at the rabbit. I let them loose one at a time to mainly run around and have some fun. They deserve it after all the hard work they did during the day. A month ago when I was overfed and fat, I hoped they wouldn't molest any animals. I held on to a lofty notion that hunting was an intrusion into this land, since I wasn't born here. I felt like my civilized upbringing meant I didn't have the right to kill animals for food. I gradually lost hold of that thought. Now with my chaffing hunger I start to relinquish this notion completely. The situation has changed and this concept doesn't seem to apply anymore. I silently chant for the dogs to catch a rabbit. I give them each one shot. And with our limited diet, I leash them back up as soon as they return so they don't take off again. The dogs come back one at a time, mouths gapping like a smile, and flop down on the ground as if they live here. But the rabbit is nowhere to be found. "Just as well," I say.

NO EASY GROUND

When I stare at Cravens Peak, I think of a science-fiction horror movie. I feel like an old crusty mansion should be sitting on the side of the peak, with gargoyles flying around the top and lizard men marching up a winding path cut right out of the rock face and leading to the front gates. From my camp, looking upriver, the gray peak stands out crisply against the gloomy, dim sky. More than all this, though, I think of loneliness when I look at that peak. It looks unearthly dark, like it belongs on an uninhabited, back-world planet.

The wind picks up again and the weather turns cold and gray, with a drilling rain hitting the land at an angle. Cravens Peak butts up against the Alatna River, and in conjunction with the craggy peak on the opposite side, it forms a giant portal. They remind me of the peaks called Boreal Mountain and Frigid Crags, the peaks I will come to in the next month of my trek that give this wilderness its actual name, the Gates of the Arctic.

These two peaks that I see comprise the final narrow pass before reaching the north side of the Brooks Range. I've been worried for several days that I would have a difficult time getting by here, but after hiking all day to reach the peak, where I set up camp to rest for a day, I see that getting by won't be a problem. There is plenty of level ground between the river and the peaks. This takes some of the eeriness away, and the peak doesn't appear so sinister when I get close to it. My first impressions soon melt away, and I begin to appreciate the height and rugged splendor of the peak and those around it. There are so many. Except for the narrow passes to the south and to the north, there are jagged rows of peaks behind more jagged rows of peaks, all around me. They are all too imposing to climb, at least in a time like this when I'm alone and working to make distance, not height. I don't have the energy to be climbing mountains anyway, or even to be thinking about it. The thought just makes me shiver. And I shake it off.

The next day I make a hard decision to stay put, taking a rest to recover for my final continuous push to Anaktuvuk Pass. Though I'm low on food, I believe my rest day is strategic. I can't let myself become totally burned out—not yet, not this far out. It would cause me to walk too slow and defeat the purpose of traveling most every day to make as much distance on as little food as possible. Not only will I lighten my load slightly by taking a rest day and eating a little of my food, but I will also be able to start out fresher. And a fresher body means better mental concentration. And mental concentration is the only thing that is going to keep me moving forward when I'm physically exhausted and out of food. Also the weather is cold and rainy, so this is another good excuse to take a day off.

I've gained some elevation since yesterday, and the river here is smaller, swifter, and half sealed in ice. I spend much of the day in my tent relaxing and reading. I'm still reading *The Invisible Man* and wondering if it's lonelier to be visible yet the only person in the world—an omega man—or to be invisible and have people around you.

My knee has begun hurting from carrying a heavy load on uneven ground for so long. The hiking here often puts my legs in an awkward position, and this strains my knees. When there is a break in the weather, I go outside with the dogs, who hit everything on the way out. I stretch my legs, build a fire, and mosey around the area like I don't have a care in the world. I feel peaceful; I think about how I like that my life is nice and simple, like nothing can warrant strife.

Even though the area is open with solid ground all around, I still manage to set my tent up behind a clump of willows to help block the wind blowing down the river. I gather up dry, dead willow branches to burn in the fire. I find them at the base of most willow bushes if other people have not already burned them, like they do around villages. People don't come here, so the firewood is all mine. I become curious when I find an old lid to a Planters Peanuts can partially buried in the soil. It must be twenty years old, but I study it like it's a rare jewel. I haven't seen another human being since April 17, or hardly any sign that humans still exist in the world. I feel a bit lonely for human companionship, so to see a little sign of human civilization makes me feel happy, like there are people around. Where there are groups of people there is usually food, and plenty of food can lead to contentedness and a stuffed belly. I laugh at the irony of wanting to trek across the Gates of Arctic alone and simultaneously wishing for a little civilization and human companionship along the middle of it, where it's the wildest. I somehow keep expecting some person to show up in this desolate land, but no one comes. I don't even hear planes. The only one I've heard since leaving Ambler in mid-April was the one that dropped my food. All I hear is the wind and my footsteps as I walk around camp. Sometimes I think I hear faint talking or a distant motor over the sound of the wind, but when I look nothing is there. There's just the wilderness and the crystalline, arctic air.

The next day I hike along the river on the ice for several hours. The surface is easier than walking on the tundra that lines the river on both sides. I get a little heedless to the dangers in order to travel faster. Sometimes I scoot over to the left side of the river, and at other times the right side of the river, depending on which side has the best ice to walk on. Once or twice I wade the river on ice-free gravel (it's not nearly as deep as the Noatak), but most of the time I cross over on ice. I don't worry too much about being trapped on the wrong side, because I'm following the river all the way to its headwaters. But there is a large creek ahead, coming in from the west, that I don't want to get trapped by. I don't want to have to hike any great distance up that creek to go across it. On most large creeks and rivers I usually can't cross at any place I happen to be. I usually have to pick and choose the right spots, where there is either stable ice all the way across or pleasant-looking gravel where the current is mild. Going up a tributary creek to find a crossing point would mean going in the wrong direction.

When I have the creek in view about a mile away it appears larger than I expect. It rumbles from behind a dark, square mountain into view like a menacing serpent winding over a granulated bottom while cutting several paths through the soiled grit of the stony tundra. It appears tumultuous so I start searching for a stretch of ice to cross back over to the east side of the Alatna to bypass the creek completely. But the ice has become unstable and breaks apart in many places. The Alatna also has a swift current flowing underneath, fed from all the snowmelt coming down. Shade plays a huge role on how much ice a creek or river will have on it. And at this point I'm getting closer to the pass where the canyon starts to open up and the mountains start to sit back farther. The river is less shaded, so the sun melts the ice faster, even at this higher elevation.

One piece of ice that I try to leap off to get across a channel gives way before I can get off it, and I float whirling on it like it's a sinking disc. I jump in the river with a full pack on before I lose my balance. The water is about thigh deep, and I land without falling. Since I'm now in the water, I wade on gravel across the channel to a large ice-covered island in the middle. I call the dogs to move quickly. "Come on, boys," I say. I don't want them in the river too long with their packs on. Their food could get wet and spoil. It doesn't matter too much what I say to them, because they don't want to stay in the water more than they have to.

The channel on the island's other side is about fifty feet wide and loaded with ice, and half of the water flows over the top of the ice. In several places the ice is caved in, forming a concave shape where part of the water swirls underneath. I avoid this area and hike a hundred yards up to the island's tip to cross to the opposite shore. It's scary because I must wade in knee-deep water that flows over the ice with those collapsed sections just downriver from me. I first take the packs off the dogs and carry one in each arm to keep them dry. It takes me several attempts to cross. I creep out in one spot and toss both dog packs to the opposite shore where I'm going. I slip a little, so I go back to the island to make a few more attempts a few feet farther up and a few feet farther down. On the last attempt I find a place where I can get my nerve up to cross. The water is the deepest and swiftest on the opposite shore, so I have to look for a place where I can leap the last few feet onto an icy bank on the other side, and I don't want to slip and fall in the last bit of water and be swept away. I'd probably be okay, but I would be taken for a ride in the slick river channel until I could gain some footing to get out. And of course there is always a small chance of being dragged under the ice through a hole somewhere. That possibility worries me the most. It's a tiny danger here since I'm strong enough to withstand the force of the current (when I have my footing), but the consequences would be catastrophic, forcing me to be careful now.

I finally get a little braver, since it takes at least a little bit to get across here. I inch my way across on the ice in water that gets deeper the farther out I go. Once I have to reach down with my hand to help keep my feet from slipping. I come to the deepest part of the current. The only thing left is to simply go for it. I lean forward, take two quick steps, and leap the last three feet across the deepest part of the channel, landing on the bank where I fall to my knees but out of the water. I put my hands down to keep myself from sliding, and after a second or two I realize I'm not going to slip into the water. I stand up and take baby steps away from the river. The dogs do pretty well. They end up sliding down the current a little, but with their four feet they seem to somehow get to where they need to be, like they always do. I watch them closely to make sure, in case I have to run down the bank to grab them if they get near a place where the river flows under ice.

With another obstacle behind me I go back to hiking on the tundra where there is less uncertainty. Icy rivers give me chills, not just from the cold, but also from the possibility of falling in and drowning. Walking on the land is slower traveling, but at least I won't have to worry about making a mistake on the river ice. I look at my GPS unit to check the linear miles to Anaktuvuk Pass. The number has gotten larger like I figured it would. It's discouraging. I have to actually head away from the village for a few days to get around the end of the Endicott Mountains, and every time I see the number getting larger I think about running out of food.

While hiking on the east side of the river, I see a caribou and yearling calf dash by on their journey north to the arctic plain. Though somewhat far, it's a straight, easy line from here. I'm hungry, so I take aim at the large adult, but at the last second I pull the shotgun up a few inches as I fire. The slug smashes into the hill just beyond them, leaving a cloud of dirt in its wake. Chances are this is the young caribou's first trek north and would be hopelessly lost without the adult. I'll shoot a ptarmigan, but I'm not at the point where I'm desperate enough to kill anything large. And though I may regret this later, I let them go, and I watch them as they increase their pace and disappear over the next hill. They travel over ground in five minutes what will take me almost an hour.

Today I don't eat breakfast or lunch so I can conserve our food. A person could starve anywhere, but while crossing the Gates of the Arctic, it's a real concern. It's at the foremost of my thoughts every day while watching myself grow thinner—while watching the dogs grow thinner. I've been expending far more calories than I've been taking in for several days, so in a sense I really am starving. It's what makes this journey so difficult. Getting a signal on my satellite phone is hard sometimes, and mounting a rescue is expensive. If I had a lot of money I would have had charter planes fly me in many more food drops at various locations. To get a drop here would cost about $2,000, which I can't really afford, but I enjoy my freedom to take on adventures like this. Being in the wild is far more important to me than working a job to provide an insignificant service or a useless product that only functions in the modern world. I care far more about wilderness and the natural world than I do for the mundane meddling in society. Nature is real; it's what will be left after human civilizations collapse or unravel. You can't rely completely on money, and food doesn't originate in a grocery store.

We humans do a lot of things that only help in the short term and are often detrimental to wilderness and the genetic diversity that goes with it; the natural net that will sustain life for eternity. Every day I grow more thankful for being able to have food. So in a sense, I'm thankful for being able to live in society, even though I'm not living in society now. It's where the food is, and finding wild food alone is difficult. Food is much easier to find with a group. And it's more environmentally sustainable to do this with a small, tight group where each individual can rely on the other, instead of being part of a large country with arbitrary rules that don't help groups of people survive at the ground level. I, too, am part of a pattern that degrades wilderness, and it takes great effort to go against the system we live in because we have grown so accustomed to it. Why collect wild nettles for you and your friends to eat when you can go to a store and buy exotic cheese and broccoli that taste a whole lot better? Most of my friends won't eat nettles anyway. I sometimes say to them, "Have you tried them?" And the ones that refuse to eat them have never tried them. "You don't know what you're missing."

They just make a grotesque face and say, "Why eat that?" Why eat local fruits when you can eat sugary chocolate imported from Switzerland? Why use common sense when no one else does? Why not live fat now while you can, high on the hog, and let posterity and the planet worry about itself later? We tell ourselves we have to take care of the planet for our children. It's the right thing to say. But I think we want to do it mostly because when we are old and feeble we want a natural world we can still rely on, when national rules have changed and we can't keep up with the system anymore. We want to know we can still gather nettles if we have to—or hunt, collect wild berries, or grow a little garden out back to eat from. We might be financially broke, and being a beggar is no fun.

During the nights it hurts to sleep. This is when I get so hungry, but I can never eat more than my allotted meal of one bowl of lentils. I usually give each dog more than I get, and since they are leaner than I am, they never eat less in a day than what I do, though this could change in the days ahead if our situation becomes bleak. I always siphon off the water I cook the beans in to let the dogs lap up. There are some nutrients cooked out of the beans that I don't want to waste. I never grow tired of lentils in my hungry state, even when I eat them plain. Sometimes I add in a packet of soup mix to increase the flavor, but I don't have enough left for every day. I need to conserve what food I have in order to ensure we make it out of here. In some of my dreams and before I fall asleep in my tent with the dogs twitching and snoring beside me, I crave chewy oatmeal cookies and thick cheesy slabs of sausage pizza. Sometimes I say to myself about my teasing discomfort, "I'm so hungry, I can't believe it, jeeze." Sometimes I say it half a dozen times in a row. But at least I'm okay and still have a solid plan.

I get so hungry as I walk along that I start thinking about the caribou and calf that passed me earlier. I've gotten even hungrier since then, and I've made a conscious decision that if I see another caribou, I will shoot with the one slug I have if I get a chance. I've decided it in advance so that when one does appear I won't hesitate with sympathy. I love animals, and I'm not really a hunter, just an observer of their habits. I enjoy learning everything I can about mammals, but if I see a large animal now, I will have to shoot to kill so that the dogs and I stay alive. Hunger has begun to suppress my sympathy for the lives of animals. I dream of chocolate bars, too, sizzling caribou steaks, and limitless dog food for the dogs. It's tough to watch them grow thin. They are the number one priority on this journey. If I think their lives are in jeopardy, I will call for an emergency pickup and pay for it by using my credit card.

Hiking is so centered on food. It's nearly impossible to hike for a long period of time unless you have a limitless amount of nutrition. While walking and burning great amounts of energy, food is everything. At home I know I will be able to get food, and I can rely on a huge supply of it at my convenience, but I have no such luxury here. In a week my body could exhaust what body fat I have remaining while walking across such difficult ground. There is no easy ground in Alaska to walk on, and there are no trails. That's what makes this place so remarkable. The tainted trails of humanity have yet to be stenciled here for the most part. I travel with my own determination, on my own course, and with my own agenda, like the old-time trappers and explorers who blazed west across North America centuries ago, just because they wanted to see new virgin land.

Later in the day I fortunately shoot three ptarmigan in a couple of hours. Hunting is a little nasty act of my journey I don't like to remember. I hit them on the ground when they are standing still, and they are all males. I load them into a plastic bag and stick them in the top of my pack to eat in the evening. Though I don't know it now, this act of killing may have just saved my life. This may keep me from starving.

While walking toward the headwaters of the Alatna River, I run across several deep gullies filled to the rim with snow. I wade a dozen of these within two hours. It's more like swimming in quicksand than hiking. When I step into the gullies, the weight of my pack contributes to me sinking to my waist. Then I have to lean forward and rock my legs loose one at a time to bring them forward, while all the time fumbling with my arms in the snow. Once I get so jammed in the snow, I have to take my pack off to release myself. Then I have to drag my pack behind me like a dead body until I get to the edge of the gully. It's just another one of the energy-consuming chores I have to execute among the actual hours of marching forward across the land, and they all require energy to perform.

Near the end of the day, we come to the pass at the headwaters of the Alatna River and sit down to rest on a low hummock. I've already walked more today than I have on most other days, and I have eaten far less. My body's endurance seems limitless. No matter how hard and far I hike, I can still get up, shake out the stiffness, and keep hiking. This isn't so much a compliment to myself but to the ability of the human body in general. It adapts when it has to, when it's thrown into a hostile environment and forced to cope. The body adjusts to walking for hours on little food. Though I got here because of my own choice, I still have to survive like I would if I had been forced here.

The ground is wide open and illuminated by space, bright grasses, soft-topped peaks, and summer arctic sun. I get glimpses of creeks that feed into the Nigu River to the west and great vistas of the Killik River draining from snow clad peaks to the southeast. I cross over the pass and head down to the Killik River. We wade across it right away without any problems, before camping along the river. The whole world opens up on this side of the pass. The mountains are more gentle and forgiving. They're not so devilish and I could climb on them without the danger of falling, if I choose to.

I roast the birds over a fire on bare earth twenty feet from the river, with miles of low tundra all around me and mountains on all sides sitting back to watch over me. I eat all the breast meat and most of the leg meat. Then I give the carcasses to the dogs. They devour everything, including heads, feet, and wings. They crunch up the bones like they're twigs, trying to fill their ravenous stomachs. We also eat a heaping pot of lentil beans—more than usual—flavored with two envelopes of instant soup mix, to go with the ptarmigan. I feel much better after the meal and sit back to enjoy the fire.

Since I'm getting far behind schedule, I fear I won't make it in time to meet my brothers and Julie at Anaktuvuk Pass. This thought has demoralized me over the past two weeks. This was going to be one of the highlights of the journey. I call Julie so that everyone can make arrangements to go ahead with their hike without me and to stick to their departure dates. "You should tell everyone to stick to their own schedule," I say somberly. "I'm not going to make it by the twenty-sixth." It's an erratic call and I lose the signal several times and have to call her back. I ask her if she can change her arrival date so we can hike together to Wiseman. "Do you think you can change your flight to June eighth?" I say. Later after she calls the airline I call her back and find out she is able to change her flight, so this makes me feel better knowing she will meet me. I should tell Julie something sincere to thank her for what she is doing for me, and to make myself look selfless. I should say something like, "You are so good at your work. I hope everything is going well." But I don't, not that I remember. With eighty-five miles to Anaktuvuk Pass, getting there by May 26 seems unlikely. I now have to concentrate on getting myself there alive, not worry about making any deadlines. I have to stay smart and travel the land as efficiently as I can, never getting off course or losing track of how much food I have left. And if I run across even anything remotely edible, I have to scarf it down like my life depends on it, because it might.

IN THE HEART OF NO MAN'S LAND

When I'm in a place where I can walk fifty days without seeing anyone and where a pack of wolves can surround me and take a long look at me, I know I'm in the wild. Where there are no roads or trails and where I'm over several mountain ranges and a hundred miles from any form of human settlement, I know I'm in the wild. Sure, I can shoot animals for food, but trying to travel this distance by walking will still leave me famished, and killing something large will cause me to waste a huge portion of it. If I didn't have any food left, there would be no way I could walk out of here before I starved to death. I will be lucky to do it with the food I have. This is a humbling experience and will make me appreciate good food more when it's available.

May 27, 2007, eighty-five miles from Anaktuvuk Pass

I shoot two rabbits. At camp I skin them, but I don't gut them. There really isn't any need to gut the rabbits unless you're trying to impress someone. I probably don't even need to skin them, but I don't want to hassle with picking through singed fur. If you're careful, the contents of the stomach and intestines won't burst and taint the meat when you cook it. Even if it did it wouldn't hurt you, so in my hungry state I choose to eliminate this step for efficiency. It's rather easy to eat around the inner organs when the meat is cooked. I lay the carcasses right on top of the fire and turn them over every few minutes as they cook. They have a lot of meat, though almost no fat. I eat the choicest parts, which are the back strap and the thighs. Then I give the rest to the dogs. They devour them in no time, including the feet, heads, guts, and bones. The only parts they don't eat are the stomach, the intestines, and their partially digested contents.

We continue along the Killik River for several more days. I cross over April Creek, which is the size of a small river. I have to search up and downstream for a way across, where the main flow of the river is dissected into several channels flowing with less depth and power. I finally find a way across by wading to a few islands spaced across the river. When I reach the other shore I'm welcomed by a tangled mass of willows that I must break through to get back on course along the Killik. I could take April Creek eastward toward the John River by way of Kutuk Pass and Shivering Mountain, but that is a higher route and I'm sure it's more rugged. It looks shorter on the map, but if I were to come to gorges and snow it could end up taking days longer, and right now I'm not sure how long my food will last. So I cross April Creek and leave it behind.

Often there are side creeks flowing into the Killik River with high water that I have to wade, and there are a few more creeks with ten-foot-high willows I have to juggle through. One creek that doesn't have a name on the map, but is a few miles north of April Creek, drains between two peaks a mile from the Killik. The peak on the north side of April Creek is dark brown and shaped like a pyramid—four sides. The other is block shaped and the start of a long mountainous ridge 500 feet above the Killik that runs for several miles to the south. Both peaks have little snow on them except for shaded slopes down in the ravine. Beyond the mountainous ridge is an upland world of tundra, rock, and lichens that stretches a hundred miles southeast to the John River where I need to get to, except

I need to travel farther north so I can take a right onto Easter Creek and follow a lower, flatter route.

Where this creek passes the peaks, it instantly fans out across the flat tundra before it enters the Killik. This alluvial fan is about a mile wide containing a microenvironment of willows amidst the never-ending tundra. It's like a dense and snarled forest with no way around. Even up near the peaks the willow forest follows the creek snuggly like a shadow. It's mind numbing to see this obstacle thrown before me after I've walked so far and endured so much hunger and fatigue. I thought this land would be easier to get by than the land with spruce trees. While coming to the willow forest, I study the fringes of it all the way around. I examine the middle and along its edges clear down to the Killik River, but the jumbled formidability is continuous. There are no breaks in the willows where I can sneak through. I have to break branches to get by, often snapping them off at chest level with my hands. If I didn't have such a huge pack I could slither through this twisted maze like a cat. The branches that don't break I bend back as I force my way past, and when they latch onto my pack I lean forward until they give or break. If they don't give or break I thrust my body against them with full force two or three times. And if they still don't give or break, I sometimes drop to my hands and knees and crawl under them. Other times I straddle over them or back up and try a different path. Every so often, I have to take off my pack to crawl through a narrow opening in the brush and tow my pack behind me.

I also have to find my way past stagnant sloughs that have penetrated in from the river, which are too deep to wade and too wide to jump. Sometimes I crash through the brush with great effort in one direction, only to find myself stopped by one of these slack sloughs. Then I have to backtrack a little to find a better route.

When I'm not breaking through brush, I'm usually marching over miles of tussock mounds that teeter over when I step on them;

however, they never lay down flat on the ground or form a steady surface to walk on. They always wobble, and this causes me to stumble a lot. Half the time, I try to put my feet on the ground between the tussocks, but often the tussocks are too close to each other, or they are too high to step over efficiently. If I try to hike too fast over them, I trip and lose my balance.

When the river turns sharply to the left, the flat, firm stretches along the river occasionally sputter out into ground covered with tussocks. It's usually faster to cut the bend and walk across tundra, taking my chances with the tussocks. Sometimes the tussocks have waist-high brush growing over them that I have to deal with. This brush is different from the willows. It clutches my legs around shin level. With the willows, I have to push my body through at chest level, but this brush is composed of small diameter branches, just smaller than the size of a pencil, which bend but never break. It's constantly snagging my pants. I have to yank my legs forward far enough until I get free of them, but there is always one bush after another, so I have to do this for about fifteen minutes at each bend I cross.

There is an undeniable beauty here along the Killik River, despite my own struggles and festering disquietude. The land has been splayed out immensely at every mile. The peaks are rounded and lack snow for the most part, and they sit back on the perimeter of this enormous valley that grows larger the farther north I go. I feel minuscule like nature knows that I could never affect its outcome. I plod on over a treeless plain unseen and unheard by everyone in the world except for songbirds and a few fleeting rabbits—an anti-hero without glory.

When you reach the confluence of the Killik River and Easter Creek, if you make it this far, you are so far into the raw cradle of wilderness that you'd better have your act together or you won't be leaving alive. Your flesh and bones will meld into the hazy backdrop as sure as the vapors evaporate over the peaks or a fleeting wolf recedes into the barren background. If you're on your own and you're not strong enough to carry a monstrous load of food and hike over incredible distances, you will starve to death before you get out. Following the lay of the land, you will have to walk well over a hundred miles without any trail to reach even the tiniest form of civilization. If you don't panic and you are strong, you just might have a chance.

If I were to walk for a few days in any direction toward distant mountain passes, I would see only more distances of endless peaks and vacant horizons. This place is so wild and so far away from any permanent human settlement, or even a seasonal camp for that matter, that no white man was ever here to have the opportunity to name the features of the land, and if they were here they didn't stay long. Many of the mountains and creeks are nameless on the maps. The few that are named, I figure have names given by the few native people known to sometimes travel this land, like Suluak and Agiak Creek, and the Killik River. The Eskimos of the coast were known to come up the Killik River and settle for brief periods of time. The Nunamiut, or Inland Eskimos of Anaktuvuk Pass, were known to travel over to this region to trade and visit with these people of the Killik River. Outside these people, though, virtually no human ever comes here. Even the Nunamiut for the most part don't come out this far anymore, at least not on foot like they used to do. It's my guess, by the absolute lack of human signs anywhere around, that the only human presence is an occasional bush plane flying over, but in all the days that I've been out here, I haven't seen or heard any aircraft flying low. Even ambitious adventurers like Bob Marshall never came out this far. Sometimes thinking about this makes my heart race, and I start to wonder what I'm doing here, dead center in one of the wildest regions on earth—in the heart of no man's land. I feel on the edge of my capabilities and at any time anything could go wrong. But I also feel flighty, giggly, and not held by any trivial restraints of modern civilization. I feel completely free for once in my life.

May 29, 2007, seventy miles from Anaktuvuk Pass

I make the great sweeping right turn onto Easter Creek from the Killik River. The water level is high and the current is torrential. It's a river itself, made by the spring snowmelt. I couldn't cross it if I wanted to. I had originally considered crossing it to hike along Suluak Creek to the north, but now I'm more content to follow Easter Creek to its source. The high water and the fact that I cannot cross it make the decision for me. The Easter Creek route is lower in elevation, so I'm not likely to run into any snowy sections, which would slow me down. This route is more predictable, and at a time when I have so little food, I can't afford surprises, which often arise when crossing narrow passes at the headwaters of high creeks. Easter Creek flows through such a wide, massive valley that I can see ahead of me for days in advance. The tussocks and boggy ground make hiking strenuous, but at least I know what to expect. I know what my pace will be, so I will be able to predict how long it will take me to reach the John River. From the John River, I'm hoping for a simple three-day march into Anaktuvuk Pass. I know I will be hungry by then and almost out of food, but I'm hoping the terrain will be no worse than what I'm experiencing now.

I see a bear feeding up on the gentle slopes leading into the mountains. Only when the animal moves can I be certain of the species. The bear is probably close to half a mile away. I often look for a light brown dot off on the distant tundra when I travel across the land—one that looks slightly out of place and well defined against the hilly background. This one doesn't know I'm around but keeps ambling along the slope, pausing now and then to dig for succulent roots or scanty rodents, oblivious to everything except eating. One of the largest predatory land mammals in the world (who also eats a lot of plants), a grizzly can afford to be unaware of surrounding life. No other animal is going to mess with this animal here, except maybe a bigger bear.

A little later I come across a lone wolf coming up from the creek. Unlike the bear, the wolf knows I'm here. When I first look up from my arduous stupor, the wolf has already stopped frozen in its tracks, looking right back at me. Then, without any half-hearted stutter steps, the wolf trots away from the creek at a fast and efficient gait, pausing at regular intervals to look back at me—to see if I'm in pursuit I suppose. But I'm weak and weary and no threat to a wolf. I'm hungry of course, so the next thing I think about is how wolves get food all by themselves. Remarkably, a wolf can vanish into the landscape when there are no trees or tall foliage for camouflage. Silvery color and my myopic human vision allows it to do this. I've never seen a wolf on this journey break into a full run. They need to be efficient in their travels. Running is saved for the final closing distance of the pursuit of prey or to evade another predator closing in on them, which for a wolf would probably only include humans and other wolves.

Like the bear and the wolf, I, too, don't run anymore on this journey. It eats up energy too fast. Back home I never think about how much energy hard running or cycling consumes (compared to here where I think about the energy I burn on every footstep) and how they require access to gluttonous amounts of food to keep up on a long-term basis. Working out must be a silly concept to those who live on the edge of starvation all the time. Now, I will only run if my life depends on it. When I get to a town and rest for a while, I might do a little bit of running, just for a few intervals of twenty seconds or so to stride my legs out, but not out here with little to eat. I can't risk it. I don't really have the zest in my legs for it anyway. It's as if my body has shifted into another mode of metabolism, conserving every ounce of energy it can. It would take a real surge of adrenaline to get my fatigued legs to move very fast. I've always been a fitness freak, and now I think I did too much intensity training over the years, when a longer, slower burn might have been more beneficial. I work out so much back home because I like to be ready for journeys like this. Fitness allows me to see the wilderness the way I want, calmly and under my own power, without the noise of a gasoline-driven machine blasting into the silent sky and hurting my head. Sometimes I wonder what our world would be like without the internal combustion engine. Besides less toxic effects on the body—benzene from gasoline combustion is a potent carcinogen—I think earth would be filled with people who are much more reflective and appreciative about nature and their own lives. A walk to the corner store or the garden to pick some food might be the highlight of their day, and when you walk somewhere you have plenty of time to think.

I have sixty miles to go to Anaktuvuk Pass and my hope that I will make it increases a little every day. By the time I get there I will probably have walked double that distance, though, perhaps even triple the distance, because I can't travel in a straight line. There are too many obstacles. For instance, dozens of times throughout the day I will come to a ravine, and to cross it I might have to veer way off course to go around it looking for a manageable way across, since there are no bridges.

The native people who lived in this region, the Nunamiut, were once nomadic and fiercely capable of survival. In 1949 a nomadic band of sixty-five people lived in the area of Anaktuvuk Pass where the modern Nunamiut still live today. They were hardy people with slight builds and great stamina who traveled across the land in search of caribou. They used large dogs to pull their sleds in the winter and to carry packs (often weighing more than forty pounds) in the summer, like I'm doing. Their lives always wobbled on the edge of starvation and survival, but they retained their humility and hospitality toward other people. I grow more interested in their history as I travel across their land in my own desperation and hunger. I'm beginning to understand the importance of getting to where food is at all cost. For the Nunamiuts getting to food meant finding the caribou so they could hunt them. For me it means reaching Anaktuvuk Pass and finding a grocery store or a kind person to sell me meat. I'm starting to know what it is to walk until you find food, no matter what the toll on the body. For the Nunamiut of nomadic times when the caribou failed to show, they turned to Dall sheep to hunt, but sometimes the sheep did not provide enough food to feed everyone. Entire bands of Nunamiut are known to have starved to death when the caribou failed to arrive.

The Nunamiut's intimate knowledge of the land was second to none. They knew which plants and berries were edible and which part of a willow bush could be used for medicine. They could make a bow out of spruce and arrows out of willows, and they were able to kill caribou with these arrows while traveling on foot. One of their methods for killing caribou involved erecting piles of rocks called cairns to direct the flow of caribou toward a certain location, like a gully, corral, or lake where they could shoot the animals with arrows. Branches could be placed on top of these cairns to wave in the wind. The caribou were fearful of the rock cairns. They didn't appear right to the caribou so they avoided them, especially when visibility was reduced by fog. Little did they know that they were being subtly directed into a strategic location where the Nunamiut could shoot them. These cairns could be set up miles in advance to slowly persuade the caribou across the land. It required great understanding of the caribou's habits and the details of the terrain to get the caribou to go right where they needed them. The caribou gave the Nunamiut life.

I remember seeing photos of human skulls lying on the tundra like stones where Nunamiut people had died of starvation. The skulls were never covered by moss or even partly buried. Some of these people who died were probably directly related to the people in Anaktuvuk Pass today. The photos never showed one skull lying by itself; the other people of the group would have buried the person it belonged to. The skulls were in groups strewn upon the tundra. That told me those bands of people were united in their struggles and that they remained together even in the face of death. They had probably been in a dire situation in which the distance was too far for them to walk for help, and by the time they decided they needed to act they were probably too weak to hike out to another village. Their dogs were probably too weak as well to carry anything. It was often that way for the Nunamiut. They had lived with this kind of uncertainty their entire lives, for many generations, where the majority of their food came from caribou. To be low on food and hoping for the caribou to arrive was not out of the ordinary. A bad situation had to get worse for them to act in order to save themselves from starving. And yet the Nunamiut chose to live this way in the wilderness of their ancestors. They chose to remain free on the land rather than live out a comfortable life in the company of sedentary people.

I don't let the dogs off their leashes anymore. They will run off no matter how hungry they get, and we don't have one calorie to spare. They grow thinner, as do I, but I think we will just squeak by. It will do us some good to suffer a little like this, to better appreciate the availability of food back home and to better appreciate the native people who inhabited this land. They are worth respecting because they respected the land they lived upon.

Sometimes the dogs cause me much frustration, and they often walk on my heels. I know this is not their fault. I need their leashes short enough so they don't get tangled up in them with their front feet yet long enough so they can lag just off my heels. But I can never get the length just right. We have many obstacles to pass by, and sometimes they need slack to get by brush. I leave Jimmy's leash a little longer than Will's leash so he can follow single-file behind Will through brush, but it never works just right and I often have to slow up a bit. This becomes a great mental challenge now that I'm getting exhausted, stumbling over tussocks, and trying to make some distance. I can count on having to stop and untangle their ropes from a bush or two that they get wrapped around, but still I cannot let them loose. There might be wolf traps around, and I don't want them to get caught in one. If they were to get caught in a trap somewhere out of my sight, I might never find them again in this vast land.

I try to walk the tundra straight as an arrow, even though the land is riddled with tussocks. I seem to start side-stepping every ten feet or so, to go around a ditch, a tall bush, or a puddle. I'm traveling about a half mile away from Easter Creek to cut part of the corner after I made the right turn off of the Killik River. It's better to pick a point on the horizon and walk straight for it rather than to zigzag to find better ground. The ground is difficult all around, and if I start swerving back and forth, it really takes away from my overall, linear mileage by the end of the day. But sometimes I have no choice.

I hear a jet flying high up in the sky. I get excited when I hear it since I haven't seen any signs of human beings in so long. Sometimes I wonder if people are still out there. I'm sure they are and soon I will probably wish I were here again, but for now I miss the comforts of home and the company of people. I miss clean, healthy food even more.

May 31, 2007, fifty-two miles from Anaktuvuk Pass

I'm still near Easter Creek heading east for the John River. There is an early-morning drizzle outside, which makes it hard to get up. The creek sounds like someone is yelling, but I know there is no one. I'm just accustomed to people, and my mind plays tricks on me sometimes now that I'm hungry, tired, and haven't seen people in so long. I feel my belly with my fingers. There's no bulge at all. It's just flat—too flat I'm afraid. I look at it, pinch the skin, and pull it. I seem to have a tinge of loose flesh yet. "Thank God," I say. Or is it just loose skin without any fat? I think there's a hint of fat yet. I hope so. I'll need every ounce to get to Anaktuvuk Pass. It's scary how quickly the two or three pounds of stomach fat I had melted away within days while trying to make miles. It's disturbing to look at my abdomen every morning and see how quickly my body is wasting away. I take photos of myself with my shirt off so I can view my body through the screen of my digital camera to get a better idea of how lean I'm becoming—to know how much danger I'm in. And I'm pretty thin. I figure I'm expending about 7,000 calories a day and only taking in about 1,500 calories a day. Each pound of body fat contains about 10,000 calories, so it doesn't take long for an emaciated body to appear on an already lean frame. I walk slowly but for a long time during the day. This is the most efficient way to travel these enormous distances when food is scarce. It's the way bears travel, when they are not ripping apart the ground for food.

My boots are wet from the previous day's hike across wet ground. It's always wet, and this often wears on my psyche. I usually use the sun in the evening to dry out my boots, but yesterday there wasn't any, so now I have to put on wet boots to start the day, and my extra socks are damp, too. Even the dogs don't want to get out of the tent. I'm drinking my coffee inside and when the pot is empty I'll have no excuse to linger. The rain patter on the tent sounds worse than it really is. I'll hike until the rain becomes unbearable today or until I start shivering from the heavy-laden wetness in the air.

During the long hours of marching I have plenty of time to think about how to make myself travel faster and more efficiently. Every day I feel more urgency to go faster. A month ago I thought I had my load as lightweight as it could be, but after so many days of struggle and pondering the size of the land and my limited speed, I occasionally come up with something new. Though this was not my plan in the beginning, today I throw away my soap, toothpaste, mirror, and shotgun to save weight. I never wanted to leave any sign of my presence on the land, but I'm starting to feel like if I don't make my pack lighter so I can travel farther with less food, I will die. I burn what I can, and what I can't I put into a neat pile, to appear less offensive I suppose. I even cut off more of the handle of my toothbrush to help lighten my load. I have to keep moving, and I'm always scheming on how to make the hiking easier, but really it can't get much easier. I just have to keep my head together and keep plugging away, like a rigid-faced automaton. I can't freak out and do something stupid, like start pacing around worrying or leaving behind vital gear. Every step I take must be in a forward direction toward civilization. Even with no food at all, I think I can still hike for a week, given a good rest each night and plenty of water to drink. My body will tear down muscle to fuel my cells when the available fat is gone, I guess. The body is amazing at surviving in a starvation situation. The metabolism slows, and you feel lethargic and weak when you're starving, like I do now. I figure this is so the body will metabolize as little energy as possible. You don't want to do wind sprints when you're starving. Your body probably wouldn't allow it anyway. Mustering up energy for a slow, continuous, ambling pace is as much as I can expect. Sometimes my breath smells funny. I think it's acidosis breath, which occurs when the body is starving and has to produce ketone bodies to fuel the brain, since the brain cannot function on body fat. It needs a more available source of fuel, like the glycogen that is stored in muscle cells after you eat. I haven't eaten enough, though, and I think ketone bodies are made for the brain and are formed when there is no glycogen left. But I'm not sure. I'm just hungry and can't think straight right now.

I dream a lot about various people, which is strange. Last night it was a couple of old friends whom I hadn't seen in years. I used to dream about adventure and nature when I was home where many people are. I've also had this recurring dream for years. I was in some remote, jungle-clad mountains searching for a lost tribe hidden from the rest of humanity. I was searching for them so I could live and roam around the forest with them. When I would wake up from the dream, I would ponder it for an hour wondering how I could get to some exotic wilderness like that and what indigenous people lived in the region. Now that I'm alone, my dreams are reversed, and people and towns slip into them. I guess I dream about things I don't have around me.

I don't eat this morning, but I give the dogs a little food. Their body fat is lower than mine, and I can't stand to see them hungry. They sniff and chew on every odd thing they wander across hoping it will be food. After I feed them, they stare at me like they are vexed by hunger, waiting for me to give them more. But I don't have any more food I can spare to give them.

I see a moose with two small calves today. She is trotting at full speed off across the tundra, heading for higher ground away from the creek. The calves are running after her as fast as their little legs can go, but they can't keep up. The mother is attentive to her calves and pauses at regular intervals to let them catch up while she looks back at me. Maybe she knows I'm hungry by the funny way I act, and that I'm searching for food anywhere I can. I would never hurt a calf or an animal so large. Or would I? As soon as the calves catch up, the mother bolts off again to encourage them to move as fast as they can.

I cross some grueling creek bogs during the day, ones that moose would love. One is waist deep. At first I search for a way around it, but then I realize it's futile to keep looking. I'm wasting too much energy going the wrong way, by not going due east—the way I need to go to cross Alaska. Finally I just wade straight across the bog and all the watery ground around it. It takes me about fifteen minutes to cross and I get soaked to my waist. My clothes will dry in about an hour in the dry arctic sun while I hike, as long as the sky is not raining. An hour later only my boots remain drenched. The ground is spongy wet everywhere, and most of my steps are in about six inches of water and on soft mossy ground that sinks when I step on it. There might be as much water sitting out on the tundra as there is flowing in the creeks and rivers.

In the afternoon, thunder clouds form on the edge of the horizon, like they often do. They look close, but they are actually rather far away. They form quickly and seemingly out of empty, blue sky. Sometimes I can see torrential rain falling in dark, undulating columns in the distance—rain so far away that it looks like it falls in slow motion, like a gray twisting veil fluttering next to a steep mountain. I always think the hard rain will come my way and overtake me, but most of the time it veers off or dissipates before I get there. Then I'm left with nothing but a misty drizzle. Sometimes I wish the rain would hit me hard so it would make me forget about my vicious hunger. Sometimes I wish I didn't have to hike anymore. But most of the time I accept the wilderness around me, and it gains more respect from me every day.

WALKAROUND CREEK

I try not to eat all day, but late in the afternoon my legs begin to feel like lead and I get so hungry I have to eat dry, raw oats that I wash down with water. I need about four days' rest and a ton of food. There are arctic grayling here along Easter Creek. It's amazing how twelve-inch-long fish can live in such a small creek and survive the winter. I try fishing, and the activity makes me forget about my hunger for short periods. I toss out a shiny lure and drag it right over the top of them several times from many different angles, but they don't react. I try a fly with a bubble and do the same, but nothing. I make a three-pronged spear out of some small willow branches. I cut each branch down to about six inches long and peel the bark off. Next I sharpen one end until they have a fine point. I touch the tips with my finger and it almost breaks the skin. Then I fasten the three prongs equally spaced around a six-foot-long willow stick and tie them securely with a shoelace. I sneak over to where the fish are swimming in place, but I can't reach them with my spear and if I enter the creek they scatter away. I see one resting next to shore under a grassy shelf. As it moves farther into the shade I creep up to it and lay down on my stomach just a foot away from the edge so the fish can't detect my shadow.

I reach my hand slowly down into the water and hold it still for about a minute. When I feel the fish brush up against my hand, I become overexcited and right away try to grab the fish, but it slips through my fingers as soon as I try to tighten my grip. Touching the fish only makes me try this technique longer. I spend an hour or more trying to grab the fish, but never manage to hold on to one. And by the time I'm finished, two hours have passed and I'm hungrier than when I started.

I hear a plane flying low, which makes me hopeful. It's the first one I've heard since my food drop weeks ago, but it flies off in a matter of seconds—just as well. I wouldn't signal it anyway. I still think I'll make it. I see a jet, too, high in the sky, and I watch it slice across the sky going north toward Barrow.

There is supposed to be a cabin at the mouth of Agiak Creek, but it probably won't be there anymore, like most of the cabins on these maps. The 1:250,000 scale maps are outdated. I look at them sometimes for an overview of my route, but I usually rely on the 1:60,000 scale maps for my exact course. I plan to walk a long day tomorrow until my body starts giving out. I need a good day. Everywhere hiking is hard; all around the terrain has tall, soggy tussocks, with brackish water in between them, and many snags of brush grow up from the tussocks. When I hike, my feet do one of three things most of the time: they sink into soggy ground, flounder on unstable tussocks, or get snagged on each step by unbreakable brush. Sometimes I get all three at once. They all drain my strength, but I have to keep moving.

I might start digging for mice. I'm not sure what species they are, but their holes seem to be scattered all over the ground. I'm not sure if the caloric benefit would outweigh the effort. It would if I didn't have to expend so much energy hiking. I don't know how bears manage it. I don't think they walk very far on a daily basis. The earth is always torn up where bears have dug, and sometimes I find fresh ruts where they have turned up the soil. Sometimes the ruts go on for a hundred yards and I peek in once in a while to see if they've left any food, but they never do. Their strength is impressive. They have an extra hump of muscle between their shoulders, which gives them more leverage. The big bears can move a 700-pound boulder with one arm.

June 1, 2007, forty miles from Anaktuvuk Pass

I skip breakfast again today, but the dogs eat some lentils. I would rather skip breakfast than dinner. If I have to suffer with hunger pains all day, I want to at least look forward to eating a meal in the evening. It's never enough food to sleep soundly, and I always wake up later hungrier than ever. I just try to get rid of the growling noise in the pit of my aching gut. It doesn't stay away long though.

I will walk today for as long as I can. I would like to leave my camp by ten in the morning and walk until nine in the evening, but my body is probably too worn out for that. I have to make more distance somehow, or face more days of severe hunger and suffering. I plan to hike by Lonely Lake today. Then I'll cross over the low pass to join up with Agiak Creek, which originates from some peaks to the north. I will follow Agiak Creek east down to the John River. A few miles north on the John River, I will have to ford Ekokpuk Creek. It will be gushing with snowmelt, and the volume of water concerns me. I don't think I will have enough food or energy to hike up to its headwater to cross.

Back home in Oregon, I used to practice hiking with little food for a situation just like this, which at the time I never really thought would arise. I just did it for an added practice to my wilderness training and spiritual growth, I guess. I would start out with no food and hike about thirty miles in two days, just eating huckleberries along the way. I did all this hiking on a trail that I knew well, so I was aware

of just how much time and effort it would take me. Here I don't know
the terrain. I've never been here before and have no idea how long
it will take me or if there is passable ground ahead. This situation
frightens me a little. Starving is not a good way to die, and I'm becoming more convinced of this after each passing hour. I've been thin
and worn out for a month and am nearing the limits of my physical
abilities. Compared with all the arduous journeys I've taken in my
life, this one is near my limits. It's humbling, but I can't afford one
mistake. I can't get injured and not be able to hike. I can't take a wrong
course and have to backtrack. I must make every right decision now,
or starve. I must get across the terrain ahead no matter what. Most of
all, I have to find the willpower to keep moving. I have to hike until
I fall in my tracks and can't get back up.

Near the upper end of Easter Creek, where it's only four feet
wide, I walk a lot in the water and cut the bends where the creek
turns. I step out of the creek onto the bank to go around a deep area
and a female ptarmigan darts out from a bush a few feet away. I know
instantly what is there, and my eyes fix to where she flew from so
I won't lose the location. I don't avert my eyes to watch her fly. I dig
my hand in the grass and find five ptarmigan eggs in a nest. I take
three without hesitation and wrap them in some cloth like jewels
and put them in my cooking pot to eat later. I start walking off,
but knowing how hungry I am, I walk back and take the remaining
two eggs as well. If I were sure I would make it to Anaktuvuk Pass
I wouldn't take any eggs. If I were only half sure, I would take only
two or three eggs. But when I think of what might happen to me, I
take all the eggs. It might be an unfair thing to do, but I don't want
to starve. Maybe it's early enough in the season for her to lay more
eggs, but with my mind locked on surviving, I don't let any remorse
creep through.

I walk in the water to save energy. The gravel bottom is an easier surface to walk on than the tussock-laden tundra. It rains again, not hard, just that kind of misty, messy drizzle that coats my glasses and makes the world fuzzy and grim. I wear a brimmed hat to shield my glasses from the rain, but it never catches all of it. I wipe my glasses off with my finger as I walk.

Then I see a bright red object in the distance as I stop to rest. I have to look twice to make sure it's really there. I think it might be someone's camp, and I begin to hope I can find food. I feel mild rejuvenation as I approach the area, but it takes me a half hour longer of traipsing through brush and across bogs to get to it because the land is so big and man-made objects can be seen from a long way off. They don't fit the color pattern of the land at all and stick out like a sore thumb. My rejuvenation disappears when I get within a few yards of the object. It's just an old gas can tied to the top of a rusty, rotten sled. Then I see a skinless carcass just a few feet away from the sled. "What the freaking hell is that?" I ask myself aloud. I walk over to it cautiously, studying it and watching out for traps. At first I wonder if I should let the dogs chew on it for some sustenance. There appears to be almost no decay, which I find strange. And there is a large amount of flesh on it yet. "Why haven't any animals eaten this thing?" It looks like a dead sled dog that had been skinned and left to lie there. All four feet had been apparently severed like a serial killer had hacked them off. All this together kind of freaks me out and I get the dogs back away. For some reason wild animals weren't coming near this gruesome thing. There are no chew marks at all on it, so no way am I going to let my dogs touch it, either. The skeleton still has a lot of meat, but this detestable carcass could be poisoned or anything else. I can't take the chance of letting the dogs chew on it. We will have to find food some other way, or just make it on the food we have left.

The terrain past Lonely Lake and down Agiak Creek is awesome yet rugged. I keep thinking I see a cabin down along the lake, but since I'm about a mile away, I can't tell for sure. It looks like just a speck, and I sit down for a few minutes studying it before heading down Agiak Creek. I don't have the calories to burn by hiking down to the lake when I'm not sure if what I see is actually a cabin. And if it were a cabin, it still might not have any food in it. My mouth waters with the thought that it might be a cabin stocked with food. But I can't take the chance, and I start hiking again, leaving the object behind. And as I walk past I keep looking over to see if I can detect any people walking along the lake. I look for tiny dots that move, like I do for bears, but I don't see any and the little hope I have about the possibility of getting more food and seeing a person fades as quickly as it came.

I cross over the pass between the headwaters of Easter Creek and Agiak Creek. The pass is wide like almost exactly how it has been along Easter Creek, and rows of peaks line each side of the valley just about everywhere. I walk for two hours to get over the pass before I realize the land has started slanting down hill into Agiak Creek. I navigate around a large hill where the ground is firm. As I descend, the terrain drops steeper. I come upon fresh green plants, some a foot high, with several species of songbirds darting between them. It's like a changed climate, as if I've come off the barren tundra and onto the lush oasis of the rest of the world south of here.

Several creek gorges enter Agiak Creek, which all take me some effort to get by. Some are several hundred feet deep. Often when I drop down into them to cross over, I descend the wall of the gorge at an angle going away from where the gorge connects with Agiak Creek because I know I won't have to descend as much if I head that way. Sometimes I encounter smaller gorges, fifty feet deep, within these larger gorges, and then I have to cross them as well. I have to cross gorges within gorges, and the straight-line distance I'm trying to make erodes along with my willpower. But I know I'll keep walking no matter what I encounter.

I'm too worried to marvel at the scenery much. I veer to the left off Agiak Creek onto the low slopes of Ursus Peak heading for Walkaround Creek and make my way north toward the John River. A frightening thunderstorm erupts, and thick, dark clouds release a deluge onto the land I'm walking on. I come to a patch of spruce forest growing on this mountain and I head into it. I get a little relief from the storm, which ends in less than an hour. Then the clouds part to let the sunlight beam through again. Many little streams trickle through the forest off the slopes, and I lie down to drink directly from one. I don't use my hands; I just put my mouth in the water and start swallowing. The walking is easier here than the days before, but I still amble on slowly. I hear squirrels nearby, alarmed by our presence, but I don't try to hunt them. I know how small they are and how much energy it takes to get one. This little forest of spruce isn't that big, though it's only a few miles from more spruce trees farther down. Squirrels live here like I've seen in every spruce forest. I never see them out on the tundra so I assume they need the trees for shelter, and perhaps food.

I would camp here if I had more food and if I had more time, but I need to keep moving. I bypass the Hunt Fork of the John River by taking this route, which is obviously the most direct way to Anaktuvuk Pass, leading me northeast. The Hunt Fork leads down to the John River, but it goes in sort of a southeast direction, instead of a northeast direction, and also there are some trees and tall willows along it that I would have to bull my way through. And I'm running out of will for that, too. I stare down the Hunt Fork for several minutes where the cabin is supposed to be, on a soft hill near where Kevuk Creek enters on the other side. To hike down there would take several hours. The spruce forest is the thickest I've seen in weeks down there, and despite my scanning, I don't see any cabin. I get a great view of Cairn Mountain farther down at the mouth of the Hunt Fork. It's shaped like a tall mound, like an eroded rock cairn with grass on it. It would be hard for anyone to miss it, and I use it for a marker to find my route northeast from here.

After an hour, the forest ends abruptly and I come back out onto the tundra. This mountain is just a deceptively large, sloping hill, and it takes me hours to get around it. I seem to hike forever trying to go up and around it. I'm starting to understand the name of the creek east of here. Maybe I was supposed to walk on Walkaround Creek to get around this mountain and bypass the brush. I veer uphill into a sea of brush that is waist high. I have to constantly move a few feet to the left and then to the right to find a path through. This lasts the remainder of the day, and towing the dogs through is exhausting, but by now they understand how to walk through brush. They try so hard, and work to keep pace with me, but the more tired I get the less I pay attention to their suffering.

After about three hours the brush finally lets up, and I camp at the base of a hillock where there are large slabs of gray rock to sit on and pools of water for cooking and drinking. I still drink straight from these pools because the water is recent snowmelt. In the coming days I won't be able to do this. The water will become rancid tasting. I've never been sick from drinking tainted water, and I've been drinking straight from the creeks in Oregon since I was a child. But here I can't afford to get sick, not now, not alone.

June 2, 2007

Today is probably the most difficult hiking of the trip. I skip breakfast again. I'm hungry of course and I stagger most of the day. I stroll along and don't try to force my pace, but I force myself to walk for a long time. It's the only way I can make miles now at this slow pace.

The tussocks are wobbly and they are everywhere. And they have knee-high brush growing out from them. There is water on the tundra that I have to walk in as usual. I curse the wicked sky with profanity several times. My body is so tired that my mind is struggling to keep control. I trip often and yell out scornfully each time. My body sways and I want to cry from fatigue and frustration.

Around two in the afternoon I stop and take off my pack, unable to continue. I drop to the ground like a corpse. I'm more tired than I realize and lie down on the tussocks to sleep for an hour, oblivious to the uneven surface below me. The dogs sleep, too, letting their bodies mold to the form of the tussocks and the pockets in between them. Jimmy has been flopping down every time I stop to bend over for the past two hours. Both dogs have become lethargic and skinny, and they have lost their animated charisma that hounds possess. (Airedales are really half otter hounds. This is what went into their breeding. Otter hounds are probably the happiest and most carefree-looking dog alive, and they can track like machines, perhaps as well as bloodhounds.) Jimmy and Will always used to look like they were smiling like hounds do. Now they appear stupefied with every exertion they have to make, like it's a bother for them. They must wonder why I don't stop for good and feed them.

I don't know what I dream about when I sleep, but when I wake up, I'm alert and clear eyed. I'm a little stiff, but I'm ready to go on. I have to go on. I've read a lot about early twentieth-century explorers, and the one that sticks out in mind the most is Robert Falcon Scott. I think about the final journal entries he wrote on his return trek from the South Pole and how he and his comrades must have suffered horrendously from hunger, fatigue, dehydration, and the cold. He and his three companions had just finished skiing to the South Pole towing sleds only to discover that the Norwegian explorer, Roald Amundsen, had beaten them there. Then they had to make the 800-mile return journey to their base camp, 800 miles more, after having already come 800 miles. All four of the men were exhausted and on limited food rations. Despite their fortitude, they were stopped by fierce headwinds and severe cold. They ran out of fuel to melt snow for water just eleven miles from their next cache that their support party had left for them in advance. Scott wrote that their chances were almost none for getting out alive. "Amputation is the best I could hope for now," he wrote earlier during the final days when they were still able to travel. But later he wrote, "Blizzard bad as ever—Wilson and Bowers unable to start—tomorrow last chance—no fuel and only one or two of food left—must be near the end. Have decided it shall be natural—we shall march for the depot with or without our effects, and die in our tracks." A few days later Scott was able to summon the strength to write one last entry. "Every day we have been ready to start for our depot 11 miles away, but outside the door of the tent it remains a scene of whirling drift. I do not think we can hope for any better things now. We shall stick it out to the end, but we are getting weaker, of course, and the end cannot be far. It seems a pity, but I don't think I can write more." These and the rest of Scott's journal entries have gone down in history as some of the greatest annuls of adventure ever recorded. All four of the men died and their remains were found in their wind-battered tent in November 1912, where they died of exhaustion and starvation.

To die of exhaustion and starvation—only now do I comprehend such a reality. Thinking about this urges me on. No way on earth am I going to let myself or the dogs starve to death. I try to make a call on my satellite phone, but for some reason I can't get reception and I worry about running out the battery's power. After a few attempts I put it away and keep hiking. I have to become bullheaded to fight through the fatigue and the haggard state of my body. It's all I can do.

I hike for nine grueling hours with a full pack over tussocks today and don't eat anything. I don't ingest one morsel of food and my gut never stops grumbling. During the last hour I bend over to rest my hands on my knees about every hundred yards, otherwise I will tip over, and it hurts me to walk more than that. The weight of my pack is torturous now that my back muscles are so sore. Looking ahead, I can see up this straight valley for miles. It's supposed to turn right at the end and connect back up with the John River, but I can't see that part. All I can see is a giant concave-shaped valley with mountains on each side, and as I walk it doesn't feel like I'm making any ground at all. In my fatigued state of mind, I want to drop my pack to the ground and leave everything behind so I can travel faster, like how an exhausted man stuck on Everest dying from cerebral edema would want to jump off to get down faster in a last-ditch effort to save himself. I toy with the idea for quite some time, not ever really intending to do it, but trying to conceive its practicality if I were to reach a point where I was certain to die anyway.

I start second guessing myself and have to keep telling myself, "I'm not going to die. I'm not going to die." I knew hunger would be bad, and I knew long before I came to Alaska that I would have to endure it, but I didn't grasp how fast it would sneak up on me and start weakening my body. I didn't grasp that I would be starving so terribly and that the land around me would be so vast and empty. Thought alone is becoming difficult. Mental anguish is reaching a boiling point as I reach my physical limits. It hurts to concentrate on walking. And the dogs don't want to play anymore.

I find a couple of caribou bones during the day and let the dogs chew on them. They chomp the bones up bit by bit and swallow them. They devour the entire things within an hour. Maybe they can get a little sustenance out of them. I consider collecting more bones and pounding them to powder to eat myself. I'm so weary and miserable with hunger that I can't enjoy the scenery here, either. I kind of regret this, but there is nothing I can do. I pay as much attention to the land around me as I can, so I can remember it, and I take some photos. I could never envision mountains as incredible as these, without having seen them with my own eyes. They line the edges of every creek and river valley I walk through. It's a shame I can't linger to lament this wild land, but I'm lucky to still be able-bodied and moving forward.

BONE HUNGRY

I arrive at the John River while a fierce wind rips through. I waver like
a stick on each gust. I think I see a camp trailer while walking down off
the pass. It looks so clear, and I start to convince myself I have come
upon people staying here. I begin to hope that someone might be here
to give me food. I stumble closer for about twenty minutes, trying to
squint and wipe my eyes to get a better view. As I get closer it turns
out to be a white patch of snow still clinging to the earth on the other
side of the river. I nearly stop cold in my tracks as my spirits sink. After
scoffing at the bushes and grasses, I grumble and grind forward.

After getting to camp and sharing a small helping of cooked lentils (a cup and a half raw, which is three cups cooked) with the dogs
while the wind bombards the walls of my tent, I begin to feel a little
better. I think we might just make it, but there is still one large creek
to cross—Ekokpuk Creek. I know it will have high water, so I'm not
sure if I can get across it. I still have seventeen linear miles to go, and
this will take at least two days, or three if I have to make a detour to
go up and around the headwaters.

Following is an actual journal entry, the way I wrote it, on June 2.

Evening—17.1 miles to go. Just arrived at the John River. No one
here at all either. Half expected a traveler at least. Just a few

cups of lentils left. I hiked 9 hours and didn't eat anything the entire day. Ouch! Stumbling along, weary. My body ain't got much left. No easy ground. Worried about being able to cross Ekokpuk Creek. It could be large and swift. Dogs found some bones today. I took a nap and let them chew them. They can chew up bone and swallow it. I was pretty beaten mentally. Near tears from exhaustion and tedious, stumbling walking. So weary and hungry today. I staggered across the land barely able to keep myself from tripping. It's so uneven, soggy, brushy and bumpy. Can't enjoy the scenery these last few days, as I worry about getting stuck somewhere with no food. Miserable. There's no easy ground here, not even when you are starving and worn out.

June 3, 2007, seventeen miles from Anaktuvuk Pass

My spirits are better this morning, but I won't eat until I get across this coming creek in the late afternoon. If we're forced to hike upstream toward the headwaters, I may need the food for a couple of extra days, but I couldn't hold out much longer than that. My body fat is pretty much all gone. My abdomen is flatter than a pancake, and my ribs stick out like steel girders.

I walk the banks along the John River. The ground is firm and doesn't have much brush. Ground squirrel burrows dot the landscape. They call out whenever we hike by, which excites the tired dogs. I'm pretty sure they would still try to dig for them if I were to let them loose, so I keep them leashed, but it's getting harder for me to concentrate and walk with them. Sometimes I see the squirrels sitting just outside the entrances of their burrows soaking up the rays of the sun. If I still had my shotgun, I would shoot one without hesitation, but now I don't even stop to look at them as I walk by. Catching one would consume more calories than we would gain, and I think it's better just to keep moving while I still can.

June 4, 2007, nine miles from Anaktuvuk Pass

When I arrive at Ekokpuk Creek, my worse fear is realized. The creek is a raging river at its confluence with the John River, and I don't dare try to cross it. I wouldn't make it three feet before being swept away into the milky water. I sit down to rest on a log and ponder this terrible scenario. I study the chocolate-colored rapids and the swift current in each part of the river hoping to see something I missed: a shallow underwater ridge I could walk across on, some boulders I could hop across on, or a root wad sticking up in the middle I could swim for, but there is nothing to help me. I get despondent and would cry if I had the energy. I just go where I have to. My only choice is to head upriver.

I rise up and hike a half mile up to where the creek branches into two smaller channels. I stop to wrap up some of my gear inside my tent. Then I put it back in my pack. If I fall in the water, hopefully some of the gear will stay dry. I tie a rope to my pack and wrap the other end around my wrist. If I go in the water, I'll slide out of my pack and make my way to shore towing my pack, but the water is so cold that I don't want to fall in. I put on my Gore-Tex rain pants to help protect my legs from some of the cold, so I can stay in the water long enough to get across before the pain becomes unbearable.

I cross the first channel without falling, and the dogs have to swim for the first time of the trek because it's swift and too deep for them to wade. Then I hike out of the creek bed to head over a point of land toward the other branch to cross. I hike up the creek about fifty yards and come back to the creek bank, where I surprise a moose with calves. I think she is the same moose I saw way back on Easter Creek. She looks tense, like she is going to charge us. In the next second, I duck back behind the embankment that I had just come over, and once I'm out of her sight, I shuffle-run for all I'm worth, with the dogs on a leash. I know there is a good chance she will be running me down to stomp me. My legs are like jelly and it's hard for me to run. There is nowhere for us to hide out here on the open tundra, and neither I nor the dogs would be strong enough to stop her attack. I wish I had my shotgun with me now.

Once we get some distance away and I see that she is not chasing us, we stop and circle around upstream. I peek back over the bank and see her leading the calves downstream around a corner. I continue on and cross the second channel. I've heard that a moose with calves will stomp you until you are a pulverized hunk of flesh, blood, and bone, but a grizzly bear will stop her attack if you don't move. So take your pick. "I'd rather not face either," I say as I climb up the other side of the creek bed. I have to climb a fifty-foot embankment of firm snow. It would have been the only place safe from a moose attack. Too bad I wasn't here when I needed it.

We walk about a mile past Ekokpuk Creek and set up camp next to the first unfrozen lake I've seen so far. Well, part of it's unfrozen anyway. I stand in it up to my knees and try to take a bath to make myself feel better. It's too cold to get all the way in, though, so I just wipe myself down with a soaked bandanna and wash my hair by hanging my head down inches from the lake's surface. My abdomen is drawn way up, almost under my ribcage it seems, and my legs have lost much of the bulky muscle I had developed from years of bicycle racing. I slide my hand over my bony hips and around to my back. My spinal bones stick out like I'm growing a prehistoric reptilian ridge—gruesome and scary. I'm wasting away into bone and brain. If this keeps up, I'll soon be merely a skull, a skeleton, and a memory of myself cast upon the northern plains, waiting to be frozen and turned to dust in the eons of time.

The tundra around here is littered with bones, sculls, and antlers. I wonder if any of the animals that the bones belonged to starved to death. I worry for a second that our bones will be added to these.

Starvation is always on my mind now. I'm somewhat mortified that I might starve. I don't have the ability or energy to even cry about it. I'm simply prodded on by the stabbing fear. There is no other way out of here. I just put my head down and grit my teeth to battle the pain. I don't have much willpower for that, either. As I stumble forward my mind starts wandering with worry. Will I collapse and not be able to move for days before the end, or will death happen right away? Who will take care of the dogs?

I couldn't handle an uncertain future for Jimmy and Will if something were to happen to me. They get reassurance and support from me. All domestic dogs seem to need this human connection; I think they become too afraid without it. I wonder if solitary wolves harbor this kind of desperate fear as they move across the wide ground looking for a pack or a companion. The morning of the day of Jonny's death when he was still able to sit up, he calmed down when I was near him, like he knew I would save him. But I wasn't able to. There were forces against him that I didn't understand—a disease I couldn't control. Maybe this is it. Maybe this is the moment of pain I wanted to happen all along, my penance or punishment for letting Jonny die. I'm weak, famished, and on the edge of my life, suffering for perhaps not just Jonny's death but for all the heedless blunders I've made. Perhaps this is what I have to go through to reach the rest of my life, my mortification to rid all guilt from my mind and reach humility. But I still have control now. I'm conscious, coherent, and able to function. I know exactly what I need to do to save the three of us. I'll propel myself along, plodding ruthlessly against failing muscles until I black out. And if I wake up, I'll prod myself onward again, stumbling and unrelenting. Sometimes you have to fight for all you're worth to stay alive.

The dogs perk up every time they see something white approaching. They stop to examine and chew on each bone. I sidestep everything white so we can keep hiking. They are strong and if I get close to a bone they will pull me right over to it, like I'm not even here. They like to stop and chew on bones because they are so hungry. Despite their suffering, they don't ever whine. I feel bad I don't have more food to give them, and I can't stop for every single bone we come across.

We come across caribou feces in the grass. Knowing the dogs will eat them, I stop, and they gobble up the pellets within seconds. They want to eat anything now that is organic, like their bodies have shifted into a survival mode. Anything goes, and if they can get it down and doesn't taste foul to them, they eat it.

June 5, 2007, seven miles from Anaktuvuk Pass

Here is what my journal says, exactly the way I wrote it, on June 5.

> I'm up early. It's five am. Didn't sleep much last night. Ducks kept whizzing over. Don't think I want to suffer through another night of hunger. Lentils just don't fill that gnawing pit in my stomach. I feel wide-awake though. The slow easy ambling pace yesterday really helped, like bears walk. It really does conserve energy. Today I'll try to make decent time just in case a store is open. I damn well don't want to miss it. Seems I always arrive to town on Sunday, when the societal folk are at church, or tucked away in their box houses eating bacon and eggs in their pajamas and slippers till noon. Birds sing all night. Sometimes waterfowl sound like yelling children. I miss yelling children. A plane flew over last night. I thought he might drop me a care package. No luck. Best weather seems to come around seven am till noon. I'll be ready. Coffee's good though. Just need a case full of biscuit mix and send me off to the mountains.
>
> It would be very burdensome to be a fugitive on the run and have to hide out like this. Couldn't come to a town to get

food or see anyone. Have to have a good friend meet you with food on a regular basis. I'd go to the Amazon and live with a lost tribe. But they are being sucked into the world web of idleness, computer games, and chocolate bars. All connected. All knowing. I wish I had some chocolate bars. Coffee doesn't stay hot long enough in my tent. And if I go out to the lake to get water, the dogs have to come, and yank out everything they touch. They wouldn't be good candidates for hauling nitroglycerin to the bombsite. I have one and a half cups of lentils left. Nothing more. I calculated this just right. I wish I had hoarded the breakfast bars. Rain comes again, always early in the morning. Never rains for more than a few minutes in one spot. Set my pot outside to fill up with water. More coffee. Nothing to eat. Just extreme hunger. Not sure if I can hike another day.

I stagger most of the day wondering where Anaktuvuk Pass is. I can't see any sign of a village ahead. I seem to be losing my ability to control my legs. They're like putty and it takes me some serious perseverance to keep them moving. I stop every couple of minutes to bend over because my back aches and I get dizzy a lot now, and if I don't stop I'm afraid I will fall down. I'm afraid I won't be able to get back up. Jimmy flops down to nap every time I stop. He's lethargic and weak, and it takes me some coaxing to break him out of his hungry torpor to get him back to his feet to start moving again. After about three miles of hiking I get so weak—weaker than hungry now—that I have to stop to cook the last of my lentils to try to regain my body composure and mental acuity. There is a cup and a half to share among the three of us. I've never been so beyond exhaustion in my life, and I'm not really sure what is keeping me moving forward. I can't possibly have any fuel left in my body.

After I eat a few spoonfuls and feed some beans to the dogs, I take a nap in hopes of regaining a little strength. It's more like a collapse into unconsciousness than a nap, though. I'm asleep as soon as I lie down and shut my eyes. I sleep hard, but I know I don't dream this time. The dogs look at me waiting for more food, but after a minute they sleep, too. I'm afraid if I don't rest now I will collapse right in town just like in the movies when the cowboy staggers in off the parched plain. I don't want to draw any attention to myself or be pitied when I walk into town. I want to look like I know what I'm doing, and I want to keep from stumbling. I don't want to be the fool who needed rescuing, though I would take a rescue right now without any hesitation if one were offered to me. I check to make sure my phone is working by turning it on for a minute. It is. I'm almost ready to call for help, but I put it away again. "A little farther," I say.

After our rest, I stretch my back and pack up my gear that is laid all around. Then we continue walking. I make a quick scan for berries, like I do sometimes, but I know it's still too early in the season. Sometimes I think I see a few but when I move closer there's nothing but willows. I think I can eat willow leaves, but I'm not sure. If I have to I will stop and start eating grass and other fresh shoots. I don't yet because I'm not sure which ones are poisonous. I'll save that for a last resort.

I have to stop every hundred feet to bend over to rest. I feel like jelly, and the dogs walk with less energy in their strides than I've ever seen in them before. I used to stroke their backs in the previous days to check their body mass and health, but now I don't because I know what I will find. Their spinal bones stick out like they could pop through their skin, like mine.

I struggle on for several hours, fatigued and mildly incoherent to anything around me. I know I'm starving, and if we don't make it to Anaktuvuk Pass today, things will become insurmountable and bleak. I might be able to walk for another few days, but the way I feel now I tell myself this is the last day I can hike with no food. The dogs look like pathetic shadows of themselves, with their heads drooping down toward the ground as they walk along. They stub their paws sometimes, and they have to take a lot of chopped steps to correct themselves.

I feel my cheeks while stroking my red, ragged beard, then grimace at the sky ahead. There's a hollow space where my full cheeks used to be. I don't even have extra flesh there, and this startles me. I've become thinner than I realized. I panic some and try to walk faster, but in about three minutes I slow back to my regular famished pace. I become irritable from my fatigue and find it challenging just to walk the dogs next to me. They want to lag back, which forces me to work more to tug them forward, and I can barely move my own body forward. I fear if I unleash them they will either run around or lie down, both of which are no good. They need to walk slow and steady like I'm doing so we can get out of here alive. I know we have to be nearing Anaktuvuk Pass, but I still can't see it over the higher ground that crosses the valley in front of us. Since my mind is under serous duress trying to keep my body together, things get a little fuzzy. I begin to wonder if there is a town at all. The horizon looks as empty as it has been anywhere. I can't imagine anyone living here. It's nothing but a vast wilderness of arctic plains and jutting mountains. "Oh, my God," I say. "What if there's nothing here." I could be a dead man if there's nothing here. "It's a damn empty wasteland."

My stomach doesn't really growl anymore. I'm just weak, agitated, and sleepy. I would stop and spend the night, but I wonder if the dogs would have a tough time lasting another day or two. They seem so listless and low spirited that it makes me sad. I force myself to keep walking, but my legs don't work right anymore. I force myself on for the dogs' sake. They don't deserve to starve. They don't deserve to die for my ambitions or for my mistake. I urge the dogs to keep walking with little jerks on their leashes, but they want to stop and sleep.

I remember when Julie and I took our first hike together, in Menagerie Wilderness in the Cascade Mountains of Oregon. We were only out for a short day hike, but she brought so much food, and I think I only had a few slices of stale bread. She always was doing things for others, and she offered me so much food that I couldn't eat it all. She had olives, a large block of cheddar cheese, turkey sandwiches with mayonnaise and lettuce, and peanut butter energy bars, and all I could offer her was some dollar loaf bread. I would take that bread in an instant right now. I think about that food and Julie's caring nature. Normal hiking can really stress a person's easygoing demeanor and good charm, but not Julie's. She would just buckle down when the hiking became difficult and keep on her smiling face every time I looked at her. I think she tried hard to impress me. I'm glad she's not here now suffering through this with me. I couldn't handle seeing her endure this. I don't think she could. I don't think anyone could endure the long days of hunger combined with the long days of difficult hiking. So at least I'm relieved about her being home and safe. The thought of her keeps me going. The thought of the dogs keeps me going. The thought of living keeps me going. I should call for help and end this struggle, if not for my own stubborn good, then for the dogs. Perhaps all my years of mental preparation and exercising made me too prepared to endure pain to dangerous brinks, like how a champion prizefighter, battered and bloodied, will refuse to throw in the towel even when he's being beaten to death. I have to think straight for the dogs' sake. I have to save enough energy to make the call and stay alive for a day or two until help arrives. I could call and tell them I will be walking in the last few miles and that they should meet me. I might as well just keep walking and not call yet. I try to tell myself that I'm still fine. I just haven't reached these physical boundaries before, which makes me assume my limit must be near. "You can hike well beyond this point if you have to," I say. "So don't worry. Straighten up and just keep going." Maybe I'm fine, maybe I'm not, but I do know I'm in a bit of a pinch, bone hungry and almost feeble-minded with several miles to go.

I stumble along another mile, grumbling softly at the dogs every ten minutes. "Get up," I say, but they don't respond or do anything differently than what they're doing, walking laboriously slow next to me however fast I go. It's my own pain and agitation that compels me to order them around, as if by them doing something differently it will ease my burden. But they're doing exactly what they're sup-posed to do. My voice is barely audible and about the only sound I can force out of myself is an infantile gripe. Once every fifty yards or so I trip and almost cry. It hurts to jolt my body like that, mainly from the effort needed to correct my balance. "Get up dogs," I say each time like they're the cause, my voice cracking in the wind. But they're not, I am.

After almost tripping again and letting out a creaking groan, and then thinking I can go no farther without food, a very faint, four-wheeled vehicle track appears off to the side from my course. Instantly I feel a surge of adrenaline pumping through my veins like fire. I study it for a moment to be sure of what it is. I don't want to waste my men-tal concentration and energy by celebrating in vain. I'll need both if it turns out I still have a long way to go. Shocked with pure hope, I look up and down the track for a few seconds with my mouth hanging open like a dull mouth-breather, my eyes wide and enlivened, but my face lacking any muscular expression at all. The faint track in either direction is just a slight depression over the rocks and grasses, but I decide it has to have been made by an ATV (an all terrain vehicle the size of a golf cart). The two winding tracks roll on parallel well out of view, and only a man-made machine could make tracks like that. After glancing at my map and taking a GPS reading, I realize all I have to do is walk a few miles more to Anaktuvuk Pass. This knowledge makes me certain I'm almost there. My despair and fatigue give way to a slight narcotic-like glee. "This track must lead to Anaktuvuk Pass," I say with only the dogs to hear me. "It must be only a few miles." I become confident we will not die from starvation now. Even if I have to rest one more day I still think we could stumble into town tomorrow, but no more, and I don't want to find out. That would be the final limits of my endurance and energy reserves until my body started shutting down and I couldn't walk anymore. And I wouldn't have any energy to look for food on the tundra, either. I've been using it all to get to the next village. I don't want to go to sleep again without food. It hurts too much, and I'm afraid I wouldn't wake up. I'm afraid one of the dogs wouldn't wake up. The dogs would probably be able to last long after I become unconscious, though they don't look like it now. After all they do retain the same genes that make a predator so resilient and indestructible, as far as mammals go. They are the perseverant lineage of wolves, and their invincibility still stirs deeply within their genetic arsenal. When I think back to this moment in the days to come, I believe I would have died long before them.

"Civilization at last," I say to the dogs to give them an emotional jolt. "We've done it, you guys. We've crossed the gates of the arctic." I become happy and hug the dogs and somehow find enough energy to keep myself upright and steady. It's the pure joy of knowing I will live and the relief of knowing I will not die that adds this extra adrenaline boost to my dilapidated body and brain. The physical pain becomes minuscule when I become sure I will survive after all. "We've crossed the freaking gates," I keep saying to the dogs while bobbing my head each time I come to the word "freaking." Sometimes I bend over and look them in the eye and pat their heads. "We've crossed the freaking gates, Jimmy," I say to perk him up. "Can you believe it, Will, the freaking gates of the arctic." It's like I'm carrying on a lavish, exuberant conversation with a group of people, but it's only the dogs and me. "Nobody does this," I say in a heightened tone of voice that had been missing for the past two weeks. The dogs glance at me once or twice, but they simply keep walking with sunken heads and dragging tails. But I'm sure my upbeat attitude now goads them forward.

After two more hours of walking, my celebratory body movements have faded. Though I'm still happy as can be, I don't have energy to show it anymore. I trudge over the high ground above town. A ptarmigan takes flight but I don't give him a second glance. I descend off the final slope trying not to fall and rest wearily on a hummock before entering the town boundary. I sag my head down mostly while I rest, but when I look up I notice the town is absolutely square shaped. There is a clear border between the gravel-surface town and the tundra, and no merging at all of the two. The town can't contain more than a hundred dwellings, and it looks like it had been plunked down randomly in this wide barren pass. I don't consider the lay of the land too much, but the town sits in the middle of a valley perhaps two miles wide. There are no trees at all, just gentle hills of short green grasses, bumps, and dark rocks scattered about. On the sides of the valley, the land gives way to unique bluish-gray mountains and high, sharp passes where wild sheep dwell.

I compose myself, stand up, and start hiking again. I'm not going to tell anyone quite how terribly I suffered. I want to be viewed like a man who thrives in wilderness, not someone who whimpers with dread when he is alone. The dogs slink immediately after my heels without me saying a word to them. Then I come onto the first gravel road, walking like I've just come home from being at sea for two months. My legs feel unsteady on the solid, flat earth, and it takes me a moment to adjust the waddling stride I've developed from walking over tussock mounds for so long. I cross the town and go to the grocery store, which I saw coming off the hill. Thankfully it's open, so I tie up the dogs next to my pack and enter, anticipating incredible amounts of food. My eyes light up when I see all the clean food stacked neatly on the shelves in their shiny packages. I buy dog food, a loaf of bread, several bags of chocolates, a bag of cookies, and a large bottle of apple juice. I pay the cashier and give a quick nod without saying a word. He seems unsure of me in my thin, scraggly state, and I'm too exhausted to talk. I walk back outside with a deep sense of urgency and dump some dog food onto the ground for the dogs to scarf up. They devour the food, and before I can sit down I have to unload the rest of the food for them. They eat ten pounds of food within a few minutes, and I'm finally able to let my crushing fear for them that was building inside of me for the past ten days, fall away like sand. They will not starve. Then I sit down against my pack around the side of the store and wolf down several portions of chocolate and bread before stopping to lie back and rest. "I can't believe I just crossed the freaking Gates."

I drink a pint of juice and shut my eyes for twenty minutes. When I open them the dogs are sacked out sound asleep. I feel I can stand up without falling over. I start to grin with jubilation, for it sinks in that I will not starve, either. "Let's go pups, you big fatsos," I say, and I strap on my pack and walk across town limping, but almost giggling. The dogs' bellies bulge out grotesquely against their bony frames. It looks funny now that I know they're fine.

The town is an almost perfect square of about half a mile on each side, and it's not hard to find the motel. I ask the first man I pass on the street. "Sir, is there a motel here?" I ask politely.

"Blue building down the road," he says. I never stop walking even to ask directions. I just walk straight for the motel with the dogs on my heels. When I get to the front door, I'm pretty much full on giggling to myself now, like I'm laughing at an invisible friend's funny joke. It's like I keep hitting my funny bone over and over again. That's what I feel like. I have pain in my body, but the deluge of hormones pumping through me drowns it out. I know my physical pain is temporary and not so terrible that my euphoric mind can't stave it off. I'm giddy and goofy with the happiness of life. I'm happier than I've been in a long time, a sort of redemption. "Jonny, you would be proud of me," I say.

"I just hiked here from Ambler," I blurt out to a man while I take off my pack.

"Ambler?" he asks sincerely. He isn't aggressive or indifferent when he speaks to me.

"Yeah, Ambler. It was a long way."

"What is that, about three hundred miles?" he asks. He waits for me to respond without talking over me.

"Pretty close," I say without any inhibition at all in my voice, though it's completely amiable.

"How long did that take you?" he asks. By this time two other men who were doing carpentry work on the motel come over to listen.

"Fifty days," I say.

"Fifty days?" the man responds in disbelief. By this time I'm smiling and beaming with the joy of being alive.

"Yep," I say. "I never saw another person the entire time, and I thought I was going to starve." The three men listen to me talk, and then each makes their own comment about the land.

"My cousin almost died caribou hunting last fall," the first man says.

"It's not easy ground to hike over," the second man says.

"You got to know how to survive out there," the third man says. I just keep nodding my head up and down while grinning from ear to ear.

"Oh, I know," I say. "I definitely know." Then I walk in to get a room. I feel I earned it.

After I unload my gear in my room, I walk over to get my boxes from the post office. Then I get a ride in the back of a pickup truck back to my room with Jimmy and Will. Some kids stop to look at them while we get out of the truck. "Can I pet your dogs, mister?" one boy asks. I tell the kids okay, but when the boy reaches out his hand Jimmy and Will start to wiggle when they greet the kids, so the boy pulls his hand back to his chest and settles for watching them instead.

I set up my tent out back for the dogs to sleep in. I tie their long leashes to a drainpipe so they won't wander off, and I give them a pot filled with freshwater and a lot of food. Then I head back inside and take a shower. I look like a prisoner of war, but I laugh and giggle at myself knowing that I have mounds of food in my room laid out on my bed so I can easily choose what I want to eat next. I know with food already in my stomach that my body is rebuilding itself. I know I won't grow any thinner. This is the most secure I've felt on the entire trek—since even before I left Portland somberly on a cold, rainy night in mid-March with Julie driving me to the airport.

I head into the lobby and call Julie. "You don't know how relieved I am to hear from you," she says. She tells me she will arrive in a few days for our trek together, so this brightens my mood even more. She also tells me that my brothers left Anatuvuk Pass the week before, which I regret a little, but I take comfort that they are on the trail in front of me. If something were to happen to them, I could catch up and help.

Next I call my parents. "We were beginning to wonder what happened to you," my mother says.

"I was trying to make it here," I say. "I knew I would be okay."

That night after I tuck in the dogs, I fade back into my room and lie down on the bed with the pile of food next to me, I kick off my shoes and flop my feet around like a cheerful kid as I snack on cheese crackers, applesauce, chocolate bars, and a quart of milk. I eat until my stomach is bloated. Then after a few minutes of strolling around my room and checking on the dogs, I eat again, stuffing myself with tuna sandwiches and raisin bagels. I turn on the television and take in some news, but mostly I change the channel until I find an old sitcom, something humorous and not too serious to ooze into my mind. The bed is level and firm, and it soothes my body like I never thought it could. After about an hour of reflecting back on my trek and thinking of home, I fall asleep while watching a rerun of *The Dukes of Hazzard*. I sleep with dreams of the future and without an ounce of worry in the world.

THE PASSING OF THE AGES

I never planned for my journey to end there high in a remote Eskimo village of the Brooks Range, but it undoubtedly did. Even though I hiked another hundred miles with Julie and spent another six weeks in Alaska, I was never again burdened by loneliness, desperation, and the dread of starving. I never felt like I was thrust out on the edge again, either, where I felt so alive. So it became the start of something new in my life—a series of reflections about what I had done in the past three months. Our hike together became a winding-down period for me where I could savor my accomplishment and think about returning home. I became content, like I often get right after the end of a hard expedition.

Quite a number of things happened to me in those six weeks, some uplifting, some disheartening, but never did I feel a sense of urgency to move on to avoid danger. I never did catch up with my brothers. They finished their trek two days before Julie and I left Anaktuvuk Pass. But we did come across their footprints over and over again as we hiked along the river bottoms. It was as if I could hear my brothers talking to each other as we walked along, like we were all together.

Julie and I saw some of the most impressive scenery of my entire trek, like we were privileged. On the upper North Fork of the

Koyukuk River where we entered the northern tree line, we sat to marvel at the two peaks that formed the actual mountainous portal the Gates of the Arctic National Park was named after, Frigid Crags and Boreal Mountain. Bob Marshall named them decades before. They represent all the splendor of wilderness that he was looking for throughout his life. Perhaps they're what I was looking for, too. The peaks are dark and dominating, and they stand out impressively against the lower mountains and hills. Julie and I could see the Gates for three days before we got close enough to make out the coarse detail of their rock faces. That's what we dubbed them, since we talked about them so often. They looked like two scraped-up cones with the tips broken off that a giant had dropped down on each side of the river valley. And in the pure air, their clean, sharp edges cut into the northern sky and into my memory. I was going to talk to Julie there, heart to heart in the shadow of those explosive peaks, about having a permanent future together. I had tentatively planned it months in advance, but the trek had dampened our good spirits so I decided to leave it for later.

Besides great vistas, Julie and I endured serious adversity on our trek together: pummeling rain, voracious horseflies, pestering mosquitoes, miles of tussock mounds, wading in creeks, fording rivers, getting lost, hunger, exhaustion, heat, illness, crossing craggy gorges, head-high brush, bears, and long hours of marching across embattled ground. It strained our bond with each other and foreshadowed our loss.

After Julie left Alaska I was alone again with the dogs to explore Alaska for another month. Instead of hiking east toward Canada—I was too thin—or going home when Julie did like she wanted, I headed down the Middle Fork of the Koyukuk River to wander a little more. I would have to complete my traverse of the Brooks Range another year. Despite being done with my trek I couldn't bring myself to leave yet.

It felt good not to have to walk so far with the village of Coldfoot only a day or two's march away. I strolled barefoot along the river and among the willows. They were the size of trees. In the warm summer sun, I searched for glittering rocks and found a fossil mammoth tooth in the gravel bank. I set it under a bush by my camp until I was ready to go home. It was too heavy to carry, and besides it belonged there. Certain things belong in the wild; certain people, too. The fossil was the size of my foot and must have weighed ten pounds. I thought how the land must have appeared when the woolly mammoth thundered across it thousands of years before, invincible and enduring before the passing of the ages. The mammoth must have had a momentous spirit knowing that it was part of something huge, a land that could not be undone. Julie and I ended our relationship the day I left Alaska over the faint buzzing of a long-distance phone call. "I don't think we should see each other anymore," she said. I wondered why things don't last forever and why we can't make things that are good, better.

On the flight home I stared out the window as awestruck as I did when I was just arriving, except there was no apprehension of confronting the unknown. I thought about my journey and how just months before I was struggling through severe cold to make miles; how I was battling to save my own life. As I gazed upon Alaska one last time, I took comfort in knowing the hard journey was over and that all the people I knew who ventured to that far-off place to hike with me succeeded on their trek. I was relieved we were safe and had completed our journey without permanent injury. I was certain we all would take something away with us. We would never doubt what wilderness could be like, what Alaska is like. It might have been either Julie or Mike who said something like, "Nothing looks as good after having been to the Brooks Range."

When I got home I returned to the room in the woods I rent a few miles outside town, where I could hear the birds sing and the insects buzz in the evenings, not the noise of motor traffic perforating my brain. I strolled out back the next morning and sat next to the dog pen, under some fir trees. The dogs were in there wrestling like our whole adventure together had been one fun game. Except for them making fake growling noises at each other, it was quiet. I could think and write about my journey. I could dream. I dreamed about true freedom for myself of course, but also for all of humanity. I felt it could only come from being in wilderness, where we as individuals or in small groups could roam the woods, creeks, and mountains at will, straining our sustenance solely from the ground we walked upon, from the primal earth. And that is the key—to be able to get the food we need right in nature without distorting it. I thought about Alaska, but also of other places I wanted to see in wild pockets of the globe. For the time being, I was staying in Oregon where I could enjoy the forest, plan for more far-away adventures, and always keep my daily life pure and cleanly simple, like the life of a four-legged friend I used to know. Then I got up to let the dogs out, and we went for our daily walk in the woods together.

SUGGESTED READING

The Songlines by Bruce Chatwin
Slaughter House Five by Kurt Vonnegut
Arabian Sands by Wilfred Thesiger
The Road by Cormac McCarthy
One River by Wade Davis
Savages by Joe Kane
The Final Frontiersman by James Campbell
The Prairie by James Fenimore Cooper
Housekeeping by Marilynne Robinson
Of Human Bondage by W. Somerset Maugham
Farewell to the King by Pierre Schoendoerffer
The Last American Man by Elizabeth Gilbert
The Beak of the Finch by Jonathan Weiner
Mountain Madness by Robert Birkby
The Worst Journey in the World by Apsley Cherry-Garrard
White Fang by Jack London
I Heard the Owl Call My Name by Margaret Craven
Lord Grizzly by Frederick Manfred
The Fool's Progress by Edward Abbey
Stones for Ibarra by Harriet Doerr
Walking It Off by Doug Peacock